DEC 2018

Praise for **Milkwood**

'From two of Australia's most energetic and capable permaculture communicators, this book gives readers the nitty-gritty for five diverse ways to nourish ourselves from stewarding nature's abundance.

A book that draws on more than a decade of passion and experience both learning and communicating practical skills powered by permaculture ethics and principles. Beautifully presented and inspiring.'
—DAVID HOLMGREN, CO-ORIGINATOR OF PERMACULTURE

'This book will change your life and your community. Pick a chapter to grow a new skill. Enjoy the ride!'
—COSTA GEORGIADIS

'Finally, the ultimate reliance manual from premier educational facilitator, Milkwood. No subscription, no interrupted streaming, no electronic subscription necessary. Just with delicious information and begin turning pages.'
—SALATIN, POLYFACE FARM

'The antidote that ails us lies within these pages. A joyful guide to how to grow, eat and live in harmony with nature.'
—INDIRA NAIDOO

'This book is an expressive roadmap to a chosen life. It is filled with fascinating and inspiring detail so that you, too, can choose and develop the simple or more complex skills you seek to nurture and make connections in your world, a world to love more fully.'
—HOLLY DAVIS

'At last! The book we've all been waiting for! Milkwood permaculture has been at the intellectual and practical forefront of all things growing, living and sharing for as long as I can remember. They have now blessed us with this stunning and knowledge-laden book that will doubtlessly become a dog-eared touchstone for anyone who enjoys getting their hands dirty and their belly filled.'
—PAUL WEST, RIVER COTTAGE AUSTRALIA

'This is a delightful book that gives permaculture-curious folk a rich place to begin.'
—CLARE BOWDITCH

D1612725

This book was written on the lands of the
Dja Dja Wurrung people of the Kulin nation,
and also the Wadi Wadi people of the Dharawal nation.
We acknowledge and pay our respects
to their elders – past, present and future.

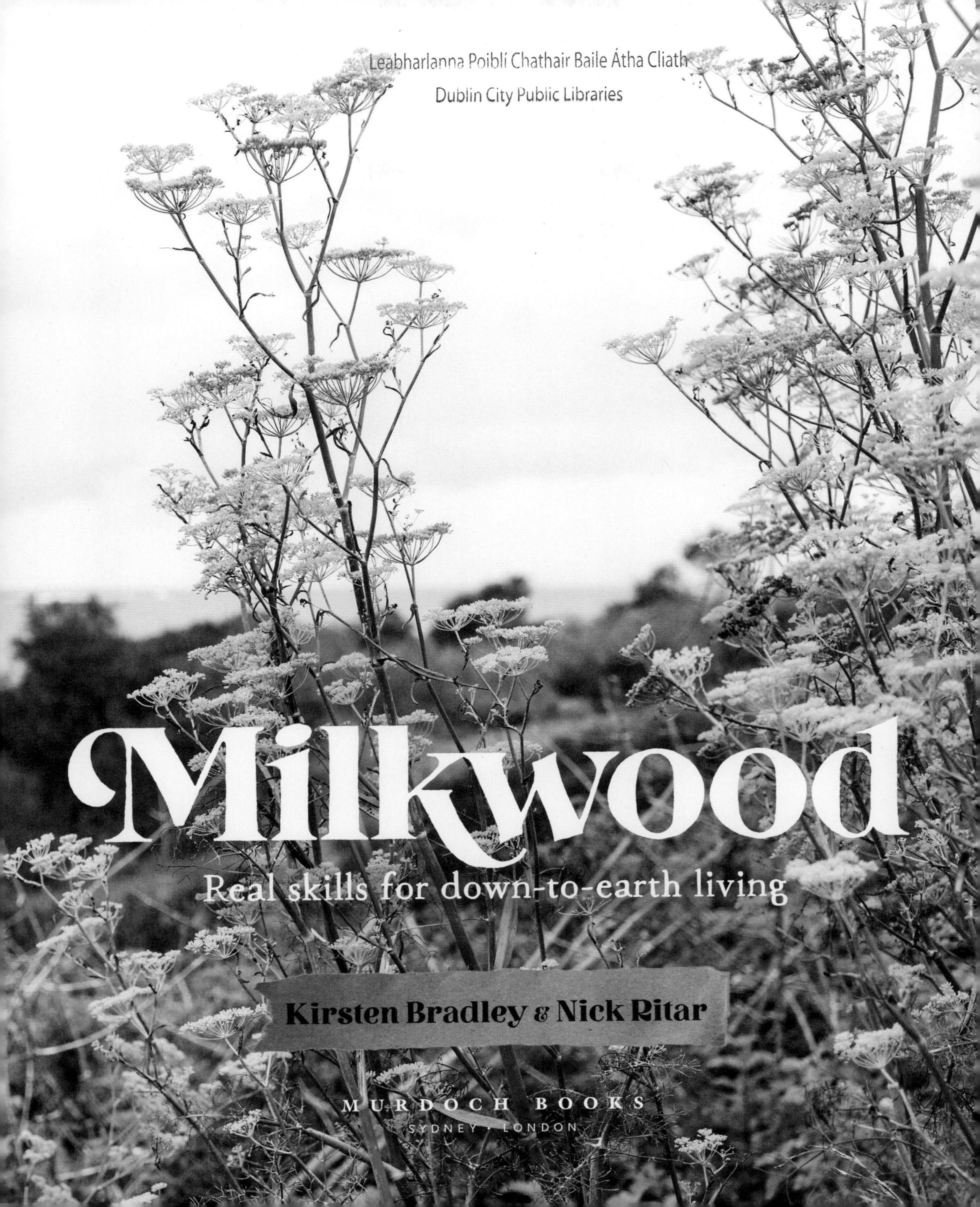

Milkwood

Real skills for down-to-earth living

Kirsten Bradley & Nick Ritar

MURDOCH BOOKS

SYDNEY · LONDON

CONTENTS

Welcome to Milkwood **6**

CHAPTER 1: **The Tomato** 🍒 **10**

CHAPTER 2: **Mushroom Cultivation** 🍄 **66**

CHAPTER 3: **Natural Beekeeping** 🐝 **122**

CHAPTER 4: **Seaweed** 🪸 **176**

CHAPTER 5: **Wild Food** 🌿 **226**

Resources **292**

Index **296**

Acknowledgements **302**

Welcome to Milkwood

This book is a gathering of skills and knowledge – five subjects to get you started on a hand-made, home-made life. It doesn't matter where you live, or what you already know or don't know. What matters is that you'd like to get started, and to dive in deep.

But, where *do* you start? So many skills and new ideas – it's all a little daunting...

We'd recommend that you start with one single, simple, doable thing. It might be learning to grow tomatoes on your windowsill, or learning which green leaves are edible in your local wild space. It might be planting a bee-friendly garden. Or gathering blackberries from the laneway, or seaweed from the beach.

Learn how to do that one thing, and make it a habit. Because what we habitualise, we take into the heart of everyday life. This is how life works, and it's how creating a home-made life works also. Once that one skill is mastered, choose one more thing. And then another. And then another.

Over time, you'll find that your newfound skills complement each other, and inform other skills and knowledge. As your confidence grows, things get interesting. You realise that it really is possible to do it yourself, or that we can do it together, and create abundance for many. Skills create strong communities, as well as tasty dinners and beehives and full cupboards of home-made goodness.

The skills in this book belong to us all, and to our grandparents, and to our grandchildren. After the screens are put away, and the busyness of modern life is paused, what are we made from? Recipes, stories, methods. Love, effort, possibilities. We are our relationships with the animals and plants that we steward, and the landscapes that we live in. The paths to the gully where we forage, the junk that we repurpose, the recipes we teach our children, the music that we make around the fire, and the food that we share across the table.

OUR STORY

We both grew up loving nature and home-made goodness – Nick lived way out west in Willandra National Park, and Kirsten by the sea in Kiama. Once grown, we moved away to cities, to make art and trouble, to organise festivals and to make a living. Just over 10 years ago we decided to jump ship from inner-city living to a bare 20-acre patch on the side of Nick's family farm near Mudgee, New South Wales, in search of a simpler life.

It was about this time that we discovered permaculture – the discipline of creating regenerative farms, communities and landscapes with good design and skills – and it turned our lives upside down. We got so excited about the implications of effective whole systems design, both for farms like ours, but also for urban and community applications, that we set aside art-making altogether. We started asking teachers in regenerative agriculture to teach courses in our family farm's woolshed, and invited everyone we knew (and anyone else, too) to come and learn with us. And people started showing up.

We called this emerging farm and education enterprise 'Milkwood' – for both softness and strength, sustenance and shelter. Over the next eight years we built a small permaculture farm from the ground up, bursting with food, earthen buildings, closed-loop systems, water, animals, friends, teachers, family and students. We all learned many things in those years.

The family farm is long since sold but our passion for sharing permaculture skills has gone from strength to strength. Watching people learn new skills that they take back to their communities, to make life truly better for everyone around them, as well as the planet, has been a beautiful and inspiring thing. And so it goes on.

We're currently living in southern Australia at Melliodora, an iconic permaculture homestead that was founded by David Holmgren, co-originator of permaculture, and his partner Su Dennett. Our days revolve around milking goats, growing vegetables, tending fruit trees and animals, pickling, making, repairing, and sharing knowledge. And it's from this beautiful place that we've finally been able to find the time to sit and write down some of the skills that we've learned and loved over these past 10 years.

It was very tricky to choose just five subjects to include in this book, so we started with some of our favourite parts of living a home-made life: bees, mushrooms, seaweed, tomatoes and wild food. We hope they become some of your favourite things to grow, make and do also.

We wish for you richness. Not of money, but of knowing, and doing. And then, the harvests of your efforts – mushroom pie, honeycomb, tomato passata, gomasio, healthy humans. The cool of the forest, and the roar of the sea. The ability to share your bounty and your knowledge forward. Into community. Into a resilient, livable, low-impact future, for everyone around you. This is richness indeed. We just need to relearn the skills to help make it happen. Let's do it.

Picking wild apples down the gully. The abundance is all around us, we just need to know where to look.

THE
TOMATO

THE ESSENCE OF SUMMER

We can't quite imagine life without tomatoes. They're such a large part of our lives in spring, summer and autumn, and in winter, too.

First, the careful seed-raising stage in early spring, in the warmth of our kitchen and then our greenhouse, as we watch closely until the first green leaves emerge. Then the potting on, and all the careful stewarding and watering through the cold snaps of spring until the seedlings are huge and it's finally time to plant them out. And then over summer the growing, and the care, and the trellising, and the feeding… and then on to the harvesting and all that autumn tomato eating. Over late autumn, winter and spring, tomatoes are central to our home kitchen in the form of bottled passata, chutneys, preserves and dried tomatoes.

Tomatoes are the memory of summer that we hold onto on a rain-whipped, frozen-fingered evening of chores done in the dark of midwinter, when we're sure that we'll never be properly warm, ever again. We thaw out by the fire with a steaming bowl of tomato-based stew in our hands – home-made and heartfelt. And then the days lengthen, and before we know it we're choosing which tomato varieties to plant, the seeds carefully stored last autumn for just this moment.

PREVIOUS PAGE, LEFT: Picking cherry and yellow pear tomatoes (indeterminate type). RIGHT: The fruits of our labour – fresh and preserved oxheart tomatoes.

LEFT: Harvesting Tommy toe and oxheart tomatoes (indeterminate type) in our garden.

THE TROUBLED HISTORY OF THE TOMATO

Tomatoes belong to the plant genus *Solanum*, and are cousins to potatoes, eggplants (aubergines) and the rest of the nightshade family. Like the potato, the tomato originated in the Andes of South America. Cultivated and eaten extensively by the Aztecs, who called them 'xitomatl' (fat water with navel), tomatoes started off as a predominantly yellow fruit. They had a fabulous ability to quickly mutate into other colours and forms, adapting to any new climate that had enough light and heat to support their growth.

The Spanish invasion of Mexico saw the tomato – an exotic, plump fruit with a wonderful scrambling vine – travel to Europe in the 1500s. It was met with some reluctance due to its similarity to other poisonous nightshade plants. The Spanish soon incorporated the tomato into their cuisine, but the Italians grew tomatoes primarily as ornamentals, using the fruit as a table decoration for some centuries before it became part of their food tradition.

The Latin name for tomato, *Solanum lycopersicum* (wolf peach) harks back to the tomato's close association with deadly nightshade. In the 1600s, everyone in Europe knew that deadly nightshade was the food that witches used to turn themselves into werewolves. Clearly the tomato was a bit more peachy-looking than the small black berries of deadly nightshade, but it was still suspicious.

The tomato made its way to the Middle East via Aleppo in the late 1700s. It then travelled to Africa, where it was quickly embraced into many cuisines that already featured eggplant, the tomato's cousin. The tomato travelled back to North America and to the Caribbean from Europe in the 1700s and became an established crop in the USA by the 1800s.

Declared 'unfit for eating' in an early British herbal, Britain nevertheless took 'love apples' into its cuisine in the 1800s, while still growing them widely as a summer ornamental.

The story of the tomato is a curious one because it is such an important ingredient in so many national cuisines. It's difficult to imagine Moroccan, Spanish or Italian food without the sweet lovin' that tomatoes bring. So it's strange to consider that the tomato effectively made the leap from a relatively unheard of, werewolf-inducing love apple to a deeply beloved ingredient – to the point of national patriotism – in just over two generations.

For us, there's no summer without tomatoes. And the first ripe, home-grown tomato of the season – filled with warm sunshine and all the care and anticipation that has gone into its arrival – is one of our very favourite things in the world.

'Red pear', an Italian heirloom indeterminate tomato, growing up a wire mesh trellis.

TOMATOES OF ALL SHAPES AND SIZES

HERITAGE vs HYBRID

The inordinate love that many people feel for the tomato, coupled with the tomato's ability to mutate readily, has led to it being carefully selected and saved to create well over 3000 different heritage varieties, not even including the hybrids.

Heritage tomatoes

Heritage tomato varieties, including some modern varieties, are bred to be true to type. This means you can consistently save their seeds for a potentially endless supply of tomatoes, year after year. Some are bred for their colour, shape or size, some for their ability to make good tomato paste and some for their resilience to drought. Some come with a story handed down through generations of home growers and some come with a taste unlike any other.

Hybrid tomatoes

Hybrid tomato varieties (often called F1 Hybrids) are most commonly used in large-scale commercial tomato growing. Often hybrid tomatoes are not bred with taste, resilience or nutritional density as the primary trait. Rather, they are bred to produce larger, redder tomatoes that transport well, are uniform in shape and colour, and can withstand many weeks of refrigeration and display without showing any spoilage. Hybrid seeds cannot be saved to grow true to type so they are not suitable for home seed saving.

TOMATO GROUPINGS

Most tomato cultivars can be grouped according to their size and shape, with a few exceptions. Some tomatoes, like green zebras, for example, exist in both large round and cherry groups. Others, like roma or plum tomatoes, exist in one main group only.

Cherry: a common name for all the small tomatoes, nearly all of which are climbers. Generally sweet, robust and disease resistant, cherry tomatoes come in many colours.

Heirloom tomato varieties Costoluto Genovese, Jaune Flamme and Thai Pink Egg.

Pear/plum/roma: larger than cherry tomatoes, and with a pear-ish or plum-ish shape. They often have dense flesh and are therefore excellent for making sauce and paste, depending on the variety.

Round and ribbed: larger tomato cultivars with ribbing on top. These are incredibly gorgeous, but are prone to cracking if they get rain at the wrong point and are sometimes prone to disease.

Round and smooth: larger cultivars with smooth skin and a round shape.

Beefsteak: a term for the large to huge tomato varieties. When cut open, these look quite meaty and fleshy, with fewer seeds than other varieties.

DETERMINATE vs INDETERMINATE

As well as the size and shape of their fruit, tomatoes are grouped by their growing habits and how their fruit ripens. It's important for backyard growers to have a sense of these groupings, especially if you want to grow enough tomatoes to bottle for winter.

Determinate tomatoes

Otherwise known as 'bush' tomatoes, determinate cultivars have a low growth habit. The name refers to the fact that each stem, once it grows a flower cluster, terminates and grows no further, hence this type of tomato does not scramble high or far. Determinate tomato plants can be either left to sit on mulched ground, or staked to allow for airflow but not for climbing. The plant will flower over a short time and then fruit nearly all at once, commonly over a four-week period. This is excellent if you're wanting to bottle the tomatoes – it's a big four weeks of picking and processing, but then all the work is done.

You do need to be prepared, though, as determinate tomatoes can be quite overwhelming when they're all ready to be picked – right now! Many of the tomatoes that are suitable for making tomato paste, such as romas, are determinate.

Indeterminate tomatoes

These are the climbing tomatoes, which need to be staked or trellised for good airflow and harvest. Their stems do not terminate at a flower cluster, but just keep on growing. Left to scramble along the ground, indeterminate tomatoes may be fine, but if it's a definite harvest that you're after, take the time to rig them up on a trellis.

As well as having a climbing habit, indeterminate tomato cultivars flower over a much longer period than determinates, and therefore they fruit over a long period – sometimes many months. They're great for a regular supply of tomatoes for salads, and in many areas will only stop flowering once cold weather and short days (meaning less natural light) overcome them.

Semi-determinate tomatoes

Of course, there are some tomatoes that defy polarities. These need to be staked or trellised but they won't grow as high as indeterminate tomatoes. They will flower and fruit over a shorter period than indeterminates, but over a longer period than determinates. If you have a shorter outdoor growing season, semi-determinates are great for supplying you with tomatoes over many weeks, but not many months.

Small climbing yellow pear tomatoes, not yet ripe.

CHOOSING THE BEST TOMATOES FOR YOUR SITUATION

If you have a sunny windowsill, a backyard, a front step or a small farm, you *can* grow tomatoes, and there's a method and a variety to suit every situation. You just need to work out what factors you have to work with and then find a cultivar and a growing method that's right for you.

Big or small?

Big tomatoes are heavy tomatoes. While this might seem obvious, until you've held a fully laden tomato vine of beefsteak tomatoes, you may not realise just how heavy they can be. This is fine if your growing space has the infrastructure to deal with such a vine – very sturdy trellises or a strong overhead pole to tie them off. If you don't, it's best to consider varieties with smaller fruit.

Smaller-fruited tomatoes are also great for kid-friendly gardens, as they are easy to pick off the vine, unlike some larger varieties, which must be picked with care to avoid damaging the vine.

Bush or climbing?

Most bush tomatoes will ripen over a short period, which can be excellent or a headache, depending on what else is happening in your house that week. Climbers will give you a smaller but steadier stream of fruit.

Climbing tomatoes are also great for making the most of limited growing space, as they use the vertical plane to maximum effect, and can climb over 2 metres (6½ feet) if allowed to do so.

Heat and light

Two things that tomatoes love are heat and light, and both are essential for a good crop. A minimum of 6 hours of direct sunlight on the plants is recommended. In temperate climates, planting them in the warmest part of your garden will definitely help – a growing space that faces the equator is ideal. Tomatoes also love heat, so in colder climates it's common to grow them in a greenhouse, which traps any available heat inside. A sunny indoor porch or a sunroom is also a great place to grow tomatoes if you live in a cold climate.

Space considerations

Do you have a small garden bed with a sunny wall behind it? Rig up a trellis and grow climbing tomatoes. Or a sunny balcony but no ground space? Grow bush or dwarf tomatoes upside down, or in pots with a stake. Do you have lots of space and are longing for a supply of home-made passata? Plant bush tomatoes in a block. What about a small vegie patch? Perhaps plant a row of well-trimmed climbers in the centre of a garden bed. Or do you have no outside space at all, but a sunny window that faces the equator? Plant cherry climbers in pots inside, and twine them as they grow, up sturdy string to the top of the window.

Climbing tomatoes can be twined around a vertical string to help encourage them to grow upwards.

GROWING GREAT TOMATOES

Once you've chosen the tomato variety that's right for you, it's time to start growing. Gather your seeds together and choose which method suits you best to raise them. Once their first leaves are up, you'll be carefully watering and watching them each day until they're big and strong – prepare to feel proud! As soon as your garden beds or pots are prepared and ready, it will be time to plant out your seedlings to grow, flower and fruit. You'll have freshly harvested tomatoes on your kitchen bench before you know it.

SEEDLING STAGE

Tomatoes are a warm season plant, with seeds that germinate best when the soil is over 20°C (68°F). Getting seeds started in early spring when the weather (and therefore the soil) is cold can be tricky, but there are some simple, low-energy workarounds that you can use.

In temperate climates, tomatoes can be started indoors so that by the time both the weather and soil are warm enough, the seedlings are big, healthy and ready to go. By getting a head start on the season, you will end up with more tomatoes.

While you can buy tomato seedlings that are ready to plant out, growing them from seed is a simple skill that isn't hard to learn, ensures resilience for future years and is much cheaper than buying advanced seedlings. And if you're growing from seed, you can choose to grow whatever beautiful variety of tomatoes you wish, including proven locally adapted varieties – not just the stock-standard seedlings at your local nursery.

Once you have your seeds, it's time to raise them. There are many methods you can use to do this, but two good options are raising the seeds in plugs and raising the seeds in trays.

Black Russian tomatoes, 'pricked out' into small seedling pots.

Plugs are great for starting lots of tomatoes, provided you have enough space, like in this large greenhouse.

Method 1: Seed raising in plugs

This method involves planting tomato seeds into individual cells or 'plugs' full of seed-raising mix in a tray. Once the seeds germinate and put out their first leaves, you can then 'pot them on' to larger pots so that the roots have more room to grow into healthy seedlings. By starting small, you save a fair bit of space until you need to progress to larger pots. This gives you more flexibility as to when and where to germinate your precious seeds and keep them warm.

You'll need a plug tray, some seed-raising mix (see page 22), a knife and your tomato seeds, as well as some larger pots and sieved compost for potting on the seedlings.

1. Fill your plug tray with seed-raising mix, patting the mix down firmly to fill all the cells. Then, use the end of a knife to make a small slit in the surface of each cell's mix, about 1 cm (½ inch) deep. Plant one seed into each slit, pressing the mix back in place with your finger to cover the seed. Label the rows of seeds with the tomato variety.

2. Keep your tray of seeds warm and moist (but not too wet – you don't want the seeds to rot). The tomato seedlings should emerge in 5 to 10 days.

3. Once the seedlings have put out their second set of leaves, transfer each plug seedling, along with its soil, to a larger pot of sieved compost so it can grow into a big happy tomato seedling, ready for planting out into the garden.

BEST-EVER SEED-RAISING MIX

Getting your seed-raising mix right is important for growing strong seedlings. Making your own is much cheaper and usually assures a higher-quality mix than using a commercial seed-raising mix.

In the past we've used a seed-raising mix recipe that was taught to us by Joyce and Mike of Allsun Farm on the southern tablelands of New South Wales. Joyce and Mike are organic growers who are famous for their fabulous tomato seedlings. We've varied the recipe slightly to use the lowest footprint and most locally available materials we can find.

You will need:

* 2 parts finely sieved compost
* 1 part worm castings
* 2 parts coir fibre (hydrated)
* 1 part coarse sand
* A suitable container for measuring your ingredients
* A bucket or barrel with a lid
* A trowel or stick for stirring

1. Measure all of the ingredients into your bucket or barrel and stir together with the trowel or stick until the mix has a uniform appearance.

2. If you can, let the mix sit for a day or so before using it, covered and somewhere out of the weather so that it doesn't dry out. This step is not essential but it helps all the nutrients and ingredients meld evenly.

TIPS

You can use whatever you like for your 'part' measure – a cup, a bucket or whatever makes sense for the quantity you're preparing.

Worm castings are the gorgeous black sludge you find at the bottom of your worm farm. This sludge is nitrogen-dense and fabulous food for young plants. If you can't lay your hands on any, just use 3 parts compost instead of 2.

Coir fibre is the pulverised husk of coconuts. It holds water very well so it acts as a wetting agent for the rest of the mix. Being a waste product, super-cheap and readily available where we are, it's great for this task. You may find another or a better material where you live. Avoid using peat/sphagnum moss. While it's often recommended for seed-raising mixes, it's harvested from moss bogs that would otherwise provide important carbon sinks. Coir is a much better choice.

A large tray of tomato seedlings creates its own microclimate, which helps maintain humidity and promotes the seedlings' growth.

Method 2: Seed raising in trays

This method is great if you want to grow a serious amount of seedlings, as it saves a ton of space and bother during the seed-raising stage. It takes a little more care than raising in plugs because it involves 'pricking out' the tomato seedlings into pots once they've germinated.

You'll need a planting tray that's at least 10 cm (4 inches) deep, some finely sieved compost and your tomato seeds. You'll also need some larger pots and some more sieved compost for pricking out the seedlings, as well as an old knife or a pricking out tool (we use a bio-intensive 'widger').

1. Start by filling the tray with the sieved compost, level the top and then make furrows about 5 cm (2 inches) apart. Place a line of tomato seeds into the furrows, then carefully cover with the compost. Don't forget to label each row with its variety.

2. Keep your tray moist (but not wet) and warm. In 5 to 10 days the seeds will germinate and the seedlings will appear.

3. Once the seedlings in your tray have their first two leaves, it's time to prick them out into pots of finely sieved compost that you have ready. Using the knife or pricking out tool, push down into the compost alongside the first seedling, then carefully lever it out. Using the same tool, make a deep slot in the compost of the larger pot that you've prepared and insert the seedling, taking care to let the roots go right down into the slot hole. Carefully press the compost back in around the seedling. Mist regularly as the seedling grows.

Tomato seedlings inside an equator-facing 'cold frame' made of wood and glass doors from landfill – the extra heat from the sun will help them grow.

It's all about the heat

The reason that it's a good idea to start in a compact space with tomato seeds all comes down to heat – soil heat, in particular. Tomato seeds need a minimum soil temperature of 20°C (68°F) to germinate, and prefer it up around 25°C (77°F) for good germination rates. And they need to sit at this temperature 24 hours a day – warm spring days with colder nights just don't cut it.

The answer to successful germination is consistent bottom heat for your seed tray. This can be achieved with an electric heating mat or pad that you can buy specifically for this purpose. However, you can also create a similar effect by keeping your seed tray inside near a source of heat that's already in use. We use a shelf above the back of our woodstove. Other heat sources include rigging up a shelf above a room heater, above an electric fridge (to catch the heat coming out the back of it) or even above your coffee machine. Find something in your house that's consistently generating heat and figure out a way to place your seed tray on or near it.

Fortunately, it's only heat that your seeds need until they've germinated – light is not necessary. So if your heat source is in a dark place, that's fine, as long as you remember to keep the seed tray moist throughout this 5 to 10 day period. We keep our seed trays in the kitchen where it's warm and we'll remember to water them. Yes, it's a bit annoying and messy, but our yearly supply of tomato passata depends on it, so we figure it's a fair trade-off.

Once they're potted on, your tomatoes will still benefit from extra heat, but by this stage they'll also need plenty of daylight.

Feed and water them well

Once your tomato plants are potted on from seedling stage into their individual pots, it's vital that you keep them well fed and watered until you plant them out. Using a good compost mix in the pots is a great start, but as you water them each day, some of these nutrients will leach out. For this reason, watering your seedlings every second day with a diluted solution of liquid fertiliser is a good idea.

Tomatoes are nutrient-hungry plants, known as 'heavy feeders'. Feeding your seedlings with some diluted home-made compost tea, seaweed tea (see page 223) or a commercial seaweed or organic plant food solution provides your seedlings with ongoing nutrients and minerals so they stay happy and healthy until they are planted into your garden.

Growing strong seedlings

Your spring tomato seedlings may still spend a few months in their pots before they're planted out, as you need to wait until the garden soil temperature is over 20°C (68°F) and all chance of frost has passed. Keeping your seedlings warm, damp, well fed and sheltered during these months is essential.

There are some different methods you can use to keep up the heat.

Greenhouse

Whether small, large, freestanding or attached to the side of a solar-passive house, greenhouses are great for keeping spring plants warm.

Cold frames

These use the sun to heat your seedlings, a bit like a mini greenhouse, but close to the ground. With the addition of some thermal mass around or inside them, cold frames are a great way to keep spring seedlings warm at night. You can open the roof during the day to ensure they don't overheat.

Equator-facing brick wall

An easy way to maximise light and heat to your seedlings is to prop an old glass door or window against a brick wall and put the tomato seedlings behind the glass.

Windowsill

Do not underestimate the power of a sunny windowsill! Yes, it may mean your living room is covered in tomato seedlings for a time. Work out which windows in your house face the equator and see if you can make room in front of them for your seedlings.

Don't forget to keep your seedlings well watered!

There are lots of ways to capture extra sun for your growing tomato seedlings.

GREENHOUSE

Brick wall absorbs heat during day and releases at night

EQUATOR-FACING BRICK WALL WITH GLASS SHEET

Glass door or panel (open at end)

Glass or plastic can be permanent or temporary

COLD FRAME

Can be propped open on hot days

Wood, brick or even straw bale walls

WINDOWSILL

Ground also absorbs some heat to release overnight; can be paved if you like

PLANTING OUT

Preparing your tomato beds, from planning to soil preparation to mulching to trellising, may seem like a big job the first time around, but once you've had a season of plentiful tomatoes and filled your pantry with sauces and preserves, you'll realise it was all worthwhile.

Planning

The first step to planting out your tomatoes is planning. Are you looking at planting them in a block or in a row? How far apart are you going to plant them? What are you going to use for your trellis?

Determinate tomatoes may be best planted in a block because when it's time to harvest, you'll be accessing them over a short period of time, all at once. You can therefore fit more plants into your growing space by reducing the number of paths between them.

Indeterminate tomatoes, on the other hand, will be harvested over a longer period of time, so access to these plants is paramount. Planting them in rows, with good access between each row, makes good sense.

Below are two planting plans for a 1.5 x 2 metre (4¾ x 6½ foot) garden bed – one is for red pear and cherry tomatoes (indeterminate) and one is for roma (plum) tomatoes (determinate).

BELOW LEFT: This planting plan maximises space for cherry or red pear tomatoes (climbing/indeterminate type), with a simple A-frame trellis and offset plantings.

BELOW RIGHT: This planting plan for roma tomatoes (bush/determinate type) makes the most of a small space, while providing access for harvest.

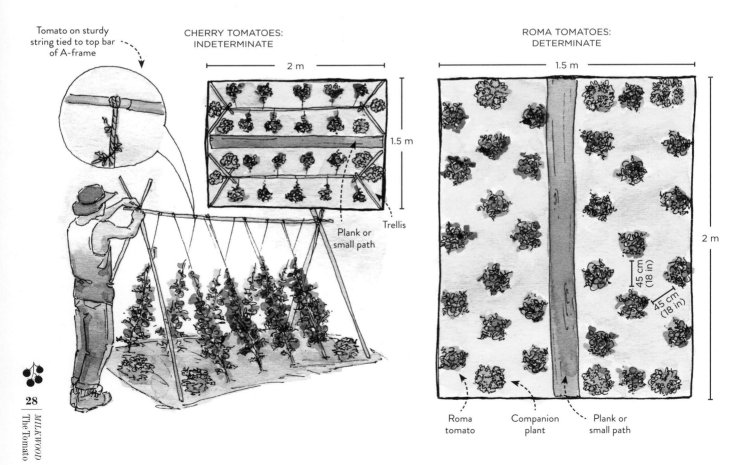

Tomato on sturdy string tied to top bar of A-frame

CHERRY TOMATOES: INDETERMINATE

2 m

1.5 m

Plank or small path

Trellis

ROMA TOMATOES: DETERMINATE

1.5 m

2 m

45 cm (18 in)

45 cm (18 in)

Roma tomato

Companion plant

Plank or small path

Soil preparation

Like most vegetables, tomatoes like fertile, well-drained and slightly acid soil, with a pH between 6 and 7. If a pH test shows that your soil is less than 6 (too acidic), you can add some agricultural lime to 'sweeten' the soil, following the instructions in the pH test kit. You can also try using a little wood ash, but be careful not to overdo it. If your soil's pH is over 7 (alkaline), you can add some sulphur or decomposed pine needles or leaf litter to help bring the pH down.

The best way to establish a good soil pH long term is usually with the addition of good compost and green manure plants in your garden bed rotation, and ensuring that your soil is well drained.

Since tomatoes are heavy feeders, your soil preparation will need to include the addition of compost – preferably home-made or locally sourced. Your bed preparation also needs to ensure the soil is well aerated, so that it has good drainage, and so that plenty of soil life can establish. The addition of well-rotted cow, sheep or horse manure is welcome at this stage also, if available.

There are many, many ways to prepare a garden bed for tomatoes. The choice depends on how you want to do it as well as what tools and resources you have available. Two options worth considering are the no-dig method and bio-intensive double-dig method.

No-dig method

If you're wanting to establish a new garden bed on compacted ground, have plenty of organic materials available and don't like digging, a no-dig garden bed is a great way to get started.

This bed-making method involves making a deep 'lasagne' of straw, carbon-rich material, compost and liquid nutrients, then planting seedlings, with a handful of compost beneath them, into that lasagne. It's a bit like making a compost pile, in situ. You may not get your best yields in the first year as the bedding material takes a while to break down into soil.

TESTING YOUR SOIL

It's a good idea to take a pH test of your soil before you begin preparing it, to ensure that it's going to be suitable for growing tomatoes. You can buy a cheap, simple soil pH test kit at a garden centre or online store. It's a good addition to any gardener's kit.

A no-dig garden plan using straw, compost, manure, seaweed and newspaper or cardboard. Water in each layer as you construct it all.

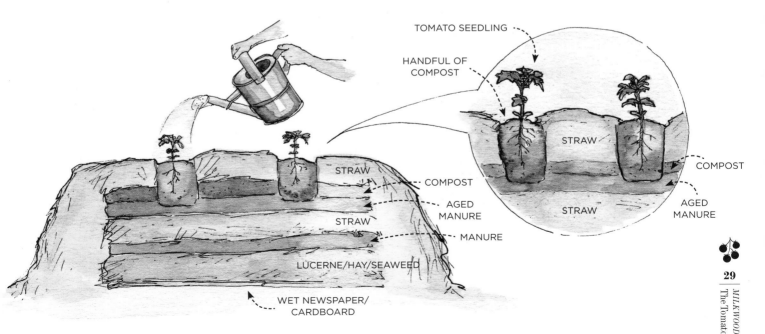

TOMATO SEEDLING

HANDFUL OF COMPOST

STRAW

COMPOST

STRAW

AGED MANURE

STRAW

COMPOST

AGED MANURE

MANURE

LUCERNE/HAY/SEAWEED

WET NEWSPAPER/ CARDBOARD

ABOVE: To make a bio-intensive bed, first remove the grass. Next, dig each trench, forking the subsoil and adding compost as you go. Once you have finished, the garden beds are ready for planting.

RIGHT: The basics of the bio-intensive double-dig process: a bunch of work at the start, for many seasons of happy vegetables thereafter.

Bio-intensive double-dig method

The double-dig method is a way of thoroughly aerating the soil to create a cake-like consistency and incorporating large amounts of compost as you do it. It takes a bunch of effort but it only uses minimal inputs: your labour and some compost. It's a good method for regenerating existing garden beds or establishing new beds on good soil. Once it's done, if you take good care of the garden bed you won't need to repeat the whole process every year.

This bed-making method is done by shovelling out rows of topsoil, then loosening the subsoil below with a garden fork before replacing the top layer with topsoil from the next row, mixed with compost. Once you reach the end of the bed, you need to rake it flat. The beauty of this method is that the plants have maximum access to nutrients and water as their roots can reach deep into the soil.

DIG A 20 CM (4 INCH) DEEP TRENCH AND
PILE TOPSOIL ON OPPOSITE END OF BED

LOOSEN SUBSOIL AND ADD
A SPADEFUL OF MANURE

PUT NEXT 20 CM OF TOPSOIL
ON THE FIRST TRENCH

PROCEED UNTIL THE FIRST PILE OF
TOPSOIL IS USED IN THE FINAL TRENCH

Mulching

Whichever way you prepare your tomato beds, mulching them to keep the moisture in and to reduce weed seed germination is highly advised. Mulching before you plant your tomato seedlings is the most time-efficient way to do it, rather than trying to mulch around your precious plants, which can result in them getting battered or broken.

Straw or similar waste products like sugarcane mulch (bagasse) are good choices as they'll be relatively weed-free. Mulching thickly ensures minimal evaporation and maximum weed control for your precious tomatoes.

Trellising

You'll need a strong trellis for your rows of climbing tomatoes. Trellising is generally easiest to do after you've done your soil preparation and mulching, but before planting. Here are some low-cost options for getting the strength and height you need for great tomatoes.

Overhead beam and twine

Take two long metal fence posts (check your local tip shop – there are often some there) and hammer them into the soil every 3 metres (9¾ feet) along each row. Then find some good long poles, such as saplings, bamboo or timber, and secure one to each metal picket with wire. (Alternatively, you can make sturdy wooden A-frames every 3 metres to do this same job, but they will take up more bed space.)

At the 2 metre (6½ foot) high mark, secure horizontal poles along the row, overlapping them if necessary. Plant your tomatoes beneath each overhead pole in a row.

Once the tomato plants are about 30 cm (12 inches) high, get some very sturdy string – a fully laden and nearly ripe tomato vine crashing to earth because its twine has rotted is a very sad thing! Cut a length of the string, allowing some leeway (if you're using jute or natural materials, consider double- or triple-folding it to ensure it lasts). Starting at the bottom, tie a bowline knot around the tomato stem, under the lowest branch.

ABOVE: Twining the tomato 'leader' up its string.

BELOW: Tying a bowline knot.

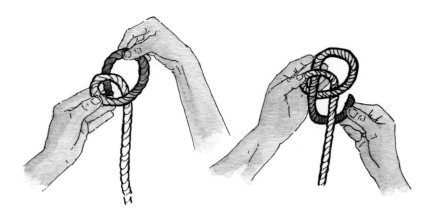

1. BUNNY RUNS OUT OF THE HOLE,   2. BEHIND THE TREE,

3. AND BACK IN THE HOLE.

PREVIOUS PAGE, LEFT: Trellising tomatoes on a top bar trellis – tie a bowline knot under the bottom branch, secure the string at the top and then carefully begin to twine the tomatoes, always twining in the same direction. This twining system is strong enough to support large fruit if done correctly.
RIGHT: Rows of happy climbing oxheart and yellow pear tomatoes.

BELOW: Twining tomatoes up a wire trellis is just as effective and better for some situations, such as exposed and windy sites.

Once the knot is secure, tie off the string at the overhead bar of your trellis. The string should be taut but not so tight that it damages the plant.

As your tomatoes grow, gently twine the central stem around the vertical string – always in the same direction – to keep the plants growing tall and proud. Check them every few days to see if they need a little more twining. When the growth of your plants get more vigorous, maintaining a consistent central stem – the 'leader' – can get confusing, as the tomato sends out shoots every which way. This is where pruning can help (see page 38).

Mesh trellis

Another option is to use a solid mesh trellis that either hangs from an overhead bar or is held up by vertical poles. If you're planting a lot of tomatoes, the stronger the mesh material is, the better. Wire fencing mesh with wide holes is a great option, as you can twine the tomatoes back and forth through it and you can use it for many years. The holes need to be wide enough to twine your plants through – we recommend a minimum size of 10 x 10 cm (4 x 4 inches). Rebar (the steel reinforcing mesh that is used in concrete slabs) is another great option as it's sturdy, with wide gaps.

You can still use mesh that has smaller holes, but you'll need to tie up your tomatoes as they climb, keeping them on one side of the mesh. Mesh trellises can also be made and/or woven using bamboo, split wood or any strong, sturdy yet flexible material you have available.

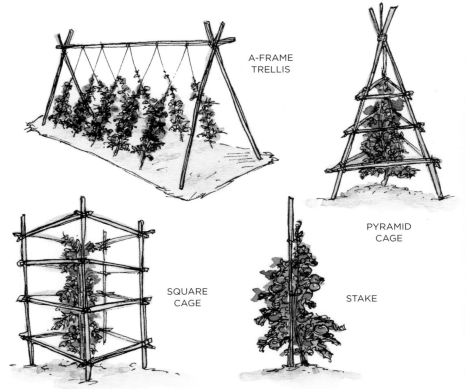

A-FRAME TRELLIS

PYRAMID CAGE

SQUARE CAGE

STAKE

ABOVE LEFT: There are lots of ways to make your own tomato cages or trellis systems.

ABOVE: Wire tomato cages can be purchased from garden stores.

Stakes

Stakes are best suited to semi-determinate or determinate tomatoes. Hammer them into the ground just before planting your seedlings. As the plants grow, tie them to the stakes to provide some structure and airflow.

Cages

There are lots of metal tomato cage designs that you can buy from garden shops to prop up your tomato plants. They're best suited to semi-determinate or determinate tomatoes, which won't grow too high. You can also make your own cages with bamboo, in a square or pyramid shape.

Time to plant

To plant your seedlings, use a garden trowel to make a hole in the mulch that's about 15 cm (6 inches) wide and one and a half times as deep as the pot. Repeat for each tomato plant, spacing them according to your planting plan.

Gently turn the pot upside down, with the seedling between your fingers and your hand flat against the surface of the soil, and remove from the pot.

Plant your tomatoes deep, covering at least the bottom sets of leaves if you can. These nodes will magically transform into roots as the tomato senses they have been buried. The more roots for your tomato plant, the better access it has to nutrients and water.

Press the garden bed soil in around your little seedling and water it in with some diluted liquid fertiliser – we use seaweed. Make sure you leave some space in the mulch around the seedling to allow for good airflow… and your tomatoes are in!

CARING FOR YOUR TOMATOES

Frost protection

While it's advised to wait until the last frost has passed before you plant out your tomatoes, figuring out that date can be tricky. If you're not sure, ask at your local plant nursery or community garden as to when folks in your area plant their tomatoes. There's likely to be a local rule of thumb, such as our one, 'not until after Melbourne Cup day', which should be a good indicator of the last frost in your climate.

However, nothing is certain when it comes to weather and it's possible to get caught out by a late frost, which will badly damage young tomato plants and set them back, if not kill them.

Be prepared to install some emergency frost protection. Putting three bamboo stakes around each tomato plant, with something wrapped around them and possibly over the top, is a good idea if you get a sudden change of weather for a day or two. We've used plastic tree guards left over from plantings, plastic bags and even pillowcases at a pinch.

Watering

Tomatoes need to be well watered, but not overwatered. Once they're planted in the ground, a good watering to the root zone once a week, or twice a week if the weather is really dry, is plenty. Once the plants are large and have fruit that is starting to ripen, daily watering may become necessary. If possible, water from the bottom, not on the tomato plant's leaves – tomato leaves that are constantly wet can lead to disease. They'll get wet in rainstorms, of course, but the less you intentionally wet them, the better.

Companion plants

Life is better together. There are many different species of plants that have positive effects on each other in terms of plant health, pollination, and disease and pest resistance. When you're starting off your tomato seedlings, consider planting a big batch of companion plants – not just one or two – all around your tomatoes. Your garden will look amazing, it will be a pollinator's playground, you'll have more good food to harvest and you may well avoid all sorts of nasty pests and diseases as a result. Happily, many of these companions happen to be the most delicious things to eat with tomatoes.

Marigolds

These are powerful plants. They repel non-beneficial soil nematodes, slugs and other garden pests, plus the flowers look great underneath tomato vines. If you plant just one tomato companion, plant some marigolds.

Nasturtiums

Nasturtiums can be used as a living mulch under tomatoes. They also ward off white flies, aphids, beetles and fungal diseases, and promote pollination.

Regularly checking your climbing tomatoes as they grow will help you keep on top of trellising and pruning chores.

Borage

Borage repels tomato hornworms and increases pollination. It can also be a helpful mulch if it gets too big – simply cut off the tops and mulch directly under your tomatoes.

Garlic

Tuck garlic bulbs into the soil around your tomato seedlings. They repel spider mites and taste great harvested along with the tomatoes.

Basil

Basil is a fabulous companion. It repels aphids and spider mites, promotes pollination, and is said to enhance the growth and taste of tomatoes themselves. It's also delicious eaten with tomatoes, of course.

Pests and diseases

Depending on where you are, tomatoes can be susceptible to a range of pests and diseases. Prevention is best, of course, so the first line of defence is keeping your plants super-healthy, well watered and well fed, with companion plants all around them and as little stress as possible.

If you do have a disease-infested plant, figure out what the problem is and if it's not a nutritional deficiency that can be fixed, immediately pull out the plant and get rid of it – preferably by burning – to prevent the spread of disease to other plants. Disease can travel fast in the height of summer so this is a good way to protect your crop as well as your neighbour's crop. It's not advisable to lay tomato prunings underneath tomato plants as this increases the habitat for possible pests. Put your prunings in the compost instead.

Below are four common tomato complaints and some advice for dealing with them.

Fruit fly

If you're in an area that's prone to fruit flies, they will likely be a problem for your tomatoes in the second half of summer. They easily get into ripening fruit through cracks and crevices, or bore holes directly, causing the fruit to rot. Cherry tomatoes are usually the least affected by fruit fly, so consider this in your planning.

Fruit fly traps, hung near tomato plants, can also help. Simply take a plastic bottle and cut a hole in the side, then half fill it with water and add a spoonful of Vegemite or another yeast extract, and a drop of detergent to break the surface tension. The fruit flies are attracted to the yeast, so they fly into the trap, then drown. You'll need to refresh the traps every other week or so during fruit fly season. You can also use 125 ml (½ cup) of urine in water instead of the Vegemite – yes, it's true!

Russet mite

This microscopic mite can suck the sap of tomato plants. Symptoms present as a bronzing of the leaves or stems, or yellowing and curling leaves that then die. Adding too much nutrient at this point can make this pest worse as it loves fresh green growth. Treating the mites with organic sprays like neem

NOT FRIENDLY!

Not-so-great companion plants for tomatoes include brassicas, corn and fennel, which do not have beneficial effects on tomato growth. Plant these in a separate bed so the growth of your tomatoes is not inhibited.

Well-mulched tomato plant with basil as companion.

Yellowing leaves can indicate a whole range of issues, from nutrient deficiency to certain types of mites – observe the plants carefully, diagnose as best as you can, and treat accordingly.

Blossom end rot presents as an indented, brownish patch on the bottom of the tomato.

oil, wettable sulphur or pyrethrum can help, as can beneficial nematodes (encouraged by marigold plants), which can also be purchased in a small box and released. It's important to remove all infected leaves. Good crop rotation and the removal and burning of badly infected plants can help reduce the likelihood of re-occurrence.

Blossom end rot

This presents as an indented area on the blossom side of the fruit, which can get watery and turn black as the fruit ripens, most common in early season fruit. It can be caused by irregular or excessive watering, but also by calcium deficiency. Balancing the pH of your soil by adding garden lime can help to make calcium more available to your plants, as can sprinkling powdered eggshells around the plants.

Root knot nematode

There are many good nematodes in the soil, but this is not one of them. Symptoms will present as stunted growth and yellowing leaves, with the roots of the plant knotted and much fatter than they should be. Unfortunately, root knot nematode also loves dandelion and purslane – two common edible weeds found in Australian gardens – which can mean that it's hard to eradicate. Your best hope is planting lots of French marigolds to repel the nematodes. Also, ensure your beds go through a good crop rotation, including green manures, to break the nematodes' breeding cycle.

TO PRUNE OR NOT TO PRUNE?

As tomatoes grow, they start off with a central 'leader' that grows upwards, with side branches coming off it. These side branches quickly develop side branches, and so on and on… tomatoes are natural scramblers, after all.

Some people pinch out these 'suckers' that develop on the shoulder of branches coming off the central stem, and some people don't. There are arguments on both sides that better growth and fruit set is promoted by either doing or not doing this job.

If your tomatoes are the determinate or semi-determinate type, we'd suggest that you don't bother with pruning – just prepare for your plants to scramble with gusto. More suckers means more branches, which means more tomatoes. As long as you've got your tomatoes staked or rigged up to allow sufficient airflow, or have lots of deep mulch for the plants to scramble over – that is, get them off the soil – pruning is not a great use of your time.

However, if you're training or trellising indeterminate tomatoes vertically, with limited space between rows, pruning can be a very good thing. This is especially true if you're in a humid climate where airflow is an issue, as fungal diseases love tomato plants that are consistently wet. Also, if you can't get in between your rows of tomato plants because they're massive, shaggy things, you can't harvest as many tomatoes without damaging your plants, which is a shame. Depending on where you live, though, this shaggy form can actually be an advantage and protect the tomato plant from heat burn, which can occur in very hot and dry areas. You'll need to weigh up the pros and cons.

How to prune

Pruning creates a more open plant structure and encourages your plant to put its energy into going upwards. Pruning climbing tomatoes also makes it easier to maintain the 'leader' – the central branch that you're training upwards. Pay careful attention when you're learning to prune, as it's possible to prune out the leader by mistake. In this case, you'll need to convince a side branch to become the new leader, which will mean a setback in the plant's growth. Go slowly and carefully until you're familiar with the plant's form.

To prune your tomatoes, you'll simply take out any suckers that form on the shoulder of a leaf branch – at the joint between the leaf branch and the main stem. When the suckers are young, you can just pinch them out with your fingers. If they're a little larger, push them to one side and then neatly snap out the shoot. If they're more advanced, you'll need a clean sharp knife or a pair of sharp secateurs.

If you have some advanced suckers that you want to remove, these can become new tomato plants. Put them in a jar of water and leave them in the shade for a week – they should send out strong roots – and then transfer them to a pot of sieved compost and coddle them for a few weeks before planting out. More tomato plants for you!

To prune your tomato plant, identify a sucker leaf at the shoulder of a branch. Pinch it out carefully to remove – and the branch is pruned!

RIPENING AND HARVESTING

Tomato plants are ruled by heat and light. The length of the day determines the rate of flowering (as autumn comes on and the days shorten, they will flower less frequently), but the ripening of the fruit is determined more by heat. This heat might be directly on the plant or on your windowsill, depending on what time of year you're harvesting.

Some folks pick their tomatoes once the first blush of colour appears and ripen them inside. Some folks ripen them on the vine and pick as they go. It's up to you, but consider the weather as a factor – a big rainstorm falling on nearly ripe tomatoes can split them, which can lead to disease and tomatoes that won't store well and need to be used pronto. We generally ripen ours on the plant but if there's big rainfall coming, we sometimes pick all the nearly ripe and semi-ripe tomatoes that we can, then finish them off inside, spreading them out on our greenhouse shelves.

OPPOSITE: Harvesting ripe
oxheart tomatoes.

RIPENING TOMATOES UPSIDE DOWN

Sometimes, at the end of the season, it's necessary to pull out the tomatoes before they're all finished – the first frost might be forecast (which will burn the plants and damage the fruit) or you might need the bed space. One solution is to pull out the whole tomato plant, roots and all, and hang it upside down under cover, preferably somewhere that gets some sun or heat. The fruit will slowly ripen over the coming weeks (and sometimes months), providing you with a slow stream of ripe tomatoes long after the tomato-growing season has finished.

SEED SAVING

When we save seeds, we are doing many, many awesome things, all at once. Saving seeds preserves great-tasting varieties and traditional varieties. Saving the seeds from your best plants also allows you to create locally adapted varieties that deal particularly well with your local soil and climate, as well as other conditions, such as late frost or early heat.

Saving seeds saves money (it's free!) and helps ensure resilience for your own vegie patch, as well as your local community network of gardens and farms. Seed saving is a valuable skill to pass on to your kids and community, as well as being a fun part of the seasonal cycle of growing good food. And saving the seeds from your best tomatoes means a potential lifetime supply of seeds.

If you just select a few fine-looking tomatoes from your healthiest vine to save seed from, without regard to their variety or proximity to other tomato types, that's okay. You will certainly be able to grow more tomatoes from those seeds. However, they may not grow true to type, meaning the resulting plants can be highly variable in taste, colour, yield, habit and health.

If you're keen to preserve and maintain the tomato varieties that you grow from year to year, whether they're heritage varieties or a local, open-pollinated tomato, plan ahead. Seed saving is a simple process, but it does require some planning in terms of where you plant and what else is flowering nearby.

Choose your best ripe tomatoes for seed saving.

HYBRID SEEDS vs OPEN-POLLINATED SEEDS

As mentioned earlier, hybrid tomatoes (often indicated with 'F1' on the seed packet) are carefully and industrially produced to be an end-game tomato. Hybrid seeds are designed to be repurchased each season, not to be saved. If they are saved and grown again, hybrid seeds will produce mongrel tomatoes of many types, with no assurance of consistency between generations.

Open-pollinated seed varieties, on the other hand, are bred to grow true to type. They have been pollinated out in the open – in a garden, not in a laboratory – with other tomatoes of the same variety to provide a consistent result, generation after generation. This type of variety can be successfully saved at home, although plenty of great seed companies produce open-pollinated varieties also.

So if you're interested in saving tomato seeds, first ensure that you have an open-pollinated variety, not a hybrid.

PLANNING FOR EFFECTIVE SEED SAVING

Happily, tomatoes are not one of those plants that need to be grown a long way apart from other varieties in order to prevent cross-pollination and grow true to type. That's because tomatoes have the ability to self-pollinate (their flowers are what are called 'complete flowers', with both male and female parts), and they will do so in the course of a normal season. Pollen-loving insects move between many flowers in a garden, though, so a little cross-pollination is possible, but there are ways to work around it.

Bush tomatoes

To get consistent results when saving seeds from a bush tomato variety, plant a block containing just one tomato variety. Then, identify healthy plants in the centre of your single-variety tomato patch and save the seeds from the fruit of these plants. The small amount of cross-pollination that will occur in this block will be with other tomatoes of the same variety.

Climbing tomatoes

Growing a single variety of climbing tomatoes that are separated from the next tomato variety by a physical barrier – trees, a row of climbing beans, a house, etc. – should be enough to provide consistent results when saving the seeds. Again, save seeds from fruit harvested from the best plants in the middle of the row or rows.

'SAVE YOUR BEST AND EAT THE REST'

This little saying pretty much sums up the way of choosing which seeds to save. Select the most perfect, well-shaped ripe fruit that you can find, from the most central tomato plants. Ripen it for a few days on a windowsill, and then get saving.

There are a few methods for saving tomato seeds and different growers swear by different methods. We use the fermentation method most often.

Fermentation method

The aim of the fermentation method is to maximise the tomato seed's viability and also protect it and its future plant against disease. During fermentation, a foamy white skin forms in the jar of tomato seeds, due to the presence of *Geotrichum candidum*, a fungus naturally found in and on fresh vegetables, which is fermenting the tomato seed pulp. This natural fermentation process introduces a protective antibiotic coating to the seeds that prevents some diseases, such as bacterial spot and canker, in your future tomato plants.

Scoop the tomato seeds into a jar of water and leave them to ferment. After a few days, strain them and then rinse to remove any remaining tomato flesh.

1. Take a few very ripe tomatoes and scoop their contents into a jar, adding a little water. Label and date the jar, then put it in a warm spot with a light covering to keep out flies.

2. Leave the jar undisturbed for a few days. Once a white foamy skin forms on top, add some more water to the jar and stir. The seeds to be saved will settle to the bottom, with the foam and remaining pulp on top. Carefully pour off the floating solids, leaving the seeds in the jar. Once you've poured off most of the gunk, pour the rest through a sieve and rinse the seeds under cold water.

3. Lay the rinsed seeds out to dry on absorbent paper, such as newspaper.

4. Once the seeds are dry, peel them off the paper and store in a labelled envelope, or simply fold over the paper and store the whole parcel in a labelled envelope, ready for next season.

Spread the clean seeds on newspaper or paper towel and leave them in the shade until they're completely dry.

Newspaper method

This method doesn't give the seeds an extra protective coating against disease, but it is a lot quicker and sometimes that's what you need.

1. Scoop out the pulp of a tomato, wash it in a sieve and apply the seeds straight to newspaper or other absorbent paper to dry.

2. Label and store the seeds as for the fermentation method above.

'Compost seedbank' method

This tomato seed-saving/starting technique came to us via a seed swap, at which someone mentioned an old tomato grower they knew who swore by this technique as his preferred way of growing strong tomato seedlings. In this method, the tomatoes are left to rot, naturally fermenting the flesh around the seeds with the same antibiotic coating as the fermentation method. The success of this technique relies largely on pest-proofing your bucket of seed tomatoes so that they don't get eaten before spring.

1. Place a few of your best tomatoes on a good layer of sieved, worm-free compost in a waterproof, pest-proof bucket with a lid. Cover the tomatoes with more sieved compost, then put the lid on the bucket. Label and store the bucket somewhere dark and cool for 6 months.

2. When it's early spring and time to start your tomatoes, take off the lid, position the bucket somewhere warm, and lightly water the compost each day until your seedlings emerge. Proceed as per the pricking out method on page 24.

STORING YOUR SEEDS

Store your tomato seeds (and all your garden seeds) somewhere cool, dry and dark – these are the big three factors in successful seed storage. A box of tins or envelopes works well, placed in a dark, cool cupboard. Always make sure your seeds are *entirely* dry before storing them.

ABOVE: Place a few of your best ripe tomatoes in a bucket of sieved compost, cover with more compost and cover with a lid. Open the bucket in spring, place it somewhere warm and lightly water each day until seedlings emerge.

OPPOSITE: Saving your own tomato seeds is a simple skill that ensures a lifetime supply of tomatoes.

TOMATOES IN THE KITCHEN

Suddenly, after so much planning, planting, watching and waiting, it's tomato season! Tomatoes everywhere, all the time, every day. Fresh tomatoes in salads, passata bubbling on the stove, racks of tomatoes drying. Tomatoes in buckets by the door, on every windowsill in the house, in baskets and trays along the top of the bookshelf and possibly even on the couch. Tomatoes for you, for your family and your friends. Tomatoes for your neighbour when he's sick. Tomatoes for the friend who's just had a baby and could do with some organic home-made love in her kitchen. Tomatoes for everyone.

And then, because of your good efforts during the crazy harvest time, tomatoes for autumn, winter and spring. Tomatoes aplenty in the dark, early evenings of winter, with garlic and beans and other wintery delights. Spicy preserved tomatoes in the frosty spring, in that gap between the winter vegies and the late-spring vegies.

Just keep that tomato-drenched utopia in mind, because things are about to get messy. If you've planted many tomatoes and the season has been kind, you will have a lot of tomatoes in late summer and early autumn.

Get sorted, get set and go hard. The effort is absolutely worth it and it's not forever.

PRESERVING ALL AT ONCE vs PRESERVING IN BATCHES

Some preserving techniques are designed, by the many generations of tomato growers and eaters who came before us, to deal with big gluts of tomatoes, often of the determinate type. But there's also the trickle (that can sometimes rise to a raging torrent) of the ripe indeterminate tomatoes – many big and small ones picked often, but not all at once.

Passata is particularly good for preserving all-at-once tomatoes, while drying and salting and pickling are good for smaller, more regular loads. That said, passata can also be made just a few jars at a time over the season. Those few jars, made a few nights a week, can lead to just as full a pantry as the epic passata-making day with all hands on deck. Once you've assessed your gear and resources, either approach can work.

If you're growing tomatoes, we encourage you to make preserving them a part of the life of your household throughout the whole tomato season – it's the best way to avoid getting overwhelmed and to ensure you make the most of this resource. Tomato preserving doesn't need to be the season's biggest project, it just needs to be done regularly – like the washing. Figure out an approach that works for you and do it consistently.

BY WHATEVER MEANS...

If you don't have an abundance of home-grown tomatoes, don't let that hold you back. Head to your local farmers' market or fruit store and organise a few boxes of great-quality sauce tomatoes. You'll still end up with a pantry full of home-made goodness.

Slicing small tomatoes in half to dry is a great way to store intermittent harvests.

MAKING PASSATA

Passata is simply tomato purée or crushed tomatoes. Some people will tell you that it must not contain skin nor seeds, but are we going to waste all that home-grown goodness? No way! Leave the skin and seeds out if you wish, but we make our passata with the whole tomato, to capture every morsel of nutrient-dense happiness.

When you're making passata on a grand scale, a motorised passata machine can help. The tomatoes go in the top, pulp comes out the side and the seeds and skin come out the end. You can then recombine the pulp with the seeds and skin for whole tomato passata.

If you're making passata on a smaller scale, a food processor is fine – whiz up the whole tomatoes and you're done. You can add herbs and garlic as well, if you choose.

Alternatively, if your tomatoes are dense, beefsteak types, you can just quarter them and add them to clean jars with basil and salt. Smash them down a bit until their liquid covers them, add 2 tablespoons of lemon juice or vinegar per 1 litre (4 cups) with salt to taste and process like that. As long as your jars of tomatoes contain enough acid for them to be safe long term, there's enough liquid to cover all tomatoes and the jars are pasteurised correctly, the options and recipes for preserved tomatoes are pretty endless. See page 52 for the basic procedure.

RIGHT: Preserving quartered beefsteak tomatoes in jars with fresh basil.

BELOW: Making passata on a large scale using a motorised passata machine.

OPPOSITE: Red pear tomatoes (an old Italian sauce variety) and basil, ready to make passata.

TOMATO PASSATA

Lots of lovely ripe tomatoes
Herbs and garlic, to taste (optional)
Salt
Lemon juice or vinegar (see Tips)

You'll also need:
A large pot for mixing the passata
Clean bottles or jars of a uniform size, with
    well-fitting metal lids
A big pot with a metal rack in the bottom, or
    similar, for pasteurising the passata bottles
A thermometer

1. Mush, crush or pulverise the tomatoes, then transfer them to a large pot. Add herbs and garlic, if you like. At this point, if you want extra-thick passata or even tomato paste (concentrated purée), simmer the mixture until it reaches the desired consistency. (We rarely do this because it takes extra time and there are just too many tomatoes. It's up to you.)

2. Once you're ready to bottle your passata, measure how much tomato pulp you have. Add 1 teaspoon of salt per 4 litres (1 gallon) of tomato pulp, and add 2 tablespoons of lemon juice or vinegar per 1 litre (4 cups) of pulp.

3. Ladle the passata into the clean bottles or jars, leaving 2 cm (¾ inch) free at the top. Tightly seal with the lids.

4. Pour water into the big pot with the metal rack in the bottom so that it will come up to the top 5 cm (2 inches) of your bottles or jars, without covering them. Heat the water until it measures 85°C (185°F) on your thermometer, then carefully add the bottles, making sure they don't touch. The water temperature will drop once the bottles are added, then slowly rise again. Once the temperature reaches 95°C (203°F), keep it at that temperature for 40 minutes, then turn off the heat (or switch your bottles for another batch). Carefully remove the bottles and set them aside to cool. Repeat the process until all your bottles of passata have been pasteurised.

5. Once the bottles of passata are cool, label them with a date and what they are. Stored somewhere cool and dark, the passata will keep for at least 12 months, although ours always get eaten before then.

Other pasteurising techniques

The rack in the bottom of the pot is there to prevent the bottles rattling against each other while they're pasteurising. Some other alternatives are to place each jar inside a sock or wrap it in newspaper and secure it with string, then put the jars directly into your pot – this will stop the rattling and prevent breakage.

On a large scale, the sock or newspaper method is sometimes used around bottles that are placed on their sides inside a 44-gallon drum of water that is heated over a fire. It's good fun but it does take a long time, so it depends on your set-up.

Fundamentally, if you can heat the passata bottles to 95°C (203°F) and maintain that temperature for 40 minutes, they should seal and store well.

TIPS

Apple cider vinegar, apple scrap vinegar (see page 240) or white vinegar will all work well.

You can buy special preserving jars for your passata, but using regular jars or recycling your old jars is also fine, as long as they have undamaged, screw-top metal lids. You can even use longneck beer bottles with caps – make sure you label and date them!

Make sure everything is super-clean. When we are making passata on a community scale using longneck beer bottles, we sterilise all the bottles by giving them a final rinse in a bucket of clean water with a few small drops of iodine in it. (You can buy iodine from homebrew stores.)

ACIDITY

Acids keep fruit, and also tomatoes, safe to eat in their shelf-stable, bottled form. When bottling fruit, you usually increase the acidity by adding sugar. When bottling tomatoes, it's more common to do this by adding either vinegar or lemon juice. Some tomatoes (especially some heirloom varieties) are more acidic than others, which is why some old recipes don't add acid when making passata. But 'best practice' says that you should add vinegar or lemon juice at a rate of 2 tablespoons (or use half a teaspoon of citric acid) per 1 litre (4 cups) of passata. This ensures that the acidity is high enough to make the passata super-safe to eat for many months to come.

Large-scale tomato passata making using a passata machine to crush the chopped tomatoes. The passata is bottled in longneck beer bottles and capped before it goes into the 85°C (185°F) waterbath for pasteurising. Don't forget to label the bottles! And enjoy...

DRYING TOMATOES

Drying is a great technique for cherry tomatoes, which ripen over a long period – you can slowly build up your stocks to jars and jars of them. Add dried tomatoes to slow-cooked stews for a tangy kick, or rehydrate them with a little water and stir them into pasta sauces, scatter them on pizzas or toss them through salads.

We usually use an electric dehydrator for drying our tomatoes, but if it's very hot and sunny at your place, putting the drying racks outside in a sunny spot (or on the dashboard of your car!) can do the trick within a few days. The low-energy methods described for drying fruit in the Wild Food chapter (see pages 282–284) can also be used for tomatoes.

To dry cherry tomatoes, halve your tomatoes (or slice larger ones into segments) and place them on a drying rack. Once they're dry, store them in sealed containers and eat them within 12 months – their flavour will taper off over this time.

OPPOSITE: Small tomatoes are sliced and spread on a rack for drying. After one day, the tomatoes are semi-dried – use them as they are, or dry completely for long-term storage.

BELOW: The final result – completely dried, shelf-stable tomatoes.

Often at the end of the season you'll have a bunch of green tomatoes that you need to pick before the frost hits. Green tomatoes are great in chutneys and relishes, but this recipe, adapted from 'Pomodoro verde sott'olio' from the book *Mangia! Mangia!* by Angela Villella and Teresa Oates, is our favourite way to preserve them. It is worth the effort. We use it on sandwiches, with eggs… with everything!

GREEN TOMATOES IN OLIVE OIL

Green tomatoes
Salt
Apple cider vinegar
Sliced fresh chilli
Sliced garlic
Dried oregano
Olive oil

1. Thinly slice all the tomatoes (if you're using cherry tomatoes, just halve them). Add the tomatoes to a clean bowl or bucket in 5 cm (2 inch) layers, sprinkling salt over each layer. Place a plate on top of the tomatoes and add a heavy weight on top of that (a big jar of water is good). Leave the tomatoes to sweat for 24 hours.

2. The next day, the tomatoes will be sitting beneath a brine. Take them out, a double handful at a time, and drain them to remove as much moisture as you can. Transfer each handful to a clean bowl. Set aside the tomato brine – we use it in soups and stews.

3. Once all the tomatoes have been drained, pour equal parts of apple cider vinegar and water over the tomatoes to barely cover them. Cover with a plate and add a weight on top. Leave the tomatoes for another 24 hours.

4. The next day, drain the tomatoes once more. Mix through some sliced chilli, garlic and some dried oregano, to taste. Loosely pack the mixture into sterilised jars (see Tip), leaving 5 cm (2 inches) free at the top of the jars.

5. Pour olive oil over the tomatoes in each jar, filling the jars to the top. Tightly screw on the lids and store somewhere cool for at least 2 weeks before using. The tomatoes will keep for up to 6 months.

TIP

To sterilise jars, first wash the jars and lids, and drain well. Then, put the jars in a 150°C (300°F) oven for 30 minutes. Carefully remove the hot jars from the oven and they're good to go – use them while they're still hot if possible.

57

MILKWOOD | The Tomato

This lovely recipe is for the height of summer, when fresh tomatoes are at their best. It's amazing in burritos or as a side salad. It doesn't store for very long, so make it in small batches and make it regularly. Probiotic goodness at its most tasty.

FERMENTED TOMATO SALSA

500 g (1 lb 2 oz) tomatoes, diced
½ red onion, thinly sliced
1 handful fresh coriander (cilantro), chopped
Pinch of cumin seeds
Pinch of dill seeds
1 tablespoon whey (the clear liquid sitting
    on the top of plain yoghurt will do)
Salt

1. Mix the tomatoes, onion, coriander and spices in a bowl. Transfer the mixture to a clean jar, add the whey and then muddle the ingredients a bit with a rolling pin or similar.

2. Make up a 2% brine solution, using 2 g salt to every 100 ml water (approximately ½ teaspoon salt for every ½ cup water). Pour in enough of the brine to barely cover the tomatoes in the jar.

3. Lightly screw on the lid. Stir the tomatoes daily for 3 to 4 days (or less if the weather is very warm). Taste them as you go and eat when they are tangy and delicious. Once the salsa is ready, it will keep for a few days.

TIPS

If you can't find any whey, you can leave it out. The fermentation process will take a little longer, but it will still work fine.

Add or subtract whatever herbs and spices you like in this recipe.

Shakshouka is a beloved Middle Eastern tomato and egg dish that is often eaten for breakfast or supper. There are a million variations. Here's how we make ours – it's an easy fireside meal that will serve two to three people, depending on how hungry they are!

SHAKSHOUKA

1 onion, finely diced
Olive oil
4 garlic cloves, crushed
Large pinch of cumin seeds
1 litre (4 cups) tomato passata or
    1 kg (2 lb 4 oz) tomatoes, chopped
1 red capsicum (pepper), sliced
1 heaped teaspoon paprika
2 handfuls of herbs, chopped (basil, oregano
    or whatever you have)
2 tablespoons crumbled feta cheese
Salt and pepper, to taste
4 fresh eggs

1. Take a cast iron frying pan or other heavy frying pan and fry the onion in a slosh of olive oil for 5 minutes. Add the crushed garlic and cumin seeds and fry for a few more minutes. Stir in the passata or chopped tomatoes, capsicum and paprika. Simmer until the tomatoes and capsicum are tender and the mixture has thickened a bit.

2. Sprinkle the chopped herbs and crumbled feta over the tomato mixture and season, to taste. Make four small holes in the surface – this will help the eggs stay put. Carefully crack an egg into each hole. Cover the pan and simmer over low heat for 5–10 minutes or until the eggs are cooked to your liking.

3. Spoon the shakshouka onto serving plates and eat with some crusty bread spread with lashings of butter, and a green salad.

QUICK TOMATO AND WAKAME SALAD

We learned this quick-to-make summer treat from Su Dennett, founder of Melliodora Permaculture, where we live. It's a great way to eat fresh tomatoes and get an extra nutrient kick at the same time, thanks to the seaweed.

Slice your tomatoes as you like to eat them and place in a bowl. Sprinkle with finely flaked dried wakame seaweed (flaked nori would also work beautifully) and stir to combine. Set aside for 30 minutes before serving. The moisture in the tomatoes will soak into the seaweed and turn the salad into a deliciously salty, umami powerhouse.

MUSHROOM CULTIVATION

PINK
OYSTER

PEARL OYSTER

LION'S
MANE

GOLDEN OYSTER

KING OYSTER

PEARL OYSTER

SHIITAKE

MAY THE MYCELIUM BE WITH YOU

Mushrooms are meaty soul food, in fungal form. They're not even in the same kingdom as plants or animals, and yet they taste like both, at once.

Learning how to grow mushrooms from scratch is a little bit like learning a magic trick. And yet, once you have the basic skills and principles sorted out, it's really very doable. Fungi are both complex and simple. They need certain things to grow well, and if you don't provide these they will sulk and produce no mushrooms. But the kingdom of fungi is also hugely generous and capable of producing incredible amounts of nutrient-rich mushrooms from simple waste substances – again, and again, and again. You just need to get to know them.

Blue oysters, garden giants, enokitake, pink oysters, turkey tail, shiitake, reishi, pioppini. A whole world of mushrooms can be grown down the side of your house. It's crazy but true.

Cultivating mushrooms is an excellent way to vastly increase both the diversity and the nutrition of your home-grown produce. And conveniently, mushrooms can be grown in disused areas with little light, so they slot into a home-grown food system without competing for the same space as your other growing projects. Down the shady, paved side of your house where not much else grows, in buckets in the empty space under the porch, under your stairs, or even under your couch can all be great places to cultivate mushrooms. Don't have much light? Mushrooms don't mind. If they have a stable temperature to grow in and can be moved to a humid environment to fruit in, they're happy.

As a bonus, home mushroom cultivation can be run mainly, or exclusively if you like, on common waste products – woodchips, coffee grounds, straw, cardboard, tree prunings, and so on. The cost for setting up home cultivation can be very small, and once you get right into it, you can harvest all year round, and each month can be packed with nutrient-dense mushroom goodness.

Don't be put off by the technical 'mushroom speak'. Generally, mushrooms are not well understood, but once you've got the fundamentals straight, the processes are straightforward. And then you'll have a potential lifetime of mushroom harvests ahead of you to nourish and heal your family, to swap and share, and you'll be able to teach others how to grow them as well. Bring on the mushrooms.

Types of fungi

Fungi are divided into two main categories, mycorrhizal fungi and saprotrophic fungi. Mycorrhizal fungi form a partnership with some plants, mostly with living trees. You can read more about these in the Wild Food chapter on page 276. Saprotrophic fungi prefer dead and decaying material. This group contains the largest number of species. If you're new to mushroom cultivation, we suggest working with a few different species of saprotrophic fungi – specifically, delicious edible ones that grow mushrooms on wood or on straw.

OPPOSITE: Some of the many edible mushrooms you can cultivate at home.

THE BIOLOGY AND HISTORY OF MUSHROOMS

FUNGI AND MUSHROOMS

Fungi are an entirely separate kingdom of life – they're not a plant, nor an animal. They're weird and amazing. Without them, life on earth might not exist.

The kingdom of fungi (*Eumycota*) encompasses yeasts, tinea, penicillium, moulds, blights and mushrooms, to name just a few. Compared to animals and plants, very little is known about this kingdom of life. It's estimated that there may be up to 6 million species of fungi, although only about 1.5 per cent of those have been formally classified – compare that with the total of 300,000 species of plants on earth!

Mushrooms are the fruiting bodies of some types of fungi. A mushroom-producing fungi spends the majority of its life cycle hidden under, or inside, other substances – substances like wood, soil or straw – in the form of mycelium, which slowly colonises and eats that substance, before fruiting into mushrooms.

It's thought that there are about 10,000 species of mushroom-producing fungi worldwide. Of these, about 30 species are grown commercially or on a home scale. There are only a handful of deadly species, and about 25 seriously poisonous species in total. Of course, these are very good to know if you're a mushroom forager. Mushroom cultivation is different to foraging, though – it's the process of growing just one species of mushroom at a time, in a controlled environment.

The parts of a mushroom, rising from its mycelial network.

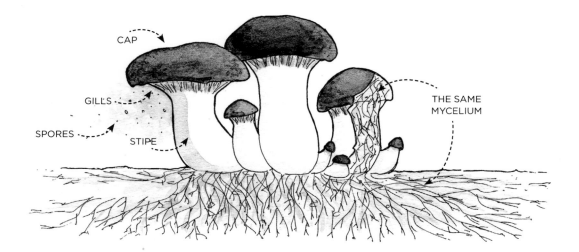

CAP

GILLS

SPORES

STIPE

THE SAME MYCELIUM

LIFE CYCLE OF A MUSHROOM

Mushrooms start off as spores, emitted from a mushroom much like seeds from a seed pod. When a spore lands on a suitable substance, it grows into a hypha – a little thread composed mainly of mycochitin, a similar substance to that which crustaceans use to make their shells.

When two or more hypha grow near each other, they bond together and share their genes to produce mycelium, a large network of hyphae, looking a little like a branching web of delicate white threads or roots.

Different mycelium eat different things. Some break down whatever woody substances they can get close to. Some mycelium have special relationships with certain tree species, sharing sugars and other nutrients with plant roots. Some mycelium eat insects, or live within them. They're truly embedded into every aspect of life on earth, in a range of symbiotic roles.

Once the mycelium has colonised and eaten as much of its chosen food as it can, and when conditions are right, the mycelium will start to form fruiting bodies in the form of mushrooms, to reproduce and extend its territory.

Mushrooms are incredible little pieces of life. They're 'anti-gravity', meaning they'll push upwards with uncanny force, through wood or soil or sometimes even asphalt in a bid to get up into the fresh air and the light, to spread their spores. Just a few days later, they're rotted and gone. Like peaches, mushrooms are a tasty, unprotected food – their mission is to be eaten. In the process of being knocked about, picked up or generally taken apart, their tiny spores spread near and far, in their millions, with some spores landing in just the right spot to begin the process of life all over again.

The life cycle of fungi, which results in mushrooms as the fruiting bodies.

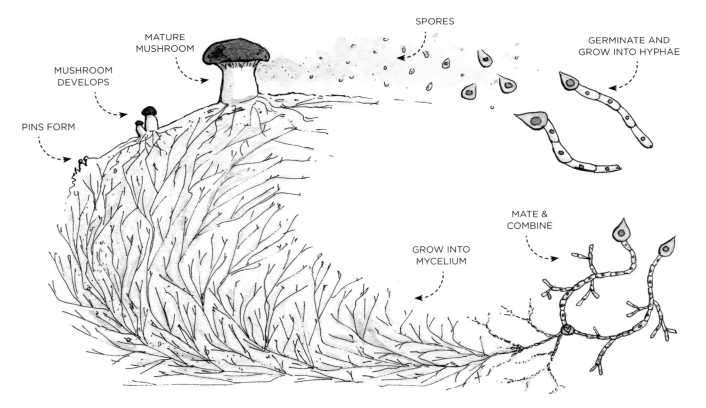

SPORES

GERMINATE AND GROW INTO HYPHAE

MATURE MUSHROOM

MUSHROOM DEVELOPS

PINS FORM

MATE & COMBINE

GROW INTO MYCELIUM

MUSHROOMS AND HUMANS

Mushrooms and humans have, in many ways, co-evolved ever since there were homo sapiens to forage, taste, eat and distribute edible and useful mushrooms across the earth. Ötzi the Iceman, preserved since around 3300 BC, was found to be carrying two mushrooms – a tinder fungus in his fire-starting kit, and a medicinal birch polypore.

There's evidence that the Romans and the Egyptians had mushrooms on their menus, and the Aztecs and Mayans used mushrooms for ceremony. Asian rulers commanded envoys to go out and seek the medicinal *Ganoderma* (reishi) growing out of certain plum trees up to 4000 years ago. And so it follows that every culture that has lived where wild mushrooms grow had all kinds of uses for them, from Australia all the way to Russia.

All these ancient mushrooms were foraged – gathered from the wild – as opposed to cultivated. Cultivating mushrooms isn't hard once you know what you're doing, but figuring out how to cultivate specific mycelium was an enormous leap forward in our relationship with fungi. The first record of edible mushrooms being specifically cultivated as opposed to foraged is in about 1000 AD, with *Lentinula* (shiitake / xiang gu) being cultivated in Qingyuan county in China.

The first European cultivation of mushrooms is not precisely known, but there's a famous story about a Parisian market gardener in the 17th century pouring wash water from wild mushrooms (which would have contained the mushrooms' spores) over some melon offcuts, and inadvertently producing a mushroom harvest of *Agaricus bisporus* (button mushrooms) soon after. The canny gardener repeated and refined the process, and was soon selling the mushrooms commercially.

Then there's another story that Parisian market gardeners noticed there were always good crops of field mushrooms found in horse manure (their main fertiliser of the era, hauled in by the tonne), and so started cultivating them that way. Then it was discovered that caves provided a stable, moist climate for reliable cultivation, and soon there was a cultivated mushroom industry for *Agaricus bisporus* across Europe.

The amazing extent of mushroom cultivation as we know it now is very recent, however. Up until the 1970s it was pretty impossible to get any cultivated mushrooms in Europe other than button mushrooms and truffles. All other mushrooms were wild-sourced, and limited to seasonal eating. As the world shrank and mycology advanced, however, the mushrooms spread (maybe this was all part of their plan) and now it's possible to get spawn for dozens of edible species on nearly every continent.

ABOVE: Shiitake mushrooms fruiting on a scribbly gum (*Eucalyptus haemastoma*) log in our shade house.

OPPOSITE: A gorgeous flush of pearl oyster mushrooms, ready to become dinner.

CULTIVATING MUSHROOMS AT HOME

Once you demystify the mushroom cultivation process, it's not unlike growing plants in many ways. You're just dealing with a different kingdom of life, which has different life cycles, needs and outputs. When you understand the basics, you can get creative. And if you get hooked, no garden or home of yours will ever be without edible mushrooms again.

Over the years we've learned different cultivation techniques from different experts, hobbyists and mad mushroom folk (there are quite a few of those). Cultivation can be done inside, outside or wherever you have some space, and requires zero specialised equipment to get started.

We've slowly developed a cultivation process that works well for us on a home scale.

Waste-free mushroom cultivation, with no single-use plastic.

SPORE PRINT OR TISSUE CULTURE

GRAIN SPAWN
(sterilised grain)

JAR CULTURE:
ALMOST ANY SPECIES
(sterilised enriched hardwood sawdust)

MULTIPLICATION OF GRAIN SPAWN

SAWDUST OR DOWEL SPAWN
(sterilised hardwood sawdust or hardwood dowels)

LOG CULTURE
(fresh hardwood logs)

BUCKET CULTURE
(pasteurised straw/hardwood sawdust)

WOODCHIP BED CULTURE
(soaked hardwood woodchips)

GARDEN GIANTS,
WOOD BLEWITS

SHIITAKE, TURKEY TAIL,
LION'S MANE, VELVET PIOPPINI

PEARL OYSTER, PINK OYSTER,
BLUE OYSTER, GOLDEN OYSTER

It is possible to cultivate mushrooms from scratch using the tissue culture of an existing mushroom. This is extremely cool but it is also extremely fiddly, with no guarantee of success when you're a beginner and you don't have all the right equipment. So we'll show you how to start at the spawn stage and work forward from there.

There are multiple paths you can take to grow your mushrooms from the spawn stage. Container cultivation (see page 81) covers growing mushrooms in buckets, jars and bags, in a semi-controlled environment. Outdoor cultivation (see page 99) covers growing mushrooms on logs, stumps and in gardens, letting the seasons do most of the work for you. Choose your own mycelial adventure. Or do both.

GROWING FROM SPAWN

Your first bag, jar or bucket of spawn will look like a white lump of mysterious goodness. It can be purchased from a mushroom supplier or, if you're lucky, a friendly mushroom grower. Spawn is simply substrate – the food that mycelium likes to eat – that has been fully colonised by said mycelium, that is, the white stuff (or possibly brown, depending on the species).

Importantly, healthy spawn is substrate that has been colonised by a single species of mycelium – the species that you want to grow. Whether it's oyster, shiitake or pioppini, that spawn will contain just the mycelium for that species, growing on a high-nutrient substrate (often grain) that makes the mycelium grow fast.

A bag of spawn can be used a bit like a bag of seeds, in the sense that you can inoculate lots more substrate (known as your fruiting substrate) with this spawn. Once that mycelium has eaten up its new substrate, the mycelium will fruit into mushrooms.

Depending on the species of mushroom you want to grow, your fruiting substrate might be logs or stumps in your backyard, or straw laid down in a garden bed. It might be coffee grounds and sawdust packed into a bucket or a jar. All these materials can be food for mycelium, although different species prefer different materials.

BELOW LEFT: Grain spawn, about to be mixed with pasteurised substrate.

BELOW: King oyster mushrooms growing on a block of well-colonised substrate/spawn mix.

BEST TYPES OF MUSHROOMS FOR BEGINNERS

Mushroom cultivation is quite different from going for a walk in a pine forest at the right time of year to gather a basket of wild mushrooms. Although, if you set up your mushroom gardens well, it can feel a lot like that experience.

Starting off with a species that will grow no matter what is a good idea. There's nothing like a feast of successfully home-grown mushrooms to spur you on to further cultivation. Of course, once you've mastered the process, you can branch out (like a mycelium!) to other mushrooms that have more specific needs. Here are the mushrooms we recommend when you're starting out on your mushroom cultivating journey.

Pleurotus ostreatus (pearl oyster)

The species we recommend starting with for bucket or jar cultivation is the pearl oyster. There are lots of *Pleurotus* (oyster) species, including *Pleurotus djamor* (pink oyster), *Pleurotus eryngii* (king oyster) and *Pleurotus citrinopileatus* (golden oyster). However, some of these other varieties are slightly more fiddly than *Pleurotus ostreatus*, so pearl oyster is a good starting point.

Preferred fruiting substrates: Oyster mushrooms prefer pasteurised straw or sawdust, but will fruit well on most farm waste products containing cellulose and lignin. They also like hardwood logs or stumps for outdoor cultivation. Waste coffee grounds are becoming popular among urban growers of oyster mushrooms, but note that they must be used while very fresh as they have a relatively high nutrient content and can be prone to contamination.

Climate: *Pleurotus ostreatus* are awesomely adaptable and will tolerate a range of growing conditions. They should fruit anywhere from 7–25°C (45–77°F).

Time from inoculation to fruiting: Quick. From 2 to 3 weeks for indoor cultivation, depending on ambient temperature and the inoculation rates of substrate.

PLEUROTUS ERYNGII (KING OYSTER)

Considered by many to be the best tasting oyster mushroom, king oysters are a meaty, full feast that can be sliced and barbecued. They crisp up when stir-fried, yet stay wonderfully chewy and nutty. They can be grown in a similar way to pearl oysters, but their superior flavour makes them worth mentioning. Once you've mastered pearl oysters, give them a go.

PEARL OYSTER

SHIITAKE

VELVET PIOPPINI

Lentinula edodes (shiitake)

Shiitake are a great species to use when you are starting outdoor cultivation. They will grow on logs in your garden. Although they're a lot slower to fruit than oyster mushrooms, if you inoculate a batch of logs every year (or even better, every season), you can soon have a regular supply of shiitakes.

Preferred fruiting substrates: Hardwood logs of almost every type, though yields will vary according to the log species. Eucalypts work well if you can't find oak, beech or alder. They can also be grown on sawdust.

Climate: There are different strains of shiitake, but the main strain that we use fruits between 14 and 20°C (57 and 68°F), which is a wide enough bracket for most temperate climates. There are both colder and warmer strains that fruit below, and above, that temperature envelope.

Time from inoculation to fruiting: Long. On logs: from 6 to 12 months (or longer), depending on climate and inoculation rates of the log. On sawdust blocks: 7 to 10 weeks. Worth the wait!

Shiitake mushrooms emerging from eucalyptus logs.

Agrocybe aegerita (velvet pioppini)

Native to poplar wood, this is a delicious mushroom with a nutty bite. It's great for stir-fries and other cooking methods.

Preferred fruiting substrates: Hardwood sawdust is best. This one is great for jar cultivation. It also does well on logs and stumps.

Climate: Keep it cool – pioppinos like to stay around 13–18°C (55–64°F), and tend to fruit in the spring, after the colder months.

Time from inoculation to fruiting: Long – 8 to 12 months for outdoor log cultivation or about 6 weeks for indoor cultivation.

Stropharia rugosoannulata (king stropharia or garden giant)

This is our favourite mushroom to grow in woodchip gardens. It's easy to grow and delicious to eat.

Preferred fruiting substrates: Hardwood woodchips are preferred, but, like oyster mushrooms, king stropharia will grow in straw and many other farm waste products.

Climate: King stropharia grow in a very broad range of temperatures, from about 5–35°C (41–95°F), so they're great for both temperate and subtropical climates. They do need good moisture, however, so make sure this is supplied consistently.

Time from inoculation to fruiting: Long. About 4 to 6 months, depending on inoculation rates and which substrate you use.

KING STROPHARIA

KEEP IT CLEAN!

Mushroom cultivation is all about figuring out a way to get only the mycelium of your choice to grow on something. That's easier said than done, as our world involves all sorts of spores, bacteria and other microbiology constantly existing on absolutely everything. Everything wants to try and grow. And it will – no matter what you do.

The key to the mushroom cultivation game is figuring out low-energy, non-toxic ways of giving your chosen mycelium a head start on all the other microbiology. The best way to do this is to keep everything as clean as you possibly can, at every stage of cultivation. This is why we pasteurise or sterilise the substrate – to nullify most of the microbial competition and give our chosen mycelium an opportunity to eat first, so it can win the race and fruit into tasty mushrooms.

Contamination will still sometimes occur. Somewhere, somehow, an undesirable mould or bacteria will find its way in and establish itself, turning your carefully stewarded bucket of substrate unsettling shades of green, pink or grey. There's nothing to do but throw it on the compost pile and start again.

Curiously, though, successful home mushroom cultivation doesn't require going into total microbial lockdown or attempting to annihilate all life. Some of the microbiology out there will actually *help* your mycelium to thrive and protect it from invasion. Think of it as being similar to creating great gut health or growing a successful organic garden. The goal is to find ways to encourage the species you want to thrive, and ensure that the species you don't want aren't given a chance to establish.

The main point is this: keep your mushroom cultivation process as clean as possible and, when you're working in the open air with a just-prepared substrate, work quickly and don't break for lunch. That's all you need to do. Formaldehyde-soaked substrates or sterile suits and hair nets aren't necessary for successful home cultivation. Between your careful hands, good technique and the friendly microbes of the world, you'll soon be on your way to cultivating many mushrooms.

RIGHT: Enokitake in their 'wild' form, grown on sawdust in preserving jars.

OPPOSITE: A home harvest of lion's mane, tan oysters, pearl oysters, shiitake and king oyster mushrooms.

CONTAINER CULTIVATION

Container cultivation is a super-flexible way to grow mushrooms, no matter where you live. All you need to get started are suitable airtight containers, some substrate and some mushroom spawn.

THE SPAWN

The spawn you use for this stage of mushroom cultivation usually comes in a bag or a jar, either from a mushroom supplier or from a friend who's already making some. As a guide, 2 kg (about 4 lb) of mushroom spawn should allow you to inoculate 50 litres (12 gallons) of substrate, and yield about 5–10 kg (about 10–20 lb) of mushrooms, which is a lot. Yum.

THE SUBSTRATE

There are many options for container substrate, and it's important for the long-term resilience of your mushrooms that you choose a source that's locally available, preferably a waste product. The best substrates for home mushroom cultivation are high in cellulose and lignin but not too high in sugars and proteins. Mycelium has an amazing ability to eat cellulose and lignin, which no other organisms can, so you can use this to your advantage. Some species of mycelium do prefer certain types of substrate, so do a bit of research first.

A good fruiting substrate is made of small pieces of either cellulose, lignin or a combination of the two – materials like straw, sawdust, woodchips, logs, wood pellets, cardboard pellets, sugarcane mulch (bagasse) or similar. It's nearly always possible to find one of these substances that is locally available, low cost, clean, fresh and, if possible, organic (and with no plastic packaging).

OPPOSITE: Re-usable food-grade buckets can be a low-cost way to grow lots of mushrooms in a small space.

BELOW: King oyster mushrooms growing out of well-colonised substrate.

MINIMISING CONTAMINATION

Although mycelium can eat just about any organic matter, for beginners it's best to steer clear of anything that includes too much sugar or protein. This includes coffee grounds, hay, chaff, grass clippings, wheat or rice bran, whole grains or seeds. Basically, if the material could be fed to animals, it's too rich to use without experienced handling. If it's used for animal bedding, it's much more likely to work for beginner mushroom growers.

If you want to use these richer kinds of materials (and their extra nutrient value can really increase fruiting), you will need to thoroughly sterilise your substrates and be extremely cautious with your cleanliness, otherwise you will get a lot of contamination from competing moulds.

HOME STERILISING

The easiest way to sterilise substrate or grain at home is with a pressure cooker, and this works well for small volumes. However, this is another reason that we use mostly pasteurisation – pasteurising substrate can be done on a much larger scale than sterilisation at home, with very simple tools.

PASTEURISATION AND STERILISATION

There are two main routes for preparing your substrate for inoculation: pasteurisation and sterilisation. For beginners, we recommend focusing on pasteurisation – the easiest way to confidently grow mushrooms. Once you've become adept at mushroom growing, you can move on to the more complicated business of sterilising substrates if you like. Refer to the Resources section on page 292 for further information.

Pasteurisation is simpler, quicker and less energy intensive. It involves removing most, but not all, microbes from the substrate before you add the spawn. It gives your mycelium a head start over the rest of the organisms in the material, while being a relatively quick and easy process. Pasteurisation is fine for most purposes in mushroom cultivation, and is the method we most commonly use. We use it to prepare substrate for bucket cultivation as well as mushroom gardens.

Sterilisation is more tricky, as it involves removing all (or very nearly all) life from your substrate before inoculation. Sterilisation takes longer, needs more equipment and also requires more fastidious cleanliness to work well. That said, once you get it right, it's a short-cut to good mushroom harvests, as your spawn has no competition from microbes to worry about when colonising the substrate. Using sterilisation, you can also use higher nutrient substrates, which will make your mushrooms fruit faster, and more profusely. We use sterilisation and nutrient-rich substrates to maximise mushroom harvests when using glass jars. Sterilised jar culture can also allow you to experiment with different species and substrate combinations on a small, manageable scale, as you can watch the mycelium develop through the glass.

FRUITING CONTAINERS

Choosing which vessels to fruit your mushrooms in will depend on the resources around you. Historically and across the world, people have fruited mushrooms in everything from boxes, bags and buckets, to clay pipes, woven straw shapes, laundry baskets, gardens, logs, jars, tins, wooden barrels and even blue jeans!

For beginners, it's best to choose a vessel that can start off clean, can be made fairly airtight until you want to let air in, and is readily available and affordable. Three of the most common fruiting vessels are bags, buckets and jars.

Breathing is important!

When considering fruiting vessels, remember that mycelium needs to breathe if it is to grow, thrive and fruit into mushrooms. There are many ways to make simple DIY filters in either the lid or bag neck of your fruiting vessel. The filter stops contaminants getting in and allows the mycelium to breathe.

The easiest way to create a filter is by drilling a large hole in the lid of your container and plugging it with something that breathes, with the fibres allowing for a hole size of under 0.3 microns – this is the established size of hole at which moulds and bacteria cannot pass through, but air still can.

While this sounds awfully technical, there are plenty of everyday materials that you can use. Poly-fil (polyester pillow stuffing), cotton wadding or surgical

THE PLASTIC QUESTION

Growing organic mushrooms in plastic might seem like a weird contradiction in terms. What if the mushrooms eat the plastic? And even if the mycelium doesn't eat it, surely it will absorb the plastic toxins?

None of us want more plastic in our lives, in our food or in our ecosystems. However, sturdy, recycled, food-grade buckets are, in our view, appropriate to use for mushroom cultivation. The mushrooms that you're cultivating prefer to eat very specific things, and the fungi we're cultivating prefer lignin and cellulose far above plastic. Fungi are pretty amazing and might, if you left them in a plastic tub for a long, long time, start to break down the plastic. But even if they did, they would do just that – chemically break down the plastic into carbon and hydrogen, to use as food.

In terms of the plastic off-gassing and being absorbed by the mycelium, it depends on the quality and grade of the plastic you use. We use food-grade plastic buckets when we cultivate mushrooms in plastic because we think it's the most inert and safe plastic option.

We use a combination of glass jars, plastic buckets and outdoor gardens for our mushroom cultivation. Use what you think is best and can easily access. If the alternative is buying mushrooms from a store, you will almost certainly be eating mushrooms that have been grown in single-use plastic bags anyway.

Food-grade buckets are stackable, while allowing mushrooms to fruit out sideways. This helps when growing in small spaces.

(micropore) tape will do a good job. Or you could use silicone to glue a patch of synthetic material cut from disposable polypropylene painting suits (e.g. Tyvek) over the hole.

Bags

You can buy a variety of plastic mushroom bags, in lots of different sizes and colours, that have a small air filter on the side. Many of them are made of polypropylene, so they can withstand the high heat of sterilisation, which means you can sterilise your substrate in the bag, before adding the spawn.

However, most of these bags are single use (although you can re-use the polypropylene ones if you're careful), so we try not to use them in home cultivation. The exception is strong recycled plastic bags or bags that are otherwise headed for landfill. Look around at what you have and also ask around – see what your family and friends buy regularly in suitable plastic bags, and get them to save the bags for you.

If you're using recycled bags, make sure they're clean and dry, and that you have an effective method for tightly closing them, while still including an air filter.

Buckets

We often use buckets for mushroom cultivation. Plastic buckets are easy to clean, re-usable for many years, easy to store (both empty and full), and are sturdy and weatherproof. Once the buckets are full of inoculated substrate, we can simply stack them in a corner out of the way (often in the lounge room under the couch because it's a stable room temperature) until it's time to check them for signs that they're ready to fruit.

After fruiting, we use the spent mycelium to inoculate our mushroom gardens, and give the buckets a good clean before storing them, ready to use again.

Jars

Jars with lids are another great re-usable fruiting vessel, and are usually used with sterilised substrate. They're easy to clean and easy to store, and when the substrate is fully colonised (which you can see, thanks to the glass), you simply take off the lid, trigger fruiting and place the jars in your fruiting chamber. If your jars outweigh the number of fruiting shelves you have, stack them on their sides with the open necks pointing outwards.

If you use solid canning or preserving jars, you can sterilise the substrate in the jars inside a pressure cooker, and then add the spawn. Or you can just pack the jars with inoculated substrate following the steps on page 86.

Of course, given that a jar has a much smaller volume than a bucket, you won't get as many mushrooms per container. But there are advantages to the small size – using jars means that if one of your vessels gets contaminated and starts growing crazy colours, you won't have lost as much of your total harvest. The jars also look beautiful when the mushrooms are fruiting.

ABOVE: Jars allow you to watch the mycelium colonise the substrate, without opening.

OPPOSITE: Blue oysters fruiting out of old preserving jars.

DIY MUSHROOM BAG AND
FILTER SYSTEM

This design is as basic as it gets, but it can still produce a very decent harvest of mushrooms. It's great for tight budgets and those without access to sturdier containers.

You will need:

❀ A clean plastic bag with no holes (column-shaped bread bags are a good choice)
❀ A small, sharp knife and kitchen shears
❀ A 1.25 litre (44 fl oz) plastic soda or soft drink bottle with a lid
❀ Inoculated substrate (see pages 90–93)
❀ A clean scrap of cotton cloth or a small piece of foam

1. If the plastic bag has been previously used for bread (or anything else with yeast in it), thoroughly rinse and dry it, then turn it inside out to remove any resident microbes.

2. Cut off the neck of the bottle to make a re-usable collar for the bag. Fill the bag with the inoculated substrate up to the three-quarter mark, and pack it down firmly. Feed the top of the bag through the inside of the bottle neck as shown. Trim the top of the bag, leaving enough plastic to fold back over the bottle neck with a skirt of about 5 cm (2 inches).

3. Take the scrap of cloth or foam and jam it into the neck of the bottle to form the air filter, which will allow a small amount of gas exchange but hopefully won't allow microbes into the bag. Make sure that the cloth or foam is not touching the substrate. Trim any excess plastic.

TIPS

Treat the filled bag like any other fruiting container – store it at room temperature and, when the substrate is fully colonised and ready to fruit, open the bag to allow good airflow.

Fast-growing species like oyster mushrooms are great for this technique – their speedy growth means there is less time for other microbes to take over.

To make your own mushroom bag and filter system, pack a clean plastic bag with the inoculated substrate, stopping before the bag is full. Pinch the top of the bag, thread it through the bottle neck and then fold back the top of the bag. Roll up a scrap of cloth and insert it tightly in the top of the bottle. Finish by cutting off the excess bag.

THE HOLEY BUCKET CULTIVATION TECHNIQUE

We use food-grade white polypropylene buckets for this system.

You will need:

※ A drill with a 10–12 mm (½ inch) drill bit
※ A food-grade bucket with a tight-fitting lid
※ Surgical (micropore) tape
※ Inoculated substrate (see pages 90–93)

1. Drill 10–15 holes in the side of your bucket, about 10 cm (4 inches) apart, out of which the mushrooms will fruit. Place surgical tape over each hole in the side of the bucket.

2. Pack the bucket full with the inoculated substrate then seal it with the lid. Store your sealed bucket at room temperature.

3. After a few weeks, open the lid and check to see how the mycelium is going. When the mycelium has fully colonised the substrate and it's time to fruit, take off the lid and soak the whole thing in a larger container of fresh water. Leave it to soak for 12 hours, then tip the bucket on its side to drain the water.

4. Expose the fruiting holes by taking off the surgical tape. Put the lid back on the bucket and move it to your fruiting area. The mycelium is exposed to fresh air via all the bucket holes, and proceeds to fruit out from there.

5. Once your mushrooms have fruited, you can seal the bucket back up and rest it for a few weeks. You can often successfully repeat the fruiting process.

TIP

If you have a supply of identical buckets, you can use a snug-fitting second bucket as a sleeve for the inner bucket, and omit the surgical tape from the side holes. Remove the outer bucket when you would otherwise remove the surgical tape. This is a no-waste option, but requires twice as many buckets.

Some species like to fruit out of side holes (like these pearl oysters), while some other species (king oyster, reishi) will do best if the lid is removed so they can fruit out the top of the bucket.

GETTING YOUR GEAR TOGETHER

The amount of spawn, substrate and fruiting containers that you have will determine the scale of your mushroom cultivation. We aim for a 10 per cent inoculation rate – 1 part spawn to 9 parts substrate. For example, if you have 2 litres (½ gallon) of spawn to work with, you'll want 18 litres (5 gallons) of substrate and 20+ litres (5+ gallons) of fruiting container space.

Higher inoculation rates will make for more mushrooms per litre of substrate, faster colonisation and less contamination, but also means using more spawn. As the spawn is usually the major expense in this stage, it's a factor you need to consider.

PREPARING YOUR SUBSTRATE FOR CONTAINER CULTIVATION

The goal in preparing the substrate for mushroom cultivation is to remove any and all spores and bacteria in the substrate that are likely to compete with the mycelium you want to grow. In order to do this, you need to take the substrate through four steps: hydrate, pasteurise, cool and inoculate.

PASTEURISING vs STERILISING

The decision between pasteurising and sterilising will depend on what your substrate is made from. If you're using a low-nitrogen substrate, like straw, sawdust, woodchips or similar, you only need to pasteurise your substrate. If you're using a higher nitrogen substrate, such as coffee grounds, wheat or rice bran, or a combination of low- and high-nitrogen materials, you'll need to sterilise your substrate.

Pasteurisation and sterilisation each require a different process for preparing the substrate as well as for inoculating it with spawn. Once these steps are completed, the process for the fruiting stage is the same for all your containers.

If you're new to mushroom cultivation, we recommend choosing a substrate that only needs pasteurising.

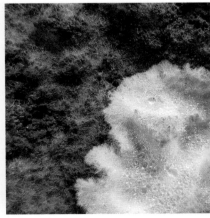

LEFT: Pearl oyster mushrooms fruiting on pasteurised straw substrate.

BELOW: Oyster mushroom mycelium colonising sterilised coffee grounds.

STEP-BY-STEP GUIDE TO
PASTEURISING AND INOCULATING

There are a few ways you can go about pasteurising your substrate, but this is the method that we've found to be the most time-, energy- and cost-efficient way for home-scale pasteurisation. This recipe will make 30 litres (8 gallons) of substrate, ready to inoculate and fruit. Do this stage once you have your spawn and your fruiting containers prepared. The process is shown on pages 92–93.

You will need:

※ Gloves, eye protection and a face mask
※ 30 litres (8 gallons) of substrate (see Tips)
※ A big tub to mix and hydrate the substrate in
※ 250 ml (1 cup) hydrated lime
※ 3 clean pillowcases
※ Rope
※ A 50 litre (13 gallon) bucket with a lid
※ 40 litres (11 gallons) of 80°C (175°F) water
※ A clean brick or similar heavy item
※ A thermometer
※ Somewhere outside to hang your pillowcases off the ground
※ A clean outdoor table or tarpaulin to work on
※ 2 kg (about 4 lb) spawn
※ Clean fruiting containers

Before you start, put on some gloves, eye protection and a mask. Hydrated lime is caustic and can burn your throat, and cause serious damage to your eyes. It doesn't produce any harmful byproducts, but it's not something you want on your skin in a concentrated form.

1. Hydrate the substrate

Put your substrate in the tub, wet it down with water (not too much – it needs to be just wet, not a soup) and then carefully add the hydrated lime. Mix it all around. The entire mixture needs to be damp and well mixed so the heat in the next step will get right into the middle of the mixture – dry substrate is a very good insulator against heat, which you don't want in this process.

2. Pasteurise the substrate

Pack the substrate and lime mixture into the pillowcases and tie them well with rope, allowing enough rope to hang them up to drain later. Put the filled pillowcases in the 50 litre bucket and carefully pour the 80°C (175°F) water over them until the bucket is full. Add a brick on top of the bags to submerge them, and put the lid on. Go and wash your hands and take off your protective gear. Then, wait, or go and make some lunch! The substrate needs to remain above 60°C (140°F) for 2 hours in order to pasteurise.

After 2 hours, use a thermometer to test the water temperature – ours usually comes out at about 65°C (150°F). Take out the soggy substrate-filled pillowcases (be careful, they'll still be hot!) and hang up to drain for at least 15 minutes. This will ensure they're cool enough to handle, but don't leave it too long, as this is still a race against other contaminants that will want to colonise your nicely prepared substrate. The aim is for all the water to drain out of the substrate. You might need to give the pillowcases a squeeze with clean hands to remove any excess water.

3. Cool the substrate

Once the pasteurised substrate has stopped dripping and you can't squeeze any water out of it, tip it out onto a clean table or tarpaulin to cool and spread it out. Leave it alone until it's just warm to the touch – about 35°C (95°F) – which means it's time to add the spawn.

4. Inoculate the substrate

Take the bag of broken-up spawn and sprinkle it along the length of the substrate. Then, with clean hands, mix well. The spawn needs to be distributed throughout the substrate as evenly as possible.

Take handfuls of the inoculated substrate and pack it into your fruiting containers until they are full. Seal your containers so that nothing else can get in, and store your future mushrooms at room temperature, out of direct sunlight. Proceed to the monitoring and fruiting stage (see pages 94–96).

TIPS

For the substrate, we recommend using one-third chopped straw and two-thirds hardwood sawdust.

Hydrated lime is sold as builders' lime or calcium hydroxide. It's great for shifting the pH of the substrate quickly, thereby killing a bunch of microbial competition.

You can use an insulated cooler or plastic garbage bin instead of a bucket.

A large urn is useful for heating the water.

In our climate, this method is enough to keep the submerged substrate at the right temperature for 2 hours. If you're somewhere colder, consider placing a metal barrel on some bricks, with a small fire burning underneath to maintain the high internal temperature.

Try to keep everything as clean as you can – clean hands, clean table, clean tools, clean rope. This will help to reduce contamination so that the fungus you want to grow is the only winner in the colonisation race. Wipe your table down with alcohol and use an alcohol-based hand sanitiser. And ensure your fruiting containers, that you're about to fill, are as clean as a whistle.

Feeling substrate with clean hands to check if it's cool enough for inoculation.

Pasteurising and inoculating

1. Mix a little water and all the lime into the substrate.

2. Pack the substrate into pillowcases.

3. Tie up the pillowcases.

4. Place the full pillowcases into the bucket, weigh them down with a brick and cover with 80°C (175°F) water.

5. Place the lid on the bucket.

6. After the pillowcases have been soaking for 2 hours, hang them up to drain.

7. Tip the pasteurised substrate onto a clean surface.

8. Spread out the substrate, to help it cool down.

9. When the substrate is cool, spread the spawn on top. Mix well, then pack into fruiting containers.

10. A few weeks later, the result: mushrooms!

MONITORING THE INOCULATED FRUITING CONTAINERS

Now it's time to wait for the spawn to colonise the substrate in your sealed containers. A stable temperature of about 24°C (75°F) is best for most species to grow well – put the containers in a closet, pantry, under the lounge or under the kitchen sink.

After a few weeks, check the contents of your vessels by looking from the outside, if possible, or by opening them up. When the substrate in the container is white and fully colonised with mycelium, you'll know it's just about ready to fruit as the mycelium is running out of food.

It may take anywhere between 3 and 12 weeks for the mycelium to fully colonise your substrate, as it depends on a lot of factors. The main ones are the spawn-to-substrate ratio and the temperature that it's held at, but the substrate type, and the species and variety of your mycelium will also affect the colonisation time. Watch and wait and watch again.

When your fruiting containers are fully colonised and fluffy white, it's time to trigger fruiting.

FRUITING MUSHROOMS IN CONTAINERS

Once you've nursed your inoculated containers to a stage where they're fully colonised and ready to fruit, creating a great fruiting environment is the key to maximum harvest.

If you've got the perfect outdoor spot to fruit your mushrooms – a spot that's very humid, cool, free of pests and with good airflow – you may not need to construct a fruiting chamber. For everyone else (and this includes us), constructing a simple fruiting chamber is the next step.

In their natural forest habitats, mycelium wait until the moment is right to fruit. When storms bring rain and wind, branches and sometimes entire trees come crashing down to the forest floor. Afterwards, the drop in temperature and increased humidity are primary triggers for many types of fungi, although the exact conditions do differ between species.

Simply put, when you fruit mushrooms, you're often trying to recreate the aftermath of a forest rainstorm, except that you might use a plastic box and a garden hose. True, it's not as romantic as the forest version, but it still results in mushrooms for your table.

Creating a fruiting chamber

There are lots of examples of DIY or low-cost fruiting chambers. One popular choice is a freestanding zippered plastic greenhouse that contains shelves. Old fridges or similar, which have been modified to allow for airflow, are also common. Some people put them outside, some put them in their bathroom. Use the most temperature-stable place you have available.

Another idea for a small and simple fruiting chamber is a 'shotgun fruiting chamber' – a big plastic tub with a lid, peppered with small holes, with a bed of clean moisture-retaining material beneath the jars and buckets. Misted regularly, this kind of chamber can keep the humidity nice and high for fruiting.

WHAT ABOUT THE SPORES?

Don't worry, they won't colonise your living room! There are no spores present at this stage of cultivation. Spores are what the fruiting mushrooms release right at the end of their life cycle, by which point your containers will be in their fruiting chamber and well away from your lounge. Fear not.

Regularly spraying water around your fruiting chamber will keep the humidity high. Try not to directly spray the mushrooms.

We built a fruiting chamber on our back verandah from old glass shower doors, with wire shelves inside that we found in a junkyard. The top and bottom are open, but screened to prevent critters entering. We have set up a small misting unit on a timer that comes on for 5 minutes every hour when our mushrooms are fruiting. This keeps the humidity in the chamber relatively high, while allowing for good airflow, resulting in many mushrooms.

Your fruiting chamber can be large or small, depending on the amount of mushrooms you're fruiting. The materials that it's made from don't really matter as much as the environment they help create.

TRIGGERING FRUITING

Being the canny organisms they are, mycelium will wait until just the right conditions are present to fruit, once they've colonised all their available substrate. You can trigger them by simulating the natural forest conditions that cause many mushrooms to fruit – a change of season, rainstorm, and so on – *but only once the substrate in your container is fully colonised.*

Below are some techniques that can help trigger the fruiting of your container of white and fluffy substrate.

Wire shelves in your fruiting chamber help maximise airflow (and mushrooms!).

* Increase the light levels (but don't allow direct sunlight, as this can quickly dry things out).
* Allow more access to fresh air.
* Reduce the temperature (e.g. place the containers in the shade on the cool side of the house).
* Soak your fruiting containers in clean water for 12 hours by filling the container with water (the mushrooms won't drown during this short time), then drain completely.

Once you've triggered the mycelium to begin fruiting, place the containers inside your fruiting chamber, mist regularly and keep watch. All being well, your mushrooms should appear in a few days to a week or so, depending on the species.

The main things to get right in this stage are humidity and airflow – the humidity needs to be up around 90 per cent in the fruiting chamber, but you also need good airflow for the mycelium to fruit. This is the magical balance of successful mushroom fruiting.

Misting

While they're in the fruiting chamber, mist your mushrooms regularly, multiple times a day. This can be done using a hand mister, an ultrasonic mister or a small greenhouse misting system, depending on the size of your operation.

Checking airflow

Some species fruit best when they're removed from the container they grew in, while others like to be left in their container and just fruit out of a few holes. The container can help provide a more stable environment if your fruiting chamber is not as stable as you would like.

King oysters pinning and starting to fruit in a bucket of substrate.

Harvesting mushrooms with a sharp knife means you don't disturb the mycelium below.

GETTING A SECOND FLUSH OF MUSHROOMS

Once your blocks of mycelium have fruited, you might be able to harvest a second or even a third flush of mushrooms. Before you do this, the mycelium will need a rest in order to digest some more of the substrate and build up its energy resources.

Remove any undeveloped mushrooms from the fruited blocks and place the substrate back in a sealed container to rest for a week or two at room temperature. After a few weeks' rest, return them to your fruiting chamber to trigger a second or third flush. Another option is to put your blocks in a moist area of the garden under soaked hardwood woodchips (not pine) to create a mushroom garden. They will slowly colonise the woodchips and fruit again, if and when the conditions are right.

If the mycelium does not have enough access to fresh air, the build-up of carbon dioxide in the chamber can sometimes halt fruiting, or cause the stems of the mushrooms to become elongated as they try to reach fresh air – make sure they've got plenty!

HARVEST TIME

The first thing you'll see when mushrooms fruit is the 'pinning' stage, which looks like a lot of tiny pinheads are emerging from the mycelium. These are tiny mushrooms, waiting for the space and right conditions to fruit. Once the mycelium begin pinning, you're only days (sometimes hours) away from full-blown mushrooms forming. An optimal fruiting environment here will make all the difference.

Harvest your mushrooms once the caps open but before they become completely flat, by cutting with a small knife at the base of each cluster of mushrooms. Store the mushrooms in a cool, dark place until you're ready to cook them. Fresh mushrooms are best eaten or processed in the first day or so after picking.

TROUBLESHOOTING AT THE FRUITING STAGE

Mushrooms pinning, but not fruiting: This can be caused by many different factors – most likely water inconsistency. Mist regularly to create the very high humidity that mushrooms need (greater than 90 per cent).

Mycelium has fully colonised the vessel, but no pins or mushrooms are visible: The temperature could be too cold for the species where you live, or they might still be digesting their substrate.

Mushrooms emerge, but they look strange: This is probably a result of inconsistent humidity or inconsistent airflow.

Mycelium has turned a strange colour (brown, pink or other than expected): Some mycelium, such as shiitake, can turn brown and velvety on the surface before pinning, but most species remain white until they fruit. If your mycelium grows a green or pink mould on the surface, this is not a good sign. Isolate it from your other containers (it could be a good candidate to fruit outside in a mushroom garden – if it does produce mushrooms, they will be fine).

Mycelium has droplets of golden or amber liquid coming off it: This is normal – it's the mycelium exuding the waste products from digesting the substrate.

A basket of breakfast: harvested king oyster mushrooms, headed straight for our kitchen.

OUTDOOR CULTIVATION

Outdoor cultivation mushroom gardens provide an easy, low-cost method of fruiting mushrooms when conditions are right in the environment. Using the seasons and the mycelium's own proclivities, you can create an effective seasonal harvest of mushrooms.

Mushroom gardens remove the need for a purpose-built mushroom fruiting chamber or room, and instead you can just grow mycelium outside around your home garden and wait for conditions to occur that trigger fruiting.

LOG CULTIVATION

Growing mushrooms on logs is an easy method of cultivation that gives ongoing, seasonal harvests of mushrooms. A single inoculated log can flush again and again for up to five years, so it's definitely worth doing.

Log cultivation requires no pasteurisation or sterilisation of the substrate. All you need is a fresh log, some spawn, simple hand tools and your fine self to put it all together.

There are many, many species of mushrooms that can be cultivated on logs and stumps, including reishi, maitake, lion's mane, pearl oyster, blue oyster, Phoenix oyster and turkey tail mushrooms. At home we generally stick to shiitake mushrooms because we love to eat them so much.

LOG CULTIVATION OF SHIITAKE MUSHROOMS

The basic process of making a shiitake log is pretty simple. The aim is to insert a small amount of inoculated material, either in the form of a wooden plug or sawdust, into holes in the log. The inoculated material makes contact with the ramial layer, which is the top layer of the sapwood, just underneath the bark. The mycelium in the inoculated material will then enthusiastically colonise and eat the ramial layer, and eventually most of the log, before fruiting into shiitake mushrooms.

Sourcing spawn

There are two main types of spawn that are used to inoculate logs: plugs and sawdust.

Plugs/dowel spawn are more readily available commercially, and don't require any specialist tools to inoculate the logs. They're made by inoculating sterile birch dowels with shiitake mycelium. You can buy them in pre-inoculated bags of 100 to 1000 or so from a reputable mushroom spawn supplier (search online for 'shiitake plug spawn' to find someone in your area).

Sawdust spawn requires an inoculator tool to get it into the log (although some folks just use a funnel). You can get bags of inoculated sawdust spawn from a mushroom spawn supplier.

Freshly harvested oak logs, waiting to become food for cultivated mushrooms.

Sourcing logs

Native to East Asia, shiitake grow naturally in the decomposing wood of *Castanopsis cuspidata* (shii), *Fagus* (beech), *Quercus* (oak), *Populus* (poplar), *Castanea* (chestnut), *Morus* (mulberry) and a few other species of deciduous forest trees. In Australia, they have been successfully grown on oak, Shining gum (*Eucalyptus nitens*), Sugar gum (*E. cladocalyx*) and Common alder (*Alnus glutinosa*). They can also grow on any other hardwoods that are fast-growing and have lots of sapwood and that hold their bark after they're dead (this gives better protection of the mycelium and better moisture retention).

If the tree is deciduous (like oak), the best logs are harvested at bud burst when the sap is rising. However, logs harvested at any time of year will usually still work.

If you have your own land and hardwood trees, sourcing wood should be fairly straightforward. We've had success sourcing logs from local arborists, who are often quite happy that someone wants to clean up and take the prunings of their work.

Look for logs that are:

- ❀ cut from a live tree (to avoid contamination)
- ❀ 750–1200 mm (30–47 inches) in length and 75–200 mm (3–8 inches) in diameter
- ❀ consistent in size (so they stack well)
- ❀ not too heavy (so they are safe to handle).

Preparing the logs

It's generally a good idea to inoculate your fresh logs as quickly as possible, although some more aromatic woods, like eucalypts, are best left for a week or so before inoculation. Prompt inoculation prevents any other mycelium getting the upper hand in eating the wood before your shiitake mycelium do.

Store your fresh logs stacked outside in the shade, but not in direct contact with the ground, if you can avoid it. A wooden pallet is a good place to stack them, or up against the side of the house.

Drilling the logs

For plug spawn, the aim is to drill a hole that's just a teeny bit wider than the plug size and a little deeper than the plug is long. Drilling the hole deeper than the plug is important for two reasons: it leaves an air pocket beneath for the mycelium to breathe, and it also ensures the plug goes in far enough to be able to seal it with wax.

There are specialist mushroom drill bits that make the drilling process much quicker. The holes should be no more than 150 mm (6 inches) apart – the more inoculation points, the more effective the colonisation.

For standard spawn plugs (the commercial plugs are pretty much the same size worldwide), use an 8.5 mm (⅓ inch) drill bit to drill 32 mm (1¼ inch) deep holes, evenly spaced around and along the logs.

For sawdust spawn, use a 12 mm (½ inch) drill bit to drill 25–30 mm (1–1¼ inch) deep holes.

To prepare oak logs for plug spawn, drill holes in the logs using regular or specialist drill bits. Insert the plugs and tap them in with a mallet, then seal the holes with beeswax. Many months later, enjoy your harvest!

TOP: Shiitake mushrooms emerging.

ABOVE: A shiitake harvest.

Inoculating the logs

To inoculate the logs with plugs, hammer the plugs into the holes using a rubber mallet until the plugs are flush or sitting just below the surface. If using sawdust spawn, pack the holes using an inoculation tool or a funnel.

Seal over the inoculation points with beeswax or paraffin wax, painted on with a paintbrush or small sponge.

Make sure you wipe your tools regularly with alcohol to keep them sterile.

Siting the logs

There's a bit of waiting in the shiitake log game. For the first 6 to 18 months, the logs are closely stacked in a suitable spot.

Traditionally, shiitake logs are stacked in forests – somewhere that's shady, cool and moist, but with good airflow. If you don't happen to live in a forest, you can stack your logs tightly on a wooden pallet, and cover the stack with hessian, shadecloth or similar to keep the humidity around the logs stable. Shiitake logs do best with 25 mm (1 inch) of rain/overhead watering once per week.

Signs of readiness

After as little as 6 months (but up to as long as 18 months), the white rot of the mushroom mycelium will soften the area directly around the inoculation points. Once this area is the size of a chicken's egg, you can initiate fruiting by shocking.

Shocking the logs into fruiting

The logs will naturally be shocked into fruiting when the weather cools or becomes more moist, so keep your eyes on your logs in autumn and spring.

You can also trigger the logs to get better, stronger flushes by doing any or all of the following:

* soaking them overnight in clean water (no longer than 24 hours)
* restacking them to provide better airflow, more light penetration and access to harvest fruit (but no direct sunlight)
* moving them to a cooler, more moist environment
* physically shocking them by hitting them with a mallet or hammer
* giving them an electrical shock using an electric cattle prod.

Once you've shocked the logs, stack them with some space between each log in a moist but open space (not tightly this time) and check daily for mushrooms. Harvest, and enjoy!

After the first flush, you can stack the logs tightly once more until their second flush. This is important as it allows the mycelium time to recover and digest more wood, giving it the energy to produce more mushrooms. The second flush is sometimes hard to predict, as it is dependent on weather and other conditions. However, you can shock the logs again to trigger fruiting.

It's a good idea to stack these older logs somewhere that you regularly check or pass by, so that you catch any spontaneous fruiting. You can get up to five years of flushes from each log in the right environment, so figuring out where the 'sweet spot' is for logs at your place is worthwhile.

MUSHROOM GARDENS

Mushroom gardens are a great way to use up odds and ends of woodchips and any spawn that needs a home, as well as creating resilience in your garden with yet another periodic, seasonal food stream that needs little attention.

There's also the input for outputs factor – considering what you put into mushroom gardens (a bunch of woodchips and some spawn) and what you get out of a mushroom garden (many flushes of tasty mushrooms, and then great compost at the end), it's a winner of a technique.

The basic processes are the same as for any other mushroom cultivation. You want to build up a large quantity of actively growing mycelium in a suitable substrate. The easiest method is to inoculate a large quantity of minimally processed woodchips in situ with grain spawn.

Pasteurising the woodchip substrate

Compared to bucket or jar cultivation, you need a lot of prepared substrate for a mushroom garden – we're not just talking about small volumes. We're talking wheelbarrow-loads of woodchip substrate. Fear not, it's entirely doable using simple tools and zero energy inputs.

This technique is a very low-tech hybrid pasteurisation / fermentation method that prepares the woodchips while effectively drowning or smothering any microbiology that might compete with your mycelium. It was taught to Nick by Paul Stamets in the USA, and we now use it at home.

To use this technique, take the required amount of hardwood woodchips and submerge them in a big drum of clean water for a week. We use a garbage can lid that fits inside the drum and place a brick on top to hold the woodchips under the water. This will kill any aerobic (oxygen-breathing) microorganisms in the woodchips. During this time, if the woodchips are fresh, they will also begin to bubble and ferment.

After a week, and once you're ready to make your mushroom garden, drain the woodchips, all in one go. Draining will flood the woodchips with oxygen, killing most anaerobic microorganisms. The woodchips are now pasteurised, and you're ready to build your mushroom garden.

WHAT'S THAT SMELL?

The fermentation process of the woodchips is the anaerobic organisms (that don't require oxygen) eating the available sugars and producing waste products. This is a good thing, as it uses up some of the available sugars in the woodchips (less sugar = less contamination) and the waste products are toxic to aerobes. This is why it smells! The anaerobes are also eating the competition directly because the water causes spores of aerobes to germinate and then they are eaten by the anaerobes.

BELOW LEFT: Fresh woodchips, ready to be fermented.

BELOW: Fermented woodchips, ready to be used as substrate.

MAKING A MUSHROOM GARDEN

You'll need to find a good spot for your mushroom garden – somewhere that's reasonably moist with dappled shade. Take advantage of places that are too shady for vegetable gardens. A blackberry patch or similar brambles makes a good choice (once you've removed the brambles, of course).

You will need:

* Corrugated cardboard to cover an area 2 x 2 metres (6½ x 6½ feet)
* Approximately 200 litres (53 gallons) of pasteurised hardwood woodchips, prepared a week ahead using the pasteurisation/fermentation method described on page 103
* At least 5 litres (1⅓ gallons) of spawn

1. Remove the grass from a 2 x 2 metre (6½ x 6½ foot) area of ground (leave any small bushes).

2. Cover the bare ground with a double layer of soaked corrugated cardboard. Cover the cardboard with a 5 cm (2 inch) thick layer of the prepared woodchips. Spread the spawn in a layer over the woodchips, then cover with another 5–10 cm (2–4 inch) layer of woodchips.

3. Periodically water your mushroom patch to ensure the woodchips stay a little moist – the equivalent to 25 mm (1 inch) of rainfall per week is a good amount.

4. Keep an eye on your mushroom patch. After a few months, the mycelium should have colonised the woodchips. When conditions are right for the mushroom species you are cultivating, they should begin to fruit.

TIPS

Woodchips from eucalyptus, willow, poplar, alder, maple, birch, ash or even fruit trees will all work.

This technique will work well for smaller areas, too – just scale down the quantities accordingly. One square metre (11 square feet) is a good minimum size to work from.

RIGHT: Cardboard, fermented woodchips and a box of woodchip spawn sourced from another mushroom garden.

OPPOSITE: The finished mushroom garden.

King stropharia (Photo: Ann F. Berger, creative commons).

GOOD SPECIES FOR MUSHROOM GARDENS

Stropharia rugosoannulata (king stropharia or garden giant)

This is one of our favourite outdoor mushroom species. It loves to live with a rich diversity of microorganisms.

Pleurotus eryngii (king oyster, boletus of the steppes)

King oyster mushrooms are from the Mediterranean and can handle slightly drier conditions. They thrive in symbiosis with *Eryngium* sp. (sea holly) and other plants from the *Apiaceae* family, so plant some sea holly, fennel, parsley or angelica in the same garden.

Flammulina velutipes (enokitake)

Enokitake grow wild where we live. In the middle of winter, they grow on all kinds of stumps and they particularly like the pruned stems of our currant bushes.

MUSHROOM SCROLLS

Our friend Paul 'Speedy' Ward showed up at our place with some mushroom scrolls one day and taught us this technique. Mushroom scrolls are a bit like seed bombs, only for mushrooms. They're a great low-input way of spreading mushroom goodness around your garden, using scraps and leftovers. Use one of the species that are suitable for mushroom gardens (see left) or wild mushrooms that you know are good to eat, if you have the right host trees about.

You will need:

* Mushroom spawn (or use a few fresh mushrooms of your chosen variety – we use wood blewits)
* Untreated hessian or cotton cloth
* String made of natural fibres
* Any root cuttings or bits of moss you wish to add
* A bucket of water

1. Roll up the spawn or mushrooms in wet hessian to make a kind of long hessian sausage. Curl the hessian into a spiral and secure with the string. Tuck in any root cuttings and moss around the edges.

2. Dunk the scroll in a bucket of water and leave for 5 minutes, until it is well soaked. Take the scroll out of the bucket and shake off the excess water.

3. Place the scroll in the preferred environment of the species you are cultivating, such as under a particular type of tree or on some wet woodchips.

4. Water the scroll periodically (when you remember) for its first year. By then, the mycelium will have infiltrated the host tree or nearby soil. Check this patch for your chosen mushrooms after rain in spring and autumn. Only harvest mushrooms you can positively identify, of course.

TIP

You might like to tuck in a root cutting from something like comfrey (a great forest garden groundcover) and maybe some moss or other support species.

MUSHROOMS IN THE KITCHEN

PREVIOUS PAGES: Nick harvesting shiitakes grown at home on scribbly gum (*Eucalyptus haemastoma*) logs, ready to head to our kitchen for drying and cooking.

Mushrooms are delicious eaten every which way, but when they're fruiting there can be rather a lot of them, all at once. As they don't store fresh for long, it's important to have a bunch of strategies up your sleeve for making the most of them, so you can enjoy mushrooms throughout the year.

Fresh mushrooms make excellent swap and barter material. If a friend came to you with a basket of fresh home-grown shiitake mushrooms and asked if you wanted to swap them for something, what would you do? We'd go running to the pantry for tomato passata, pickles, eggs or honey – whatever we had on hand that we could swap. Or maybe we'd offer seedlings or firewood. If you know you've got a flush of mushrooms coming on, ask around and see what you can swap.

Harvesting

Harvest your mushrooms with a small knife, at the base of the stem. By cutting instead of tearing the mushrooms from your jar, bucket, log or garden, you'll ensure minimal damage to the mycelium, which will in turn maximise the second, third and even fourth flushes of mushrooms.

USING FRESH MUSHROOMS

A fresh mushroom pie or pasta made from home-grown mushrooms is as good as it gets, in our view. Mushrooms are also wonderful in soups, stews, stir-fried or stuffed, or barbecued with lots of olive oil and lemon.

Our favourite way to cook mushrooms is to sauté them in butter until they're soft, with some garlic, herbs and cracked pepper, then deglaze them with a little wine once they're nearly done. They're amazing mixed through some great-quality pasta or piled on toasted sourdough.

We always cook our mushrooms and never eat them raw. This is partly because mushrooms, being fruiting bodies designed to be tasty so that their spores will be spread, can be quickly colonised by all forms of microscopic and macroscopic life. If you eat mushrooms raw, you're potentially eating a lot of other unfriendly microbiology that can make you quite ill.

Also, mushrooms contain mycochitin in their cell walls (unlike plants, which contain cellulose). Mycochitin is not easily digested by humans, but it's broken down during cooking. Since mushrooms are full to the brim of so many awesome nutrients, we want the full benefit of all that goodness. And so we cook our mushrooms.

Cultivated lion's mane (*Hericium erinaceus*) mushroom, ready for pan-frying with chives, garlic and butter.

ABOVE LEFT: Sliced shiitake mushrooms, ready to be dehydrated.

ABOVE: Slices of dried shiitake.

DRYING MUSHROOMS

Drying the excess of your mushroom harvest is an excellent and versatile way to enjoy mushrooms all year round. It's important to dry your mushrooms when they are as fresh as possible – the day that you pick them. The longer you wait before beginning the drying process, the poorer the resulting dried mushrooms will be.

You can dry mushrooms whole or in slices. For larger mushrooms, dried slices are easier to use in future cooking, but we love drying the smaller mushrooms, particularly shiitakes, as whole mushrooms. Brush off any dirt or other debris on the mushroom, slice them if necessary, and proceed directly to your drying set-up.

We use an electric dehydrator set to 52°C (126°F) and spread out the mushrooms on each shelf. If you don't have an electric dehydrator, there are plenty of other options (see pages 282–284 in the Wild Food chapter).

Once your mushrooms are dry, store them in an airtight jar with a sprinkle of salt at the bottom. Don't forget to label them!

Dried mushrooms store well for 6 to 12 months. We rehydrate them and add them to our pastas, soups and stews. They're also excellent if you pulverise them into a powder and use the powder as a flavour kick in a similar way to seaweed sprinkles (see page 209). With the addition of a little salt, dried mushroom powder can become a umami sensation that's great for garnishes, adding to savoury crackers and sprinkling over rice and anything else you can think of, including popcorn.

Rehydrating

When you're ready to use your dried mushrooms, pour over enough boiling water to barely cover them, and stand for 30 minutes. If they were dried when they were super-fresh, most mushroom species will bounce back well and become slightly chewy slices or whole mushrooms. The mushroom soaking liquid is also great for cooking.

SUNNY SIDE UP

When exposed to sunlight while they're drying, it seems that some mushrooms experience a marked increase in their level of vitamin D. It soars to 460 times the level found in mushrooms that aren't exposed to the sun. Hello, sunshine!

PICKLING MUSHROOMS

There's a grand tradition of pickling foraged mushrooms that comes to us from the cultures of Poland and Russia. There are so many ways to do it, so many delicious options.

Some folks salt their mushrooms in a crock with spices, some folks lactoferment their mushrooms in brine with herbs and garlic, some pickle their mushrooms in vinegar. The options are many and recipes are easy to find with a little research. Start with a good resource on Polish cooking and take it from there.

Many of the recipes we've come across, though, call for cold storage of the finished product. If you have a traditional underground cellar, this presents no problem. But most of us don't have one of those, so these cold-stored mushroom preserves end up in the fridge, which means an ongoing use of energy to store the preserves. This isn't ideal, if you can avoid it. Mind you, pickled mushrooms are so delicious that we never end up storing them for long. On the following pages are two delicious ways to pickle mushrooms in order to ensure maximum shelf-life and delectability.

OPPOSITE: Pearl oyster mushrooms fermented in brine, with three-cornered garlic leaves sitting above and below for extra flavour.

BELOW: Clusters of pearl oysters, ready for pickling.

These probiotic mushrooms make insanely good bruschetta with good-quality butter and herbs, or you can serve them as a side dish with just about anything. The one trick with this recipe is not to pack the mushrooms into the jar tightly – there must be plenty of brine around them. If you have too many mushrooms, find another jar. While this method flies in the face of the 'always cook your mushrooms properly' rule, the fermentation does a similar job of breaking down the mycochitin as cooking does.

FERMENTED MUSHROOMS

Mushrooms
Good-quality non-iodised salt
LOTS of fresh garlic
Some fresh, tannin-rich leaves: grape, oak,
    cherry or horseradish
Spices, to taste, such as dill, fennel, coriander
    and pepper
A few big edible leaves (see Tips)

1. Slice your clean mushrooms into slices about 1 cm (½ inch) wide.

2. Bring a large pot of water to the boil. Add the sliced mushrooms and wait for 2 minutes, then drain and set aside to cool.

3. While the mushrooms are cooling, make up a 2% brine solution using 1 tablespoon salt to every 1 litre (4 cups) of water.

4. Chop up the garlic – you can just halve a whole head of garlic crosswise (without peeling it) so you end up with a bottom half and a top half that look great and hold together in the jar.

5. Add a few of the tannin-rich leaves, the garlic and the spices to the bottom of your clean jar. Once the mushrooms are no longer hot (warm is fine), get them into the jar, leaving the top 10 cm (4 inches) empty and being careful not to pack them down too tightly. Pour in the brine solution to cover the mushrooms. Add a few big leaves to help the mushrooms stay below the brine, then top up the brine so it comes to the top of the jar. Lightly screw on the lid.

6. Leave the jar to ferment at room temperature for 7–10 days, with a plate sitting underneath to catch any dribbles. After a week, taste the mushrooms. They should be garlicky, tangy and lightly sour – if not, put them back on the bench for another day or so.

7. When the mushrooms taste good, tightly seal the jar and place somewhere cool (either in your fridge or cellar) and eat with gusto. The mushrooms will keep for a few months.

TIPS

You can use either wild or cultivated mushrooms in this recipe. We use shiitake, oyster and pine mushrooms.

If you can't find any tannin-rich leaves, green tea will do (at a pinch).

The outer leaves of brassicas like cauliflowers or cabbages are perfect for submerging the mushrooms so they are covered with the brine solution.

This is a foolproof, shelf-stable mushroom pickle. You can make it using fresh, foraged or bought mushrooms of any type. Our favourites are wild saffron milkcaps and cultivated oyster mushrooms. Experiment with some different spices and herbs – the possibilities are endless. The mushrooms are excellent served with a sharp cheese and home-made crackers.

VINEGAR-PICKLED MUSHROOMS

Mushrooms
Good-quality vinegar (we use apple cider vinegar)
A sprinkle of spices for each jar (we use dill, coriander seeds and juniper seeds)
A few slices of garlic for each jar
Good-quality non-iodised salt

1. Put your washed jars and lids in a 100°C (200°F) oven to sterilise while you prepare the mushrooms.

2. Wash all the mushrooms. Slice any large ones into 1 cm (½ inch) wide slices. If they're small and the width from cap to gill is around 1 cm (½ inch), you may not need to do this.

3. Bring a large pot of water to the boil. Add the mushrooms and cook for 2 minutes, then drain.

4. Meanwhile, make enough pickling liquid to fill your jars by adding equal quantities of vinegar and water to a small pot. Bring the liquid to a simmer.

5. Take the jars out of the oven. Add the spices, garlic and a pinch of salt to each jar.

6. Fill the jars with the hot, drained mushrooms, up to the neck of the jar. Cover completely with the hot pickling liquid. Wipe the jar necks with a clean cloth. Tightly seal with the lids, then turn the jars upside down on the bench and leave to cool (this will help to seal them).

7. Store the pickled mushrooms out of the sunlight in a cool place for a good few weeks before digging in – they'll store on the shelf for at least 12 months, but ours never last that long.

TIP

If the jars, lids, mushrooms and liquid are all nice and hot, we don't bother putting the filled jars in a waterbath. You can if you like, though.

This condiment uses up all the wonky dried mushroom bits and turns them into a umami powerhouse of nutritious sprinkle flavouring, but you may love it so much that you use all your dried mushrooms to make it. The recipe is super-simple. It just requires an equal weight of dried sliced shiitake mushrooms (shiitakes are our go-to, but do try others if you like – we sometimes use foraged saffron milkcaps) and salt. We're lucky enough to have a local salt lake to harvest from – we harvest a few buckets a year to use on our farm. If you're buying salt, make sure it's non-iodised and of the best quality you can find.

SHIITAKE SALT

Equal weights of dried sliced mushrooms and good-quality salt

1. The dried shiitakes need to be crispy and dry. Either use them straight after they've been dehydrated or, if they've been in the cupboard for a while, put them on a tray in the oven at a low heat for 20 minutes to crisp them up.

2. Once you've got your crispy shiitake bits, blend them in a food processor, just for 10 seconds. Add the salt and whiz again until the shiitake pieces are about the same size as the salt grains.

3. Store the shiitake salt in an airtight container or in small jars (shiitake salt makes an awesome gift or bartering material). Use it to garnish anything for a salty, smoky, earthy kick – roast meats, roast vegies, pasta, rice, eggs, home-made crackers… you name it. If it's savoury, it can be improved with a little shiitake salt.

NATURAL
BEEKEEPING

THE WAY OF THE BEE

Waking up to the soft hum of the beehives outside our back door is a special way to start the day. There's so much to be learned from, and about, bees.

In spring, we watch the activity at the hive's entrance, as the bees begin to fly and bring back pollen to feed their new babies. In summer, we take a quick peek inside the hive to check that all's well, and give the bees the space they need to expand. In autumn, we harvest surplus honeycomb, if there is any – sometimes yes, sometimes no, depending on the season. And in winter, we render the spare wax down into candles, protect and support our family's health with honey, propolis and bee bread, make mead, and clean empty hive boxes, ready for the season ahead. We protect the hives from heat, cold and curious cows. We disturb them as little as possible.

The importance of honeybees in productive backyards and small farm systems cannot be overstated. If you keep bees, you receive many gifts other than honey. The apples eagerly set fruit, the pumpkins are everywhere – all your vegetables and fruit harvests are enhanced. And it's not just your patch that receives the benefits, of course. Every garden or farm within a 5 km (3 mile) radius is visited by these incredible little creatures, who bring life wherever they go. Add to that abundance the occasional harvest of honey, bee bread, propolis and wax, and you have… heaven. Sweetness and light, for real.

Our ancestors understood the importance of bees – most cultures have kept, or had relationships with honeybees. To ensure our grandchildren also receive these gifts of pollination and occasional harvests, it's up to us to steward honeybees well. We can keep them in well-crafted hives, with minimal intervention and a lot of observation. We can support local bee populations by planting for pollinators and preventing habitat loss. And we can lobby our councils and national authorities to halt toxin use that adversely affects bees in agricultural and garden settings.

In return, the gifts the bees give us – all of us – are many. They deserve our care and our utmost respect. We cannot do without them.

Inspecting a Warré U-bar frame of natural comb and brood.

THE HISTORY OF BEEKEEPING

The historical relationship between humans and bees could well be called a co-evolution. When you think about a prehistoric diet, with only the occasional and highly seasonal sweet and sour tastes of berries and fruit, the experience of biting into honeycomb would have been the ultimate explosion of both sweetness and tightly stored energy. It's likely that we have loved bees from the start, despite the danger and pain that comes with robbing a wild hive for its treasure.

Honey hunters

There are records of honey hunters from many continents. The First Australians would tie a feather on a thread to a *Tetragonula* bee (a native, stingless, social bee) in order to follow it back to its hive to rob the stores. In parts of Africa, the greater honeyguide bird has a long history of guiding hunters to beehives in return for a share of the hive's spoils. Cave paintings from 15,000 BC in Valencia, Spain, depict a honey hunter robbing a cliff-face hive for honey. And in Nepal and parts of India, the Asian honeybees' combs, which hang free under rocky overhangs, are still collected in the traditional way, as they have been for centuries.

As for keeping honeybees, there's evidence that the Ancient Egyptians, Greeks, Chinese and Mayans, to name but a few civilisations, all began to keep species of their native honeybees in ancient times. The oldest records of clay and log hives date from 6000 years ago.

The keeping of bees

Up until the 18th century, beekeeping was a very context-driven practice and hive designs and materials depended on climate and local resources. Some Europeans used skeps – large thimble-shaped structures, woven from reeds. Some regions used log hives, like the karakovan hives of Turkey, or integrated tree hives, like the Bashkir forest hives in the Urals. In the Middle East and the Mediterranean, clay or mud hives were common. And it's probable that the Greeks were doing top bar beekeeping in similar hives to what we now call a Kenyan top bar hive, starting 3000 years ago.

In the 19th century, however, alongside the industrial revolution, a 'more is more' approach to beekeeping as a commercial activity came into play. This marked the move from managing honeybees as a whole colony to managing them as a series of boxes with removable frames of comb. One of the hives that rose to prominence in the USA was the Langstroth hive – a box-and-frame system with dimensions based on the empty champagne crates Mr Langstroth had in his shed at the time. This basic hive design and the subsequent use of foundation and extractors increased the ability to maximise honey yield, and it has become one of the default hive designs of modern western commercial beekeeping.

At a similar time, different hives with a different goal were being designed. In the early part of the 20th century, a French monk named Emile Warré

Skeps are traditional European beehives woven from rushes.

A pollen forager honeybee (on the left) returning to her Warré hive, fully laden with pollen to feed the colony's brood.

developed what he called 'The people's hive'. His aim was to design a hive that was focused on bee colony health by mimicking a vertical tree hollow, while still allowing for a minimal-intervention honey harvest. And while also being small enough (and therefore light enough when fully loaded with honey) to be workable by anyone. As it turned out, he did a pretty stellar job, and the Warré hive is now popular across the world with backyard beekeepers wanting a minimal-intervention, bee-centric approach to beekeeping.

The future

The future for honeybees is uncertain. Between various bee diseases that have spread worldwide, environmental pesticide use, mismanagement and habitat loss, bee populations in many parts of the world are strung-out and struggling. Keeping bees on a small scale in a naturally bee-centric way with minimal intervention, and putting colony health first before a honey yield, can help a lot. As Simon Buxton, beekeeper and author, said, 'The future of bees is not in one beekeeper with 60,000 hives, but with 60,000 people each keeping one hive.'

BEE BIOLOGY

Worldwide, there are thousands of species of bees – they're found on every continent except Antarctica. Some bees are social and live in a colony with other bees, and some are solitary. Some bees produce honey, stored in combs of various constructions, and some just eat the nectar from a flower and move on to their next meal. All are important for pollination, and there's evidence that all have co-evolved with the flowering plants of their native habitat.

The species that we're looking at in this chapter is *Apis mellifera* – the western honeybee. After originating in either Africa or Asia (there's still debate around this), *Apis mellifera* has become the most common honeybee used for beekeeping worldwide. Some of its biology is common to other bee species, and some is not.

As a natural beekeeper, it's important that you understand the life cycle and natural behaviour of honeybees, so that you can do the best thing by them and respond to their needs.

A fully built-out comb in a Warré hive, containing brood with a wreath of capped honey above it.

The super-organism

A honeybee colony is considered to be a super-organism. It's made up of many female worker bees (who undertake different tasks throughout their lifespan), male drones, one mother queen, and the wax that the bees secrete from their own bodies and construct into hexagonal comb, on which they all live. A honeybee colony is also a warmth organism, so it needs to maintain a core temperature of 35°C (95°F) to remain healthy and free of disease.

Queen bees are often portrayed as being the boss of the hive, but the opposite is actually true once you know how the colony works. In a wild hive, the collective super-organism, composed mainly of worker bees, makes all the big decisions – when to raise a new queen, when to swarm, how many drones to produce and maintain, and so on. All of these decisions are determined by environmental and internal factors that we are only just beginning to understand. Bees know stuff – big stuff. In natural beekeeping, we defer to their knowledge as much as possible and try not to impact on their decisions unless we have to.

The comb

The wax comb that the bees live on is an intrinsic part of the super-organism, given that it's made by the bees, of the bees, for the bees. The comb functions as a 'social uterus' – it's the bees' collective womb, as well as their larder for food storage. The comb is essential to the colony's communication, too, as the bees use it to vibrate messages throughout the hive.

The bees construct their comb as a two-sided hexagonal array of cells made of pure white beeswax. They start at the top of an available cavity and draw the comb downwards. In a naturally managed hive, the queen consistently lays her eggs into fresh, virgin comb that the colony draws for her, in an ever-descending pattern. This virgin comb is the cleanest possible space for baby bees to grow, ensuring peak colony health. Directly above this ever-shifting brood pattern, the bees store a tight wreath of pollen, topped by a dome of honey.

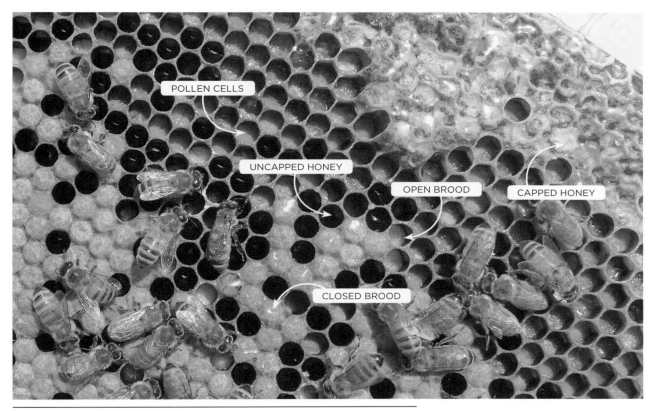

POLLEN CELLS

UNCAPPED HONEY

OPEN BROOD

CAPPED HONEY

CLOSED BROOD

A natural comb is a truly multi-use space. This one contains brood, pollen and honey cells, arranged in a descending pattern.

BEE SPACE

'Bee space' is a special measurement of between 6 and 9 mm (¼ and ⅓ inch). It's important because bees leave gaps of one bee space all around the hive, allowing all the bees in the hive to travel easily. Combs will generally be built one bee space apart, on the wide side and at the top and bottom, so that the bees can work around the combs every which way. If the bees encounter a gap of more than one bee space (at the bottom of a comb, for example), they will fill in the difference with comb. This is important to note when constructing frames and beehives.

The life cycle of a honeybee. Workers, queens and drones all progress through this process at slightly different paces (with slightly different food), but they all go through each separate stage before hatching.

1. Queen lays egg into cell
2. Brood nurse feeds larva
3. Larva reaches full size
4. Brood nurse seals cell
5. Larva spins cocoon and pupates
6. New bee emerges

Life cycle of a worker bee

Worker bees begin as all bees do, as an egg laid by the queen into a comb cell. Genetically, a worker bee egg receives half its genes from the queen bee and half from the dozen or more drones the queen has mated with. Over a 21-day cycle, that worker egg grows into a larva and is fed both royal jelly and 'bee bread', which consists mainly of pollen plus microflora added by the bees. Once the larva transforms into a pupa, the cell is capped (day 9). On day 21, the new bee eats through its capping and emerges.

Newborn worker bees go straight to work and progress through a range of roles in the hive, including cleaning cells, becoming nurse bees, comb constructors, guard bees and, finally, foragers that fly out of the hive into the big outside world and come back with nectar or pollen. Until they are foragers, they live completely in the dark of the hive, communicating through comb vibration, pheromones and physical contact.

Life cycle of a drone bee

A drone bee is a male bee, and his purpose in the colony is a bit like community service – his main objective is to diversify the overall honeybee genetics of the wider area, which in the long term is good for his own hive as well. A drone life cycle starts off like that of a worker bee, except that a drone egg contains only the genetics of the queen, not the genetics of the drones she has mated with. Drone brood cells are larger than worker bee brood cells, and have an extruded cap. They take 24 days to emerge into drone bees. Once hatched, they load up on honey and prepare to fly out to what is mysteriously known as a Drone Congregation Area or DCA. It's an area about 100 metres (110 yards) from the ground, often kilometres away from the hive. A DCA is where local drones gather to await virgin queen bees from colonies within the area, with the goal of inseminating them and passing on their hive's genetics. If they have no luck, they fly back to their hive and return to the DCA on the next day to try again. This continues for months until the drone either manages to inseminate a virgin queen (at which point they die, as their genitals are ripped out in the process) or dies of natural causes. In colder climates, where bees cease to fly over winter and there is no need for the drones until spring, the drones may also be turfed out of the hive entirely at the end of the mating season. Being a drone bee is a bit of a thankless job, but the resilience and wild genetic diversity of honeybees depends on them. Thanks, drones!

Life cycle of a queen bee

A queen bee grows from an egg that the worker bees select as being a future queen, for one of a variety of reasons. To transform that egg into a queen, the nurse bees feed the larva copious amounts of royal jelly, which the nurse bees produce from their own heads. This substance changes the morphology of the larva into a queen. The new queen hatches after 16 days. What happens next is complicated and depends on why the colony raised that new queen. Generally speaking, if there are any other queens in the hive (or queen cells that are soon to hatch), the new queen will try to kill them. She then flies out to the local DCA on what is called the 'nuptial flight'. While at the DCA, the new queen will mate with up to 20 local drones before returning to the hive full of locally adapted and diverse bee genetics. She then proceeds to lay eggs into the comb the workers build for her and never leaves the hive again (unless the hive swarms). She can live for up to three years until she's usurped by a new queen that the colony produces when they see fit.

BEE PHEROMONES – CHEMICAL COMMUNICATION

In the warm, dark heart of the hive, bees use chemical pheromones to communicate all sorts of messages, as well as temporarily change the behaviour of other bees. Pheromones are emitted by one or more bees (either in liquid or vapour form) and received by other bees via their antennae or via direct contact. Bees use pheromones to sound an alarm, specify what to do next, give orientation, leave trails, mark egg cells as ready or not ready, hide things, reveal things and for possibly thousands of other reasons. It's pretty wild stuff.

A natural brood comb showing drone brood cells to the left (the protruding, lighter ones) and worker brood cells to the right.

WHY BEES RAISE NEW QUEENS

It's important to understand why bees raise new queens, as there are a few contexts and indicators, and it helps to know what you will see on the comb. The bees create three different types of queen cell shapes and place them in different areas of the comb, depending on why they're raising a new queen: swarm cells, supercedure cells and emergency cells.

Swarm cells

Swarm cells are cells containing a growing queen that are built when the colony is confident, healthy and ready to split via swarming. These cells look like a thimble hanging off or near the bottom of the comb. Only once these baby queens are in the final days of gestation will the colony swarm, with the existing queen flying off with the swarm. The swarm cells then hatch and whichever queen emerges first will kill the others in their cells. Conventional beekeepers sometimes prevent swarming by squishing swarm cells (this isn't recommended in natural beekeeping) because the colony will generally only consider swarming once they know they're leaving behind viable queens that are about to hatch.

Supercedure cells

A supercedure cell is a normal brood cell that the colony has decided to convert to a queen cell because the existing queen is sick or old. They appear on the face of the comb and look like a crooked little finger – a thimble with a right angle in it. The bees mask this cell with pheromones so that the existing queen doesn't recognise it as a queen cell and attack it during its brood phase. When the new queen hatches, the workers continue to mask her presence with pheromones until she has flown out, mated, returned to the hive and is laying successfully. Only then do the worker bees dispose of the old queen.

Emergency cells

Emergency cells are normal brood cells (in early stages of development) that the colony has belatedly decided to transform into queen cells. They do this by enlarging the brood cell to a round pot shape (sometimes called a queen cup) and backfilling it with royal jelly. Often these are made because the queen has suddenly died or left the hive. The colony can sense this turn of events almost immediately and responds accordingly.

OPPOSITE: Protect the queen! Can you see her? She's the extra-long yellow bee in the centre. Here she's laying eggs into a frame of fresh comb that the bees have just drawn.

BELOW: Here are a few distinctive queen brood cells, on the edge of the comb. Figuring out which type of queen cell they are can be tricky, though.

WHAT IS NATURAL BEEKEEPING?

The term 'natural beekeeping' is an oxymoron in some ways, in the same way that 'keeping' any wild thing is. The act of hands-on stewardship means that the organism (or super-organism) is no longer completely wild or in its natural state.

Honeybees are wild creatures in a super-organism form. They are neither pets nor livestock. Unless disabled or prevented, they will do as they choose, each and every time. The trick to natural beekeeping is learning to work with the bees for a mutually excellent result.

So the term 'natural beekeeping' is really a term of comparison. In relation to conventional beekeeping practice, in which the hive design and management techniques are aimed at maximising honey harvest for the beekeeper, natural beekeeping aims to put the bees first, and honey harvests second.

There are many beekeeping traditions across the world that strive to keep bees in a way that honours and respects their wildness, while enabling a honey harvest. And harvesting is really the crux of the issue – finding a way, through good hive design and management, to harvest with minimal disturbance or manipulation of the colony so it can live on, from year to year, happy and healthy in the space we've provided for it.

OTHER SUPPORT STRATEGIES

The alternative to natural beekeeping could simply be honeybee support – maintaining bee habitats in the backyard in the form of a pollinator garden, and at a community scale in the form of meadows and forests. Putting up logs or other structures for wild hives to colonise, without interference, is also a great support. But the benefits of delicious and medicinal hive products like honey, wax, bee bread and propolis are all things that we want in our lives. And so, we keep bees – naturally.

OPPOSITE: A gorgeous full box of Warré comb that the bees have built. Note how they've maintained the bee-space between combs.

LEFT: Planting favourite plants for bees (like this borage) is another way to support and steward both bees and honey production in your area.

RIGHT: A wild colony will sometimes decide that the underside of a branch is the best they can do for a new home. This colony stayed for a few months, before swarming onward.

OPPOSITE: A wild colony up inside an old tree stump, making the most of the space it could find.

HONEY
STORAGE

PERIPHERAL
GALLERIES

POLLEN
STORAGE

BROOD

DRONE CELLS

QUEEN CELL

The hive in its natural state. (Illustration after T.D. Seeley and R.A. Morse's *The Nest of the Honey Bee,* 1976.)

THE HIVE IN ITS NATURAL STATE

When wild bees are seeking a new home, they'll look for a protected space with a small entranceway and a large, preferably well-insulated, internal cavity. Often this is a tree hollow or a rock crevice, but it can be anything from a letterbox to a roof cavity. The bees will work with what they can find.

In a typical tree hollow, the bees will first clean out all undesirable material. They will then proceed to start drawing long, vertical comb from the top of the cavity for their queen to lay into, storing honey around the central 'brood nest' of cells containing baby bees. They plug and cover the walls of the cavity with propolis, an antibacterial and highly medicinal substance that they make from collected tree resins. When the bees feel a comb is getting too big to be stable, it will be cross-braced in whatever way they see fit, which creates the amazing crenulated patterns we see in wild comb hives. Holes and peripheral galleries are created wherever needed to allow movement between combs.

As the queen lays successive generations of brood, each one below the previous generation, the generation in the cells above hatches. Once each newly hatched bee vacates its cell, that cell is immediately packed with pollen to support and feed the brood below. When that pollen is eaten, the cell is packed with honey and then capped. In this way, the pattern continues – a descending brood nest enclosed by a wreath of pollen, topped by a growing dome of capped honey. The bees will continue this pattern until the end of the season, when it becomes too cold to fly. They then stay inside the hive, tending the remaining brood, eating their honey stores and keeping their core temperature stable until spring. In warmer climates, honeybees may not go broodless nor stop flying over winter, but instead maintain a smaller brood, which expands again in spring.

Simply put, natural beekeeping is the practice of managing a bee colony as a whole, in a tree hollow or, more often, a simulated tree hollow.

TOP, LEFT: Bees love our *Eryngium* patch. TOP, RIGHT: Observing at the hive entrance. ABOVE: A top bar Kenyan beehive can be great in colder climates – there are many ways to keep bees naturally.

NATURAL BEEKEEPING: A BEE-CENTRIC APPROACH

As a beginner beekeeper, it's very easy to get confused about different hive designs, management techniques, plastic inserts, taps, queen excluders and all the rest. If you're interested in keeping bees in a way that puts the bees' needs first (which doesn't necessarily mean a lessened harvest, because healthy bees are productive bees), start by doing a bit of research, and consider a principles-based approach.

Natural beekeeping principles encompass the basics of what bees need to thrive, and so they're excellent principles to guide a beginner natural beekeeper. With proper care and attention, they can be applied to a range of different hive designs.

Some hives used in natural beekeeping are box hives, kept in a vertical stacked format. There are also various horizontal hives that mimic a horizontal tree hollow. And there are actual log hives, and neo-skep hives… and so many others. For the purposes of this book, we've used the Warré hive (the one made by the French monk Emile Warré) as the default hive design. It's a vertical box hive that has top bars in each box. There's a rundown of this hive design on pages 148–149.

Once you get your head around the fundamentals of what bees need to be healthy, you can make your choices accordingly, and get hold of (or make) a hive and gear that's right for you, your context and the bees.

UTILISE LOCAL KNOWLEDGE

When it comes to bees and natural beekeeping, there is so much to know and learn. The first resource you should look into is your local beekeeping club or apiarists' association. Although some of the folks attending may practise a very different style of beekeeping to that described here, there will be all sorts of local and hard-won knowledge to absorb. We suggest you follow your own path – use whatever advice and knowledge you can, and leave alone anything that runs contrary to bee-centric beekeeping.

A Warré apiary in Bathurst, New South Wales, maintained by Malfroy's Gold.

NATURAL BEEKEEPING PRINCIPLES

These principles can be applied to a range of countries and contexts. They include the essentials of what a honeybee colony needs to thrive and create long-term resilience for bees as a species, and for us, too.

Natural comb

Allowing bees to build their own comb is essential for long-term colony health. Natural comb is literally made of bee. The bees secrete flakes of wax from the underside of their abdomens and then shape it into cells in a collective construction operation, and these cells are then used successively to harbour babies, pollen and honey. Classed as part of the super-organism, the comb is the bees' womb, home and larder. The bees vary their comb's cell size according to their needs (drone cells need to be bigger, for example), and draw comb at different speeds according to the season's attributes.

By drawing their own comb, rather than being forced to use plastic, pre-made or re-used comb, the bees can ensure that the queen is always laying into fresh, virgin comb, which makes a big difference to colony health. The wax comb is lipophilic, and like the fat stores of any organism, accumulates any toxins that the bees come into contact with, building up over time as the bees work that comb. This is part of the reason that comb renewal is so important.

Comb renewal

Comb renewal happens naturally in a wild hive. When the bees deem a comb to be old or contaminated, they will cut it out and either dump it at the bottom of the cavity or fly it out the front of the hive and drop it there. In conventional beekeeping, the bees don't have this option. They're stuck with the fixed comb they're given, and must re-use it as many times as the beekeeper sees fit – both for brood and honey storage.

In natural beekeeping, facilitating comb renewal is paramount. Having your bees cycle through fresh comb cleanses the hive, drastically limits toxin build-up (both for the baby bees and in the honey you eat) and means the hive is as healthy as it can be, even in the face of widespread environmental chemical use.

Comb renewal is helped along by providing ongoing space beneath the colony, allowing the bees to continue to draw new comb downwards. This beekeeping process is called 'nadiring' – placing an empty hive box under the existing colony, which gives the colony space to grow with minimal disruption (see page 145). In this way, the colony can draw comb endlessly downwards. And excess honey can be harvested periodically from the top box, at the top of the honey dome, with minimal disturbance to the hive.

The comb renewal process is also helped along by the fact that in natural beekeeping, the whole honeycomb is harvested – this 'flushing' effect further limits disease and toxin build-up, as no old comb is returned to the hive.

ABOVE: A Warré box and a frame of natural comb all in the process of being built by the bees. Their natural U-shaped comb will slowly be built out to the sides of the frames and naturally secured.

OPPOSITE: A full box of natural honeycomb, showing the different colours of nectar that the bees have collected.

SWARMING IN THE SUBURBS

Swarming bees are one of the first things your neighbours may ask about when you tell them you're planning on getting a backyard hive. However, when bees swarm, they're at their most gentle, as their mission is to protect the queen and find a new home as quickly as possible.

When bees swarm they take to the air in what looks like a loose cloud (the buzzing noise is incredible) and cluster in a tight group when they rest, usually on a tree branch. The colony alternates between flying and resting until a new home is found, confirmed and accepted.

As a potential suburban beekeeper, putting up a bait hive in the hope of catching a local swarm is a great idea. One box with a good lid and some frames with starter strips in a likely place should do the job, and a bit of 'slum gum' (the gunk left over after rendering beeswax) can help, too. Bait hives typically do best when placed a few metres high, as the bees are looking for a home up off the ground – on top of a carport is a popular spot. If a swarm finds and accepts your hive, you can then move it to your chosen apiary site.

If you come across a swarm in its resting state but don't have a box or hive to put it in, contact your local beekeepers' association or local council.

Natural reproduction: swarming and re-queening

In terms of a honeybee colony, natural reproduction happens on two levels. The first is reproduction of the super-organism as a whole, when the colony splits via swarming. Swarming is an optimistic act in which a colony chooses to split in half to reproduce itself. The existing queen flies out with the swarm, while a portion of the colony stays behind with a new queen. Often bees will swarm if environmental indicators point to a good season ahead. Sometimes a hive will swarm because it has completely run out of space in its hive cavity. This allows the halved colony that's left behind to rebuild its numbers.

The second form of natural reproduction is on an individual level, allowing the bees to raise a new queen when they choose and allowing that queen to freely mate with local drones. A honeybee colony may decide to raise a new queen because the existing queen is old, sick or injured, or laying poorly. When this happens the bees will change the diet of a chosen egg or eggs to create potential new queens.

Allowing bees to swarm and/or raise their own queens means that the hive itself chooses the next queen. They choose the timing of when she is produced and, importantly, her genetics. In the process of conventional 're-queening', a commercially produced queen bee is typically mail-ordered and then added to the hive. This queen will usually be bred to focus on traits like golden colour, quietness and honey production, traits favoured by commercial beekeepers. In a natural beekeeping system, however, there are other important traits that are valued in a queen and the genetics that she passes on – local disease resistance, strong comb-building abilities, strong foraging and successful swarming abilities, to name just a few. Natural, locally adapted genetics are vital to ongoing colony health. The bees know what they need. Let them decide and reproduce accordingly.

Natural reproduction is important not just for individual colonies but also for the 'super-super-organism' that is the community of bees in a given area, all interacting and swapping locally adapted, resilient genetics to ensure long-term colony health for all.

Natural food: honey and pollen

Bees eat honey and pollen. These are both food and medicine to them, and represent a complete diet throughout an adult bee's life.

The thousands of species of beneficial microflora found in both honey and bee bread are largely a result of the honey-making process. As the bees eat and regurgitate the nectar many times between its arrival at the hive and its eventual packing into a cell, layers and layers of microflora are introduced. By the time the nectar becomes honey, it is a serious probiotic powerhouse and the perfect food for bees.

The pollen that bees collect in baskets on their legs from millions of flowers is similarly processed inside the hive, becoming 'bee bread'. This is stored in cells both to feed baby bees and to provide protein for adult bees as well. It's another dense food and medicine for the bees, containing many species of microflora.

When you understand what honey means to bees, it's pretty easy to see why it's so important to ensure they have the food they need, especially through cold winter months, for optimal colony health.

Beekeeping practices that harvest too much of the honey from hives over the summer create a situation where the bees do not have enough stored food to make it through the winter. It is then common to feed the bees on sugar water. It's a bit like us living on white bread alone for six months. Instead of a wholesome, balanced diet, sugar water provides empty carbohydrates with none of the probiotics or medicinal aspects of honey that bees need, especially when they are stressed, cold or sick.

In natural beekeeping it's essential to ensure the bees have enough honey stores at all times. In a crisis, feeding starving bees clean honey, preferably in the form of honeycomb and always from a disease-free hive, is the best substitute for their own honey stores.

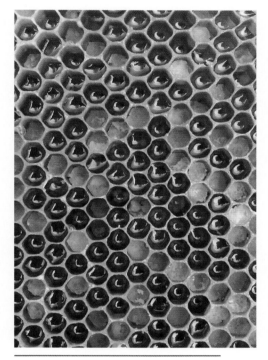

ABOVE: Cells of pollen, the foraging work of many hundreds of bees, interspersed with cells of uncapped, glistening honey.

OPPOSITE: A swarm of bees, resting on a branch before flying onwards. The queen is in the middle of the cluster.

Minimal intervention

A minimal intervention approach towards beekeeping limits hive opening and disturbance of the colony. Minimising intervention doesn't mean ignoring your hive, however. If anything, your relationship with the hive is enhanced and more nuanced.

Since a bee colony is a warmth organism, maintaining the colony's internal heat is crucial. Bees are not warm-blooded by themselves, so they create this collective heat through friction. Heater bees buzz their bodies at a frenzied rate, generating heat for the benefit of the colony and the health of both brood and adults. Along with the 'nest scent' (the environment of pheromones actively used for communication within the hive), maintaining this core temperature is intrinsic to colony health and disease suppression. Limiting the times you open the hive from the top to two to three times per season is a big help in retaining this heat and scent.

Another way to check on the bees throughout the season is to observe the entrance activity. Bees bringing in pollen means the queen is laying well. Bees flying in low and crashing onto the bottom board (or below it, and crawling up) can mean that there is plenty of nectar around and the bees are coming back fuller than full. Bees landing light on the bottom board can mean that nectar foraging is sparse. Different smells also indicate different things. Read the signs (and good books on the subject) and you will learn a lot from what happens at the hive entrance.

Nadiring is yet another way to minimise intervention. Until a hive is many boxes high, getting a friend to help raise the hive as a whole and slip a box underneath is a great low-intervention way to add space to the hive without opening it up.

Natural management

In an age where bees on many continents are routinely dosed with chemical treatments, either to control existing disease or in anticipation of infection, the idea of natural management flies in the face of much conventional beekeeping practice. However, a dedicated focus on good hive management, natural husbandry and disease prevention are key to healthy bees, in the same way that these techniques are key to growing healthy food or keeping healthy animals.

The principles outlined above, particularly ensuring natural comb renewal and natural reproduction, have been shown to greatly lessen bee colony diseases over time. With lots of research and careful observation, good management and prevention can be your key tools for hive health.

NADIRING

Nadiring is the process of adding space to a hive from below, in the form of an empty bee box. It allows the bee colony to expand downwards whenever it's ready, with minimal disturbance. Adding space to a colony only from the bottom ensures the integrity of the colony's natural structure is maintained: a brood nest topped by pollen cells, topped by capped honey, in a close, continuous pattern, with no big gaps.

Nadiring runs contrary to many conventional beekeeping practices, where empty boxes that contain pre-formed comb are added on top of the colony, above the brood nest. Along with queen excluders, these techniques are aimed at maximising honey production. However, they can also encourage disease and bee stress, as they add empty space (that will need to be heated) and unpatrolled comb (that will need to be kept free of pests) above the very centre of the super-organism.

Adding space to the bottom of a hive allows for the colony to grow at its own rate, with all the comb in the hive being able to be patrolled by bees for disease and pests. Adding this space at the bottom and harvesting from the top of the colony also 'flushes' the hive of disease and chemical build-ups that can reside in the older comb. Each season new comb is built underneath and older comb is harvested from above, full of that year's honey.

Observing entrance activity can tell you many useful things about the health of the hive and its current foraging patterns.

FOUR SEASONS OF BEEKEEPING

Although every year is different, you can generally expect each year to follow a similar pattern. Here is an example of how a year of natural beekeeping in a temperate climate might look.

Spring

As the weather warms up and plants start to flower, bees are flying and foraging and building new comb, to expand their colony. It's a good time to check entrance activity to ensure that the queen is laying (look for pollen coming in) and that your bees seem strong and healthy. No hive check is generally needed.

Summer

As things heat up and the bees are flying strongly, early summer is a good time to do a hive inspection and nadir an extra box (see page 145). Wait for a sunny, calm day that's about 27–30°C (81–86°F), and open the hive in the late morning when the majority of foragers have left for the day. Check for capped brood, eggs and honey stores, as well as any unusual activity. There won't be any harvest at this stage.

If the bees are flying very strongly, which indicates that there's a lot of nectar around, or are crowding on the front of the hive due to heat (bearding), nadiring a second empty box underneath can help with airflow in the hive as well as allowing for extra comb building.

Autumn

Early autumn is a good time to do a second hive check, and possibly harvest if it's a very good season and there is a lot of honey and a strong colony. Always leave a box of honey on the hive because you never know what the weather may bring.

In mid to late autumn, before the weather gets too cold, choose a warm day for the final hive inspection of the season. Again, check that the queen is laying, that there are no pest problems, and so on. If there's a lot of honey, this is the year's main harvest, while leaving the bees a full box of honey for the winter. At this time of year we 'pack down' the hive as much as possible, reducing the boxes to a minimum of two (or three if there's a big brood nest). This helps the bees throughout winter as they're not attempting to warm such a big space.

Winter

Winter is the time for processing, researching, resting and remaking. The only hive work is watching the entrance and keeping an eye on the general apiary area. Back inside our home, honey is pressed, wax is rendered, candles and soaps are made, and spare hive boxes and frames are scraped clean. Sometimes new boxes are constructed. There's time to read new beekeeping and bee biology books. And there's mead to be made.

And then, the weather slowly begins to warm up once more, and it's time to cycle back through the seasons.

SPRING: Bees bringing in pollen is a good sign that the queen is laying well.

SUMMER: Hive check – honey stores are looking good.

AUTUMN: Harvest and honey pressing.

WINTER: Repairing and top-bar frame making with starter strips.

SPRING

SUMMER

AUTUMN

WINTER

BACKYARD BEEKEEPING WITH WARRÉ HIVES

The Warré hive is a simple box hive that you can make yourself, or even buy as a flat-pack from some beekeeping suppliers. It's designed to provide a bee-centric approach to beekeeping while being easy to make and easy to work with, and allowing for a honey harvest if the season is bountiful.

The hives we use at home are Australian Warré hives. They're a variation on the classic Warré hive that have been slightly adapted to meet Australian conditions and regulations by full-time Warré beekeeper, Tim Malfroy. The hive's dimensions aim to mimic a vertical tree hollow that's not too big and not too small. Composed of a series of square boxes containing top-bar frames, the Warré hive looks simple. And it is. But as is often the way with good design, it's a simple solution to a complex challenge.

Warré hives on simple hive stands – facing east to catch the morning sun, and sheltered from the west.

THE WARRÉ HIVE: FROM TOP TO BOTTOM

Roof

The traditional Warré roof is gabled to shed both water and snow, ensuring no moisture pools above or inside the hive. A flat roof board covered in metal sheeting to reflect heat also works well.

Top board

The top board rests on the quilt box and provides insulation, protection from critters and a handy place to record the goings-on of the hive, at the end of each hive inspection.

Quilt box

This is a shallow box cut to the dimensions of the hive. It contains a removable cotton bag filled with a clean, dry, absorbent material (wood shavings are a common choice). The bag acts as the 'quilt' above the colony, insulating it from heat and cold while also wicking excess moisture out of the main hive space. It can be taken out at each hive inspection, checked, plumped up and then put back in place before the hive is closed.

Screen

The screen tops the hive space so the quilt box can be removed without disturbing the bees. It's cut to size from inert material, such as fibreglass flyscreen, allowing air to pass through freely. The screen also lets air and moisture come through without letting bees into your quilt box.

Boxes

The hive is made up of a series of vertical square boxes of a width that promotes straight comb building and easy management. When completely full of capped honey, one of these boxes will weigh no more than 15 kg (33 lb), which is safely manageable for most people.

Frames

The frames in a Warré hive are designed to allow the bees to draw their own comb, while also being removable and manageable for the beekeeper. The classic Warré design involves just top bars, with a small strip of wax to guide the bees' comb building. This design can result in the bees building and attaching their combs to the sides of the hive box, which means that removing a single top bar can be difficult when the box is full of comb.

The variation we use is a 'top and side bars' format – a U-shaped open frame with a starter strip of wax secured along the top bar. This variation allows the frames to be removable, as the bees will naturally build the comb downwards first, and then to the sides of the cavity to secure the comb. By providing a false 'side wall' to each comb, the bees build their combs securely to the U-shaped frame, leaving the usual bee space of 6–9 mm (¼–⅓ inch) at the bottom of the comb to allow them to move about, before starting again on the frame in the box below.

In Australia, regulations require that all hives have removable frames for disease inspection, so Tim Malfroy's variation on the traditional 'just top bar' is a great solution.

Base board

The base board is the solid bottom of the hive, with a 'landing board' at the front for the bees returning home from foraging. In colder climates, it's made of solid wood to insulate the colony. In warmer climates, especially where bee pests like small hive beetle are a problem, the base board may contain a metal trap to catch pests. The base board has a 10 mm (½ inch) 'riser' that keeps the bottom box up off the bottom board.

Hive stand

Getting your hives up off the ground ensures good airflow and minimal moisture for the hive, two factors that help prevent disease and bee stress. Hive stands can be made out of any solid, weatherproof material. Making a solid wooden stand that allows a space for hive work beside each hive is great if you can manage it, but a stand made out of solid bricks will also work well.

Always make sure that your hive stand is level in both directions, because the bees will build their comb in the direction of gravity. A crooked hive stand will make for crooked comb, tricky hive work and a grumpy beekeeper.

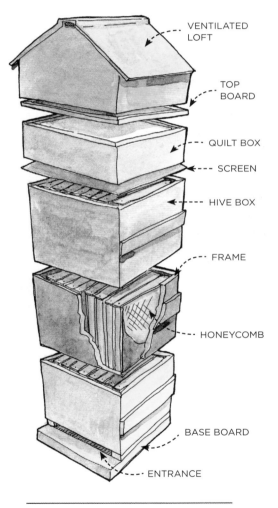

VENTILATED LOFT

TOP BOARD

QUILT BOX

SCREEN

HIVE BOX

FRAME

HONEYCOMB

BASE BOARD

ENTRANCE

The Warré hive, expanded.

Other hive designs for natural beekeeping

There are many, many hive designs, both traditional and recent, that are used across the world for bee-centric beekeeping – from Japan to Nepal to Bolivia to Croatia to Kenya and back again. Here are a few: the Kenyan top bar hive, a modified Langstroth hive, a karakovan log hive, a skep hive and the sun hive. There are some resources on page 292 to aid further discovery in hive designs, if you like.

A few of the many hives used for natural beekeeping around the world: skep hive, Kenyan top bar hive, karakovan log hive, modified Langstroth hive and sun hive.

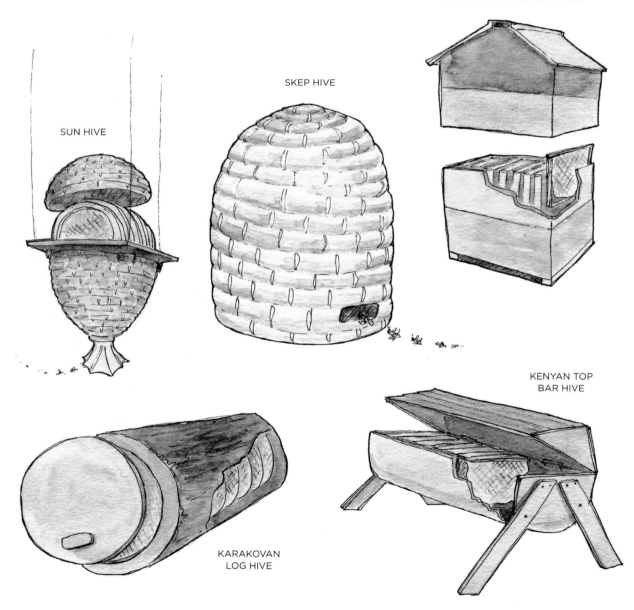

MODIFIED LANGSTROTH HIVE

SKEP HIVE

SUN HIVE

KENYAN TOP BAR HIVE

KARAKOVAN LOG HIVE

ABOVE LEFT: Dry pine needles are a great choice for smokers – they light easily and blow a very cool smoke.

ABOVE: Having all the tools and gear you need on hand is a huge help in ensuring quick and successful hive checks. Better for the bees, as well as for the beekeeper!

THE GEAR

Smoker

Smokers are used to repel bees, either from the comb or from beekeepers themselves, and can be used judiciously as an excellent hive management tool. If you overdo it, you'll stress the bees out, but a little smoke can be very helpful when things get tricky.

There's a saying that if you ask three beekeepers a question you'll get five answers back, and many keepers prefer using different materials in their smokers. Dry pine needles are a good option as you'll find them somewhere nearby in most places. They smoke for a long time at a low temperature and blow a cool smoke (hot smoke is not recommended as it further irritates the bees). It's a good idea to gather a sack of your favourite smoker material and store it somewhere dry so that you've always got some when you need it.

When checking our bees, we use just a few small puffs of smoke when taking the screen off the topmost box. After that we don't use smoke unless we need to push the bees down into a box, for example, when we're putting the screen back on the top box. It's always a good idea to have your smoker lit in case you drop a comb or otherwise mess up and get the bees highly annoyed. Smoking bees off yourself can limit stings in such a situation.

Hive tool

All hail the hive tool! It's a simple piece of metal with so many uses. A good hive tool is a wedge, jimmy bar, scraper and knife, all in one. We love hive tools that have a hook on one end, great for hooking up the end of a frame to help take it out of the hive with minimal disturbance.

A hive tool is especially useful when the bees have glued their boxes together with propolis. A gentle levering of all four corners can unglue the box without too much disturbance of the bees. It's a good thing to have in your hand whenever you're inspecting a hive.

Suits, veils and gloves

Most people start their beekeeping practice fully suited up and protected, but some prefer to have less barriers between them and the bees. It's true that the less gear you're wearing, the more respectful your attitude tends to be towards the hive. However, not having much gear on can make some people nervous about getting stung, and a nervous attitude is not a good thing when you're working with bees. Wear whatever makes you feel comfortable enough to get in there and work with the bees.

Over time, your attitude will probably change and you will wear less gear as you learn to smell, listen and read the signs of the hive as you work with it. As long as you're not suiting up for battle with an attitude that bees are the enemy and you can do whatever you want with the hive because you're protected, you'll be fine.

Practice, thoughtful observation and choosing the right day to open the hive will slowly get you to a place where you feel comfortable with your bees, and you'll find yourself wearing less protective gear accordingly.

Water

It's great to have a small bucket of water on hand for when things get sticky. And it's also good to have around in an emergency.

Empty hive box

An extra empty hive box is good to have around during a hive inspection. You can rest a full bee box on it if needed, keeping the hive box off the ground, or place frames in it, if you need to put a frame or two down while you deal with issues in the hive.

KEEPING THINGS CALM

When you go to open up a hive, make sure things are calm so the bees don't become agitated – no lawn mowers nearby, no shouting, no crazy actions. And being bees, this means keeping things calm in terms of smell as well (remember, pheromones are the bees' main communication tool). Strong artificial smells like hairspray and perfume should be avoided when working with bees.

ABOVE: A hive tool with a hooked end is very helpful for raising frames out of a full box for inspection.

OPPOSITE: Ashar carefully holds up a full comb of healthy, closed brood from one of our Warré hives.

SITING YOUR HIVE

Selecting a good site for your apiary can make a huge difference to honeybee health, and to your hive's honey harvest, too. A single, permanent site for your hive will cause the least stress possible to the bees, rather than moving them around.

Consider the factors described below and prepare your site, the stand that the hive will rest on and the access to it before you purchase or catch your bees. The day you come home with your bees is not the time to decide where they should go.

Aspect

Ideally, a north-east facing site (or south-east facing site, if you're in the northern hemisphere) will be best for your bees. Honeybees will start flying when the temperature reaches around 10–12°C (50–54°F). If your hive is somewhere that gets the early morning sun, the bees will fly out first thing to go foraging.

Shade

Protect your bees from the hot afternoon sun if you possibly can, especially in summer. The colony actively regulates its core temperature to 35°C (95°F), night and day. A hive doesn't want to be too hot any more than it wants to be too cold. A hive sitting in full summer sun, after midday, is going to get hotter than it wants to be.

Some aspects of an ideal backyard apiary site: protected to the west and south from cold winds, summer shade to the north, early sun to the east, and good access. Flip north to south for northern hemisphere apiaries, of course!

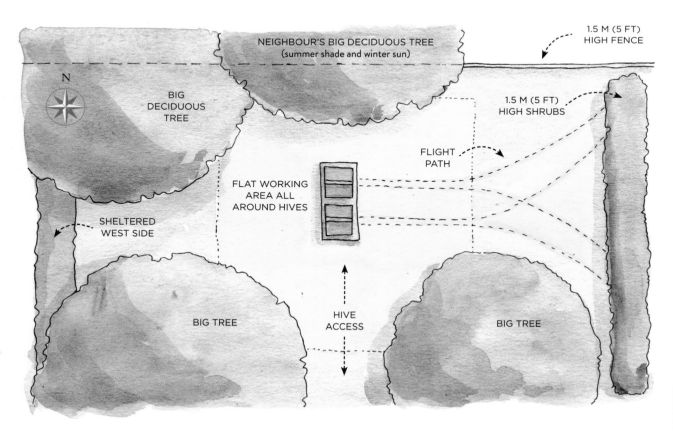

N

NEIGHBOUR'S BIG DECIDUOUS TREE
(summer shade and winter sun)

1.5 M (5 FT) HIGH FENCE

BIG DECIDUOUS TREE

1.5 M (5 FT) HIGH SHRUBS

FLIGHT PATH

FLAT WORKING AREA ALL AROUND HIVES

SHELTERED WEST SIDE

BIG TREE

HIVE ACCESS

BIG TREE

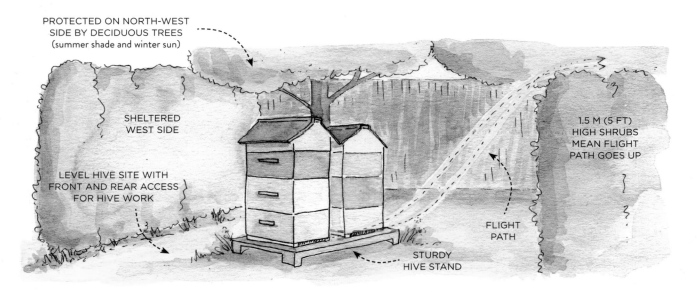

PROTECTED ON NORTH-WEST
SIDE BY DECIDUOUS TREES
(summer shade and winter sun)

SHELTERED
WEST SIDE

LEVEL HIVE SITE WITH
FRONT AND REAR ACCESS
FOR HIVE WORK

1.5 M (5 FT)
HIGH SHRUBS
MEAN FLIGHT
PATH GOES UP

FLIGHT
PATH

STURDY
HIVE STAND

Access

Access to your hive is really important. The easier your bees are to access, the more time you will spend observing them. If you can, site your bees close to somewhere you go every day so you form a natural habit of checking the hive regularly. Good, flat access will also make harvest days much easier when you're wrangling full boxes of Warré honey that can weigh 15 kg (33 lb) each.

Nearby nectar sources

Honeybees have a 5 km (3 mile) foraging radius, so before you site your hives, check your local environment to see if they will have enough to eat, over as much of the year as possible. While year-round flowering patterns are pretty much a given in most temperate urban or suburban areas, it can be a different story on rural blocks.

Foot traffic

Honeybees are very adaptable, but they prefer a clear flight path for at least the first few metres directly in the front of their hive.

While it's true that if you keep bees naturally and well, they're far less likely to be angry and stressed out, there's no point siting them in a way that may antagonise them.

Keep the area around your hive calm. A site that faces walkways where people come and go throughout the day or a driveway with loud vehicles moving by, is not your best bet.

Other disturbances

In an ideal world, your hive would never be bumped or knocked over. But reality is often different. Hive disturbance can take many forms, from errant soccer balls and cricket games in urban settings, to curious cows, horses and random trail bikers in rural settings.

A knocked-over hive is not something you want to encounter. It's terrible news for the bees and their natural comb, and not much better for the beekeeper who has to try to fix it. So do ensure your hive site offers protection.

An uninterrupted flight path that also encourages the bees upwards with bushes or a fence is a good way to ensure minimal disturbance to your neighbours.

SHELTERED BEES ARE HAPPY BEES

Sheltering your hive site from cold winter and hot summer winds will help greatly with colony health, so try to find a site that's not too exposed. While honeybees are highly adaptable, a sheltered hive will be much happier for your forethought.

HARVEST DAY: THE PRODUCTS OF THE HIVE

When you open your natural hive on harvest day, it's not just about the honey. You're also harvesting honeycomb, beeswax, bee bread and propolis. All of these are useful and exceptional bounty, in different ways.

HONEY

This incredible, medicinal, almost mythical substance has been sought after ever since humans have inhabited the earth. It's even been found, untainted, in Egyptian tombs – thousands of years old and still perfectly edible.

So what is honey? Honey begins as nectar from flowers. Foraging bees drink the nectar, store it in their honey stomach and deliver it back to their hive. Once at the hive, they regurgitate the honey and pass it to other bees. The bees continue this process of regurgitation until the nectar is partially digested and contains a huge amount of microflora, thanks to the stomachs of all the bees it's just passed through. This half-cured honey is then packed into cells and fanned by the bees' wings until its water content reduces to less than 17 per cent. The cells are then capped with a layer of wax and the honey is stored until it is needed as the super-probiotic, energy-rich bee food that it is. Or until the honeycomb is harvested, of course.

HONEYCOMB: THE LIGHT AND THE DARK

In a natural hive, you'll notice that the honeycomb has wildly different colours, sometimes in bands of colour on the one comb, from lightest yellow through to dark red and brown. Sometimes this is due to the different colours of the nectar, but most likely it's because some of that honeycomb is 'post-brood honeycomb' – comb that has had a cycle of brood pass through it, before being repurposed to store pollen and honey. In many cultures, this is the really good stuff, valued far more than virgin honeycomb, which has only ever had honey stored in it. In preparation for the queen laying into the comb, the bees line each cell with a variety of antibiotic and generally helpful nutrients and substances, to keep their babies healthy. After the brood hatches, these cells get re-used and filled with honey, but the cells still contain residues of the antibiotic compounds. Hence the post-brood honeycomb is considered (correctly) by many cultures to contain more goodness than the virgin honeycomb, and is sought after and priced accordingly.

The light yellow honeycomb is virgin honeycomb, which has only been used to store honey, and nothing else. The walls of the cells in this honeycomb are usually thinner as the cells haven't been reinforced for holding baby bees. For some people's tastes, this is the best honeycomb to eat whole.

Any and all types of honeycomb are great for crushing and straining into honey, as long as all the cells are capped. Uncapped honey cells are best cut out and crushed or eaten separately, as the uncured honey is not finished and may ferment in the medium to long term. It's best not to combine it with your finished honey.

Harvesting honeycomb

Harvesting honeycomb from a naturally managed hive is a relatively simple process. Just remove the honeycomb from the hive and that's it – honeycomb for you! There are a few ways to remove the honeycomb safely, outlined below.

Before harvesting, you should carefully check the honeycomb for remaining brood cells. If there are still brood cells in the middle or at the bottom of the comb, put that frame back in. The nurse bees will not leave their brood easily, and of course you don't want to kill the brood. Just put the box back on the hive and check again in a week.

Clearer board

If you live somewhere that has cool nights, you can place a 'clearer board' (available from beekeeping stores) between the top box to be harvested and the box below. Leave the clearer board in place for 24 hours. The bees should retreat to the boxes below to cluster around the brood at night time and the clearer board, with its one-way passages, means they can't get back up into the box of honeycomb. The next day, the top box is harvested, the clearer board removed and the quilt box and roof placed back on the hive. If your nights are not much cooler than the days, many bees may stay up on the honeycomb as they are not needed to warm the brood, so you'll need to choose another method.

Shaking

This is a remarkably effective method of harvesting honeycomb. Take out each frame of capped honeycomb and give it a short, sharp shake in front of the hive entrance. The bees will fall off and crawl back into the hive.

Chop and drop

If you're planning to harvest honey and also nadir another box underneath your hive on the same day, you can use the chop and drop technique. Take out each frame of capped honeycomb from the top box and give it a sharp shake or two outside the hive entrance to remove any bees on the comb. Using a sharp knife, cut the comb from the frame into a bucket with a lid, leaving a top strip of honeycomb to function as a 'starter strip' for the now empty frame. Once the whole box of frames has been harvested, the box of empty frames, with its sticky starter strips of honeycomb, is nadired underneath the hive. The small amount of dripping honey will soon be cleaned up by the bees.

ABOVE: The 'chop and drop' technique of natural comb harvesting allows the frame to go straight back into the hive with a sticky honeycomb starter strip – great for large honey harvests.

OPPOSITE: Checking a honeycomb – you can see the middle portion of cells is still uncapped. We'll put it back in place and return to this hive in a week's time.

ABOVE: Honey harvesting from natural comb can be done with simple kitchen tools – just your hands, a sieve and a bucket.

OPPOSITE, TOP: Pressing natural honeycomb into honey. LEFT: The light and the dark – the different flavours of honeycomb. RIGHT: Post-brood honeycomb, stored for eating whole.

Processing honeycomb

Once you've got your honeycomb back to your kitchen or shed, it's time to decide how to process it. If you have combs of capped honey that are entirely intact, one option is to store and eat them as whole honeycomb. While this is certainly a chewier option than liquid honey, honeycomb is a taste sensation unlike any other. The wax can be chewed and then removed like a glob of chewing gum, but it's fine to swallow, too.

Whole honeycomb as a food

If you're storing whole honeycomb, first ensure that it is completely free of pests – wax moth, small hive beetle, and so on. Find a container with a tight-fitting lid that's deep enough to store your combs vertically, if you can. If the combs are stored on their flat sides, the cappings will crush. An insulated cooler box with a good seal can be a good solution. When stored in capped natural comb, most types of honey can potentially keep, without crystallising, for many, many years. (There are a few exceptions, as some nectars have different sugar structures.) If you do intend to store honeycomb long term, freezing it for 24 hours first will kill all stages of wax moth and small hive beetle, which is good insurance for successful long-term storage.

Crush and strain

If you're after honey in a jar, simply crush and strain the comb. You don't need any special equipment to do this, especially for smaller batches. A good sieve over a bowl or bucket is all you need if you're crushing with your hands. Leaving the wax in the strainer overnight is a good idea to get the last drips, or even in a sunny inside place where the wax will be warm (but not too warm) and so will release the remaining honey from its crevices.

If you're working on a reasonable scale, a honey press is great. You can use either a home-made version or a bought one – they're often sold as a small-batch fruit press. We'd recommend one that has holes no smaller than 7 mm (¼ inch) so that it doesn't get clogged up, and that's made from non-reactive metal that's easy to clean.

Once you've crushed your comb, store your honey in a bunch of clean jars or a container with a well-fitting lid. Lids with a good seal are important here, as ants in your honey is a very sad situation. A honey bucket with a honey gate at the bottom (taps clog too easily) are easily sourced from beekeeping stores.

Don't throw away the wax once you're done – beeswax has so many uses.

SLUM GUM – ALSO USEFUL!

The blackish goop that's left in the sieve after the wax has been rendered is known as 'slum gum', and it's amazing, too. Roll it into lozenges for the best-ever firelighters, or store it to place inside bait hives in spring – it's great for attracting swarms.

A few ways to process beeswax at home, using simple everyday materials.

BEESWAX

Once the honey is removed from the comb, you are left with gorgeous, sticky beeswax, which can be cleaned and used. Beeswax is incredibly useful stuff and represents an enormous amount of care and energy from the hive. It should be processed just as carefully as your honey. You can use beeswax in cooking and to make medicines and balms, candles and soaps, and even no-plastic lunch wraps. It's great for plugging shiitake logs, keeping wooden furniture glistening and whole, and a thousand other uses.

Processing beeswax

When your beeswax has had all the honey strained out of it, it's ready to render down into pure wax. Rendering is the process of removing the non-wax materials with which the bees have lined the walls of their comb cells, along with any last skerricks of honey.

The first step is to get the remaining honey out of your wax. Luckily, honey is water soluble, so this part is easy – plus you can make mead and other drinks from the left-over honey-infused water (see page 170). Dump

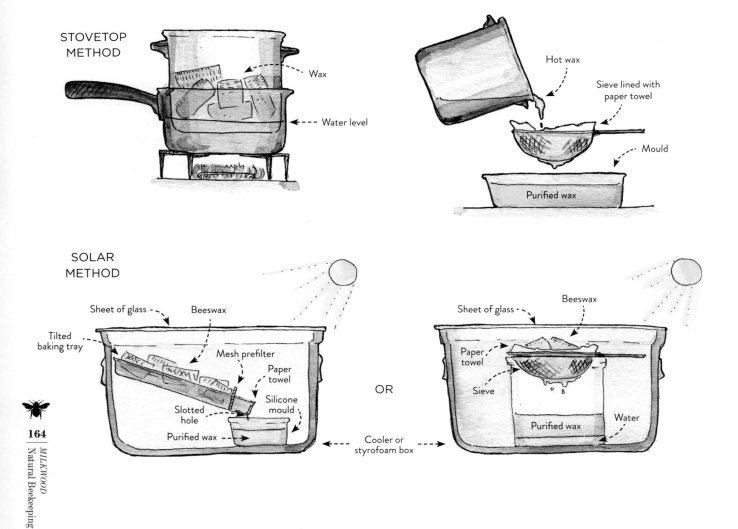

STOVETOP METHOD

Wax

Water level

Hot wax

Sieve lined with paper towel

Mould

Purified wax

SOLAR METHOD

Sheet of glass

Beeswax

Tilted baking tray

Mesh prefilter

Paper towel

Slotted hole

Silicone mould

Purified wax

OR

Sheet of glass

Beeswax

Paper towel

Sieve

Purified wax

Water

Cooler or styrofoam box

all the waxy bits in a clean bucket and break them up into small chunks, then cover it with clean water that is double the depth of the wax. Use unchlorinated water if you plan to use the wash water for making honey-flavoured drinks (which you definitely should do).

Using your hands, swish all the water around and rub the chunks of wax together to release the remaining honey. Once the wax no longer feels sticky, pour this mixture through a fine sieve or a piece of muslin (cheesecloth) and reserve the sweet water for making tasty things. The wax in the sieve is now ready for rendering.

Rendering beeswax

The basic process of rendering involves heating the wax (gently, so that it doesn't burn) on the stovetop or in the sun until it is completely liquid. Then you simply strain out the bits, leaving behind golden, pure beeswax to set into a block.

Beeswax is very difficult to get off utensils and pots, so consider making a beeswax processing kit with all the bits you'll need to use over and over again. We buy everything we need from local op shops or thrift stores.

Stovetop method

Place the wax chunks in the top of a double-boiler arrangement. Either use an actual double boiler or use a big pot of water with a smaller pot sitting snugly inside (but not touching the bottom), with the water coming up the side of the smaller pot.

Heat slowly until the wax is completely liquefied, then pour the wax through a sieve lined with paper towel into your mould of choice. This is the messy part, so make sure you've got everything you need on hand before you begin.

Solar method

This method is the most fun method and uses the least energy. It's also the least messy as everything happens outside, in one container. Get a 5 litre (1.3 gallon) bucket and a styrofoam box (or an insulated cooler) that can comfortably hold the bucket. You'll also need a sheet of glass or perspex to place on top of the box, a sieve that will sit in the bucket and a piece of paper towel.

Place the bucket in the cooler box, with about 2.5 cm (1 inch) of water in the bottom. Line the sieve with the paper towel and place it on top of the bucket, then place your wax in the sieve. Put the glass or perspex on top, and place outside in a sunny spot. Over the course of a hot day, this method should render as much wax as the sieve can hold into a nice round block of clean beeswax inside the bucket. You can tilt the box towards the sun throughout the day and prop it up with a brick or chunk of wood. The water in the bottom of the bucket will help to dissolve any remaining particles of honey, and also makes it easier to pop the block out at the end of the process as the block of wax will float on top.

Variations on this theme include creating a DIY solar wax melter (perhaps like the one shown left, which is what we use at home) or using an existing solar cooker.

Purified beeswax blocks with their characteristic 'bloom'. Such useful stuff!

MAKING BEESWAX WRAPS

Every kitchen should be full of these re-usable wraps. Use them in place of plastic wrap, but also to wrap bread and vegetables to keep them fresh. Beeswax wraps are washable and can be used again and again. Clean them with cold water and gentle soap as necessary, but we usually just rinse them in water and hang them up to dry. When the wax wears out, the wraps can be re-infused.

You will need:

- ❈ Thin cotton cloth of various sizes
- ❈ A hand grater
- ❈ Beeswax
- ❈ Metal baking trays
- ❈ Jojoba oil
- ❈ A wide paintbrush
- ❈ Pegs and a drying line

1. Cut the cotton cloth into squares or rectangles of your preferred size – we make them from 15 cm (6 inches) wide to about 40 cm (16 inches) wide.

2. Preheat the oven to 100°C (200°F). While it's warming up, grate the beeswax.

3. Place a cotton square on a baking tray and sprinkle it with some drops of jojoba oil, then sparsely sprinkle the grated beeswax over the top, all the way to the edges. Less is more – if the wax is too thick, the cloth won't be able to absorb it all.

4. Place the tray in your warm oven and watch closely – remove it as soon as the grated wax has melted, about 5 minutes at most. Use the paintbrush to ensure the whole cloth is covered with the melted wax, all the way to the edges.

5. Pick up the wax-covered wrap and peg it on a line until cool and dry. Repeat, repeat and repeat until you've used all your wax. If there's excess wax on the baking tray, just press the next cloth into it to absorb it, and reduce the amount of grated wax you add.

TIPS

Use scraps of cotton fabric, old skirts or pillowcases to make the wraps.

Choose a paintbrush that you're happy to get wax on, because you won't get it off again!

The jojoba oil helps the wax to spread evenly through the cloth. An eye dropper is useful for sprinkling the oil.

When you've finished making wraps, scrape any excess wax from your baking trays and add it to your spare wax supply.

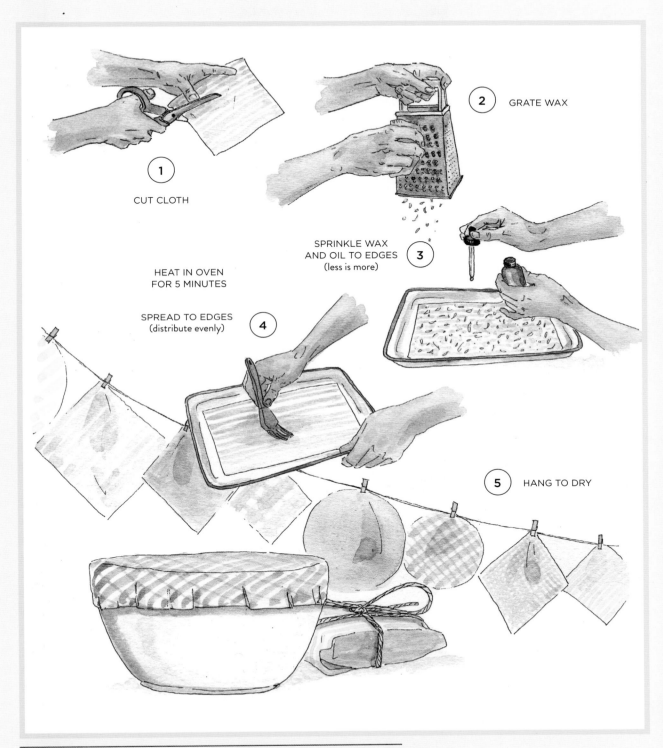

1 CUT CLOTH

2 GRATE WAX

3 SPRINKLE WAX AND OIL TO EDGES
(less is more)

HEAT IN OVEN
FOR 5 MINUTES

4 SPREAD TO EDGES
(distribute evenly)

5 HANG TO DRY

The process of making beeswax wraps, using everyday kitchen equipment.

PROPOLIS TINCTURE

You will need:

- ✺ Propolis
- ✺ Coffee grinder or mortar and pestle
- ✺ A small jar
- ✺ Vodka (minimum 40% alcohol – 80 proof or higher) or a similar spirit
- ✺ Muslin (cheesecloth)
- ✺ A dark glass jar

1. Collect your propolis over the course of the season and keep it in a jar that's not exposed to light. When you have enough to get started – 3 tablespoons of small pieces is a good amount – roll all your bits of propolis into a clump and freeze it overnight.

2. Grate or grind the frozen propolis to a coarse powder using either a coffee grinder or a mortar and pestle. Add the propolis to a small jar, filling it one-quarter full.

Pour in enough vodka to fill the jar to the top. Seal and label the jar. Store it in a warm, dark place, agitating it daily for 4–6 weeks.

3. After 4–6 weeks, strain the liquid through a piece of muslin, pressing firmly to extract as much liquid as possible. Compost the solids.

4. Pour the completed tincture into a dark glass jar and seal. Label and store the jar in a dark place. Decant the tincture into smaller bottles as you need it. It can be taken orally as a few drops in a glass of water or sprayed directly onto the skin.

TIP

Small bottles with eye droppers in the lids are useful for storing and dispensing the tincture.

Removing propolis from the tops of Warré top bars.

Small shavings of propolis, carefully harvested from the hive. Over a year you can build up quite a store.

PROPOLIS: TREE MEDICINE

The bees gather various tree saps and resin to turn into propolis, the dark brown, grainy-looking substance you'll often find along the tops of frames and in any nook or cranny of the hive. Highly medicinal and antibacterial, propolis is used by the bees to seal the hive's cracks and to coat the cavity of the hive, as well as for lining their brood cells. It's a medicinal coating that contributes greatly to colony health. Propolis is powerful stuff.

You'll harvest bits of propolis here and there. Carefully scraped into a jar, this is strong medicine, full of antibacterial compounds. You can roll propolis into a small ball and chew on it for hours for a medicinal kick. It's strongly flavoured, though, and not for everyone.

Propolis also makes an excellent tincture that's great for treating cuts, burns and scratches; sore throats, colds and flu; cold sores and some other viruses; and dermatitis and some skin rashes. It's also good as a preventative tonic when everyone around you is getting sick.

BEE BREAD: PROTEIN OF A MILLION FLOWERS

Bee bread is cells of pollen that the bees have collected to feed their brood. Sometimes they have an excess and it's left behind in the honeycomb. It's a probiotic treasure trove with a full-on taste. Bee bread is one of the best aspects of harvesting natural comb.

You can leave these cells in the comb to be crushed into honey (they'll add complexity and goodness). Or you can cut them out and store them separately to eat sparingly as a pick-me-up when your health and vitality is low.

If you opt for whole honeycomb, eaten in chunks, you'll get the full effect when you hit a cell of bee bread. Ever wanted to eat the goodness of a thousand flowers at once? This is how you do it.

RIGHT: Can you see the many layers of bee bread laid down by the bees in this cell? The bees ram it into the cells with their heads!

OPPOSITE: Mead on the make. The airlock ensures no competing microbes enter, and allows the mead to off-gas during its fermentation process.

MEAD, METHEGLIN AND MELOMEL

Wild fermented mead, in its purest form, is made with honey, water and time – that's it. It's perfect for making from your wax washing water, with some more honey added.

In a wild fermentation approach, this process can be as simple as adding honey to water in a suitable container, covering it with a cloth and stirring regularly until it bubbles – the raw honey provides all the yeasts necessary to ferment this mixture into mead. At this point an airlock is added (to help prevent other microflora entering the container and spoiling the mead) and the mead is fermented until you choose to drink it, after anywhere from a week to a year.

Melomel is mead to which fruit has been added in order to aid the fermentation process and to complexify the flavour. There's a recipe for making blackberry melomel in the Wild Food chapter (see pages 246–247).

Metheglin is mead to which herbs and spices have been added. The possibilities are only limited by your imagination, your garden and your spice rack. You can add the spices and herbs at the beginning, or when you airlock the mead. Ginger metheglin is amazing, as is metheglin made with orange zest, star anise and a vanilla bean. Actually, we vote for any metheglin – it's all good. And if it's not good (wild fermentation can be a variable practice), at least you made some spiced vinegar!

SEAWEED

TO THE SEA, TO THE SEA...

When the surf is booming from the big seas that spring storms can bring, there's almost always seaweed to be gathered along the shoreline. Down we go at low tide with our baskets, bags or sacks, sometimes to the beach and into the waves, sometimes along the rock shelf. We pick and choose the freshest pieces of seaweed for eating, and other pieces to make into nutrient-rich teas for our vegie garden. It's a seasonal ritual, of sorts – a time of the year that we look forward to, when we restock both our pantry and our garden shed.

Seaweed is downright amazing stuff. If you're looking for an easily accessible wild food and nutrient resource that can grow metres in a single year; draws in goodness from sunlight, air and water; and is jam-packed with minerals, protein and nutrients, it's hard to go past seaweed. Add to that impressive list of features a compulsory trip to your nearest beach or rock shelf to gather it, and you might just have the perfect wild resource.

Seaweed comes in all sorts of colours and shapes, all with different features, tastes and nutrients. Some are big and some are small. Nearly all are edible, and most are very tasty.

In Australia we generally don't, for some reason, have the same excitement and reverence for seaweed that you'll see in many other coastal nations. As a kid growing up by the beach in Kiama on the south coast of New South Wales, Kirsten recalls only once seeing a family gathering shoreline seaweed. When she asked them about it, they turned out to be a visiting Japanese family. They were quite perplexed that all this goodness was just sitting there, unloved and uneaten, on the clean yellow sand.

Fast forward a few decades and we were farming in the dry hills of inland New South Wales, on inhospitable soil. Gathering enough nutrients to feed the vegetables in our market garden was a problem, so we were using a fair bit of Seasol (a liquid seaweed product) to keep the vegies happy in between rounds of compost. During a visit to Kirsten's parents' house in Kiama, she was sitting on the beach, surrounded by seaweed, when the light bulb went on: seaweed – it's right here!

And so the shift in our thinking occurred. What seaweeds do we have here? Which ones are edible? Which should we use on our vegetable garden? Which ones should we feed to our family? We started gathering, researching, experimenting, making, using and eating. And we haven't really stopped.

Our pantry always contains three to four types of seaweed in various amounts. They get used in stews and broths or as sprinkles over vegies and rice. Seaweeds make their way into our sauerkrauts and kimchi, and there isn't a bean that gets boiled without a piece of kelp in the pot.

The garden gets its share, of course – seaweed teas are a great way to grow strong seedlings or cheer up stressed plants. And they're a great way to get new minerals into our homestead's system that the land wouldn't otherwise provide.

Right now we're living a few hours from the ocean, but that's fine. Spring seaweed-gathering road trips, here we come. A chance to explore new beaches, gather new tastes and make dinner in the dunes – our kind of weekend.

PREVIOUS PAGE: Harvesting cast-off golden kelp and crayweed from the beach.

LEFT: Harvesting golden kelp.

SEAWEED THROUGH THE AGES

Seaweed and people: we go way back. Before we were making wheels, developing complex systems of agriculture, or building ships and empires, coastal peoples were eating and using seaweed.

The earliest evidence we have of seaweed consumption is 14,000 years ago in the mountains of Chile, from an excavated home hearth. But given that seaweed decomposes easily, our relationship with seaweed probably goes even further back than the available evidence. Seaweed has been many things to many peoples apart from a nutritious food source. In northern Europe, seaweed has been an important animal fodder since the Middle Ages, if not before. Dried seaweed is also, because of its salt content, excellent as fire-proofing, insulating and soundproofing material. Dried seagrass was used as a mattress and pillow stuffing for many centuries, as well as a building material in a cob-like mix, with added mud. It's also been used as an insulating layer to keep blocks of ice cold in summer, and to prevent root vegetables from freezing in winter. In parts of the British Isles and beyond, seaweed has been layered under potato plantings to add much-needed and diverse nutrients, usually with manure added.

The use of seaweed as an animal fodder might have come from farmers watching their coastal herds self-medicate. Our friend Jane, a Scottish-born organic farmer, tells childhood tales of watching the neighbour's sheep trip-trap their way down to the rock shelves to graze on the seaweeds at low tide.

In New Zealand, bull kelp (*rimurapa*) was harvested for making light, strong bags – the fresh pieces of kelp were split and hollowed out, inflated like a balloon, and sewn up tight until they dried as a roundish bag. This type of bag was also used for preserving salted muttonbirds. In Australia, bull kelp was traditionally sewn into water carriers and baskets in Tasmania and the southern states, and seagrass was used for basketry in the north.

In the past, seaweed was also used to make a 'black salt'. This involved burning the seaweed, then leaching out the salty ashes in seawater, followed by an evaporation process that resulted in a not-perfect, but definitely better than nothing, salt for using in food preservation.

In terms of eating seaweed, every continent has its own living history. While considered in many countries to be a crisis food, to be drawn upon in hard times when harvests failed, there are plenty of places where seaweeds were, and still are, an everyday food.

In indigenous Australia, rolled and dried bull kelp was traditionally used as an endurance food when travelling, in times when stopping to find or prepare food was not an option. Many different seaweeds (and samphire) were eaten raw as well as being used in cooking.

In Ireland, seaweed has been everything from a traditional breakfast on the west coast (laver in milk) to an important food during times of both crisis and plenty – for eating and for animal fodder, as well as for fertilising gardens and crops.

In Japan, it's estimated that seaweed makes up as much as 10 per cent of the average diet, between the various types of nori, kombu and salad seaweeds. In Hawaii, over 40 varieties are traditionally eaten.

And in Korea, China, throughout Africa, North America, Iceland, Greenland, the British Isles and beyond, seaweed has been used for everything from food to fibre to fodder to ceremony, and it still is.

An essential part of the ecosystem

Seaweeds, as nutrient-rich algae, are essential to their ecosystems as food for many types of marine life, and also as shelter and habitat. Even when they're washed up on shore, the old crusty, dried and smelly seaweeds are life-rich communities for all sorts of seashore microorganisms, and hunting grounds for shorebirds.

And then there's the oxygen factor. Algae help the ocean stay oxygenated by converting sunlight into oxygen for healthy marine life and, in turn, for life on the land. It's estimated that marine algae contributes up to 80 per cent of the oxygen in our atmosphere.

Looking to the future, seaweed stands out as a sustainable solution to many challenges, from biofuel production to food production to integrated regenerative ocean farming.

On a home scale, seaweed is something we love to have around, in both our kitchen and our garden. You just need to know what to gather, when to gather it and what to do with it.

Neptune's necklace (*Hormosira banksii*) seaweed, sheltering an entire rockpool ecosystem below.

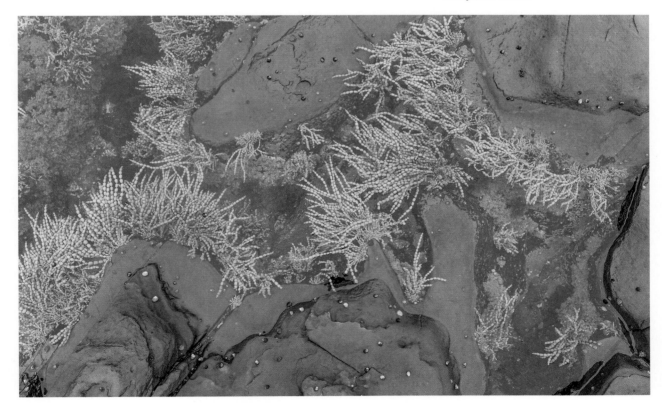

GETTING TO KNOW SEAWEED

OPPOSITE: Brown, green and red algae – the seaweed rainbow.

COLOUR CHANGELINGS

Drying or cooking seaweed can significantly change its colour, which is why nori sheets are green, not red, in their dried form. Many kelps also turn from brown to bright green when they are dried or cooked. When you're cooking with fresh seaweed, be prepared for magic.

TYPES OF SEAWEED

The word 'seaweed' is used to refer to most of the macroscopic algae that you'll come across in the intertidal region of beaches and rock shelves. There's also a whole world of microscopic algae, but it's the big ones that are referred to as seaweed. Bearing that in mind (and understanding that there are various exceptions, because the classification of life on earth is like that), seaweed is generally separated into three main groupings based on colour: brown algae, red algae and green algae.

Brown algae

This group includes the kelps (*Laminaria* spp) – the long, thick, belt-like seaweeds that we know on our plates as kombu, wakame, *rimurapa* etc. It also includes the seaweeds often called wracks (mainly *Fucus* spp) – the leafier, smaller-bladed brown seaweeds that we know as things like knotted wrack and crayweed.

Red algae

The red algae group includes laver/nori (*Pyropia* spp), carrageen and dulse (*Palmaria* spp). The red seaweeds are generally much smaller than the brown, and are sometimes only one cell thick, as in the case of laver.

Green algae

This group includes sea lettuce (*Ulva* spp) and many of the more hair-like seaweeds you'll find on slippery rocks at low tide.

GUT WEED

SEA
LETTUCE

WRACKS

NORI/LAVER

DULSE

WHERE THE DIFFERENT SEAWEEDS GROW

Here is a rough guide to where different seaweeds can be found in the tidal zone. Some of them, like wracks, can be found from nearly high tide down to below low tide. Others, like sea lettuce, have a smaller range. Keep in mind that many may be just beneath your feet, hidden by the tide – another reason why low tide is the best time for exploring. Spring tides occur twice a month, around the new and full moon.

SPRING TIDE – HIGH

HIGH TIDE

LOW TIDE

SPRING TIDE – LOW

ALWAYS UNDER WATER

SEA
SPAGHETTI

SUGAR
KELPS

FOREST
KELPS

SEAGRASS

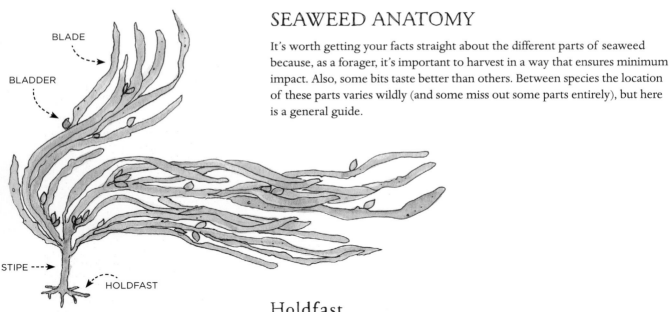

BLADE

BLADDER

STIPE

HOLDFAST

ABOVE: The basic parts of seaweed. The 'holdfast' secures it to a rock (or another seaweed). The 'stipe' is usually very solid and strong, and the 'blades' and 'bladders' (if present in that species) grow from the central stipe. Because the world of seaweed is so diverse, many species miss out on some or all of these parts. Don't worry, you'll soon get to know your local seaweeds.

OPPOSITE: Searching for cast-off seaweeds on the rock shelf (and finding a small octopus in the process).

SEAWEED ANATOMY

It's worth getting your facts straight about the different parts of seaweed because, as a forager, it's important to harvest in a way that ensures minimum impact. Also, some bits taste better than others. Between species the location of these parts varies wildly (and some miss out some parts entirely), but here is a general guide.

Holdfast

The holdfast is the part of seaweed that attaches to the rock (or to other seaweeds, if it's a free-loading epiphyte), and it does just that – hold fast, through stormy seas and wild swells. It may look like roots, but seaweeds get all their nutrients from the surrounding water and sunlight, so the holdfast is more like a hand than roots.

Stipe

The stipe of a seaweed is similar to the stem, out of which grow single or multiple blades. The stipe is usually quite stiff and strong.

Blades

The blades are like the seaweed's leaves, and these are the main parts that break off and regrow each year. As they're the youngest part of the seaweed, they're also generally the tastiest.

Bladders

Some seaweeds have air bladders to help hold the seaweed upright, or to help it float on or near the surface of the water. Bladders may be big or small, and attached to the blades or to the stipe, depending on the species.

If you live somewhere where live harvesting is allowed, generally only the blades of seaweeds are harvested. It's important that the stipe and the holdfast are left intact to enable growing for the next season.

NUTRITION SCORECARD

The nutritional benefits of seaweeds are quite enormous, and in the past seaweed has been the one food that has pulled whole communities through in times of hardship or famine. Seaweed is amazingly nutritious stuff. Some seaweeds contain all the elements and trace minerals required for healthy human bodies.

Seaweeds often contain large amounts of protein, as well as potassium, calcium, magnesium and dietary fibre. Species like sea lettuce also contain large amounts of chlorophyll. Many other species specialise in extra levels of nutrients, such as manganese, protein, iron or iodine.

Iodine is present in many seaweeds and is in highest concentration in certain kelps, especially kombu. While iodine is fantastic in small amounts, this has been a cause for concern for some people eating kombu (or products containing liquid kombu) as too much iodine can lead to thyroid problems. If you've got any concerns, stick to other seaweeds.

In addition to choosing your species carefully, we suggest that the best way to approach eating seaweed, like any food, is to use it in its simplest whole form – raw, home-dried or dried from a reputable supplier sourcing good-quality seaweed from clean waters. It's much easier to moderate your intake in this way, according to your needs.

CONTAMINATION

In an age of radiation leaks, nutrient plumes, industrial agricultural runoff and a bunch of other things we'd like to keep out of our kitchens and off our plates, sourcing clean food is an important concern. Sourcing clean seaweed is no different to sourcing clean spinach, fruit, grains or any other food. Do your research, make informed choices and find the cleanest and hopefully most local seaweed you can – whether it's on a nearby beach or in a box from a great seaweed supplier.

FORAGING AND HARVESTING

Most seaweeds are short-lived perennials, and new growth emerges each year in the early spring as the water warms and the days lengthen. Therefore seaweed has its biggest flush of growth in spring and summer, so the weed that you collect in these seasons will generally be the youngest and most palatable. That said, if you're collecting wrack or kelp to turn into a powder or flakes for home use, the age of the weed isn't as much of an issue. Some kelps are actually considered better quality if they are second-year blades. It all depends on the species and your tastebuds.

LIVE SEAWEED vs BEACH-CAST SEAWEED

Your location will determine which seaweeds you're able to forage. Some parts of the world allow live seaweed collection – cutting seaweed tips from its holdfast. Some places specify that you can only collect beach-cast seaweed – seaweed that has been ripped from its holdfast by the waves and washed up on shore. In some places it's technically illegal to harvest any seaweed at all.

These regulations are usually in place to protect biodiversity, which is great. However, in many places, authorities mechanically scoop up beach-cast seaweed after a big storm and take it to landfill, which benefits nothing in the biosphere and results in waste, and sometimes harmful outputs like methane. When we choose where and when to harvest seaweed, it's based on balance and responsible foraging.

If you do live somewhere that live seaweed collection is possible, take a sharp knife with you and always harvest the seaweed's tips, not the whole plant, so that the seaweed can regrow easily. This goes for laver, dulse, kelp,

FORAGING SEA LETTUCE: A SPECIAL CASE

Sea lettuce (*Ulva lactuca*) is a green, lettuce-like algae that is found all over the world on rocks in intertidal zones, and it is delicious. Known as *aonori* in Japan, it's one of the only seaweeds that you can harvest live (i.e. while it's still attached to its holdfast) in most parts of Australia. Make sure you use a sharp knife and harvest the tops only, leaving the holdfast intact. It's a perennial organism, and will regrow quickly.

Sea lettuce particularly likes to grow in nutrient-rich waters, so do check, if you find a good patch, that you're not harvesting near an ocean outfall or industrial runoff. It's also perfectly possible to find sea lettuce growing happily in clean waters.

OPPOSITE: Foraging for seaweed as a family is an opportunity to discover all sorts of treasures (as well as seaweed).

LEFT: Bull kelp, washed onto the beach, ready for us to take home and use.

sea lettuce and wracks. Think of it a bit like foraging leaves from a plant – don't disturb the roots (holdfast) or main stem (stipe), just harvest the leaves (blades). And take only a bit from each plant, if you can. Spread out your impact, so that the forest of weed will continue to grow happy and strong.

If you're foraging seaweed in Australia, your main option is beach-cast seaweed. Check the local regulations where you live – in some places, collecting beach-cast seaweed is fine, but in others it's not. Once you've got the all-clear, it's time to pack your kit and head for the beach.

There's an assumption with some folks around foraging beach-cast seaweed that it's only good for fertiliser and not for eating, since technically it's no longer alive. But beach-cast seaweed can be a free and valuable food, if you can get it when it's fresh enough. And given that this is the only way we can legally get hold of local seaweed without a permit where we live, beach-cast seaweed it is.

The best way to get fresh beach-cast seaweed is, of course, to harvest it from a rock shelf or beach near where that seaweed grew, as this will be the freshest. Head to your local rock shelves at low tide and check out what's growing around the edges, in the subtidal zones. It follows that the seaweed that's washed up on that beach (or rock shelf) will often be from the kelp or wrack beds nearby. Low tide is best for harvesting, as the waves often leave behind wracks and kelps that have come off their holdfasts in the last tide.

When collecting beach-cast seaweed, always practise responsible foraging and harvest lightly from within the tidal zone – there are lots of animals, birds, insects and other organisms that also consider that seaweed valuable, so leave more than enough to go around.

Some foragers prefer to wait until a big batch of seaweed comes in on the tide, brought by currents from a recent storm, and harvest the seaweed in the breakers, as it rolls in on the waves. Whichever way you like to collect your seaweed, it's a wild, fast-growing, renewable resource that's an incredibly useful addition to both your kitchen and your garden.

OPPOSITE: Harvesting golden kelp as the tide brings it in.

BELOW: Small harbours often have lots of seaweed nearby, as it grows on the breakwalls – it's always worth checking, especially if you have a bag or a basket with you.

Harvesting sea lettuce.

CHOOSING WHAT TO HARVEST

Unlike plants and fungi, the overwhelming majority of seaweeds are edible and there really aren't many that are inedible. There are a few exceptions on each continent, so do some research and find out which ones to avoid.

Generally speaking, the different types of seaweeds are used for different things. There are plenty of great resources that cover specific species and their uses (see Resources on page 293). It's a bit tricky to talk about algae types and groupings in a non-botanical way (apologies to our botanist friends), but here's the general rundown of a few common types, in plain English.

Wrack (mainly *Fucus* spp)

The wracks are particularly high in alginates and are commercially harvested all over the world to make agar. Wracks are mostly edible and quite nutritious, but their taste is often considered less than inspiring. They are usually eaten cooked, or dried and crushed.

Kelp (*Laminaria* spp)

Kelp prefers colder waters, so is found in temperate and colder seas and oceans all across the world, in the subtidal zone. The kelps are generally fabulous for eating when blanched or dried – wakame, kombu, bull kelp, golden kelp and sugar kelp, to name but a few. They can also be eaten fried or flaked.

Laver/nori (*Porphyra* spp)

Laver can be found clinging to rocks around the high-tide mark. It looks a little bit like draped cellophane when dried up between tides. Porphyra of various species can be found across the world, where it is variously called laver (Europe), nori (Japan) and karengo (New Zealand). It can be eaten blanched and added to laverbread, dried and eaten as is, or made into nori sheets.

Sea lettuce (*Ulva* spp)

Sea lettuce is a common bright green, lettuce-like seaweed that you'll find across the world on rocks in the intertidal zone. It's delicious and is often used fresh or blanched, or dried for delicate flakes and garnishes.

Dulse (*Palmaria* spp)

Mainly considered a northern hemisphere species, dulse is another intertidal species that hangs in long ribbons from rocks or sometimes on *Laminaria* species. It's a prized dried seaweed and tasty eaten fresh too. Known as dillisk in Ireland, dilsk in Scotland and söl in Iceland, dulse is typically dried and eaten much like chips as a snack, or flaked into cooked dishes.

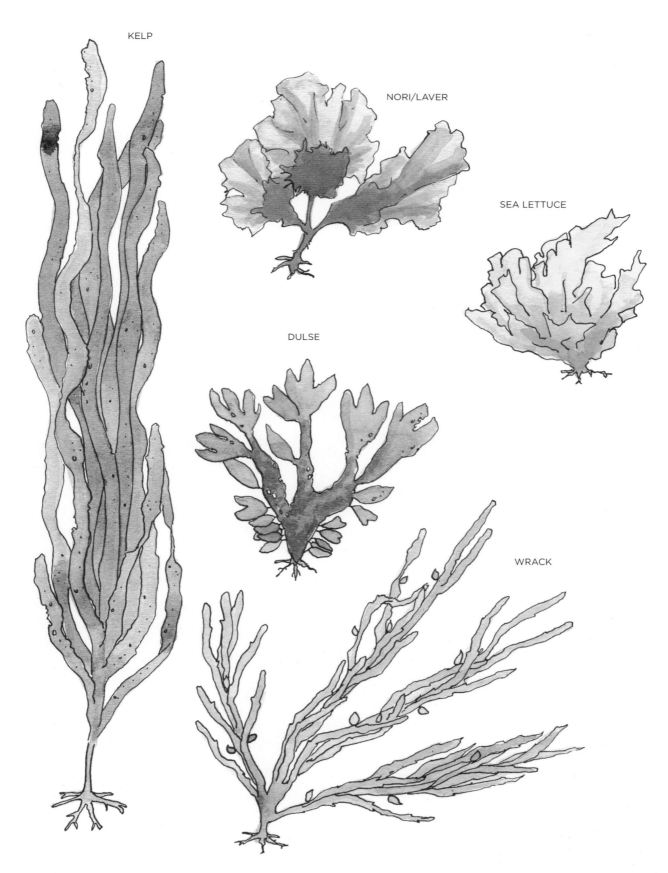

KELP

NORI/LAVER

SEA LETTUCE

DULSE

WRACK

HARVESTING WITH THE MOON AND THE TIDE

Before you set off to harvest seaweed, check the weather reports for surf conditions. Sometimes the seashore can appear calm, but a big swell is due – if this is the case, you will want to know about it before you hit the shoreline.

Low-tide harvesting is best done on a spring tide, which happens twice a month (not just in the spring) when the water is 'springing' due to the moon's gravitational pull. At this time, the high tide is higher, and most importantly the low tide is lower, than other times of the month, which is ideal for harvesting. Spring tides generally occur around the full moon and new moon, but check the tide using a tide chart.

Follow the tide out and come back in with it or, preferably, a bit before it. Take extra care on rock shelves, where surges on the rising tide can be quite sudden. Always tell someone where you're going and try not to go foraging alone.

SEAWEED HARVESTING KIT

Take a basket or bag that lets water out but keeps seaweed in, plus a smaller bag or bowl for smaller species. Slip-proof shoes are a great idea if you're heading to the rock shelf, as well as a tide chart and a foldable sharp knife. Foraging with a friend is always a great idea!

As with any type of foraging, being mindful of your environment is key, in multiple ways:

※ Only forage from somewhere that's relatively clean and non-toxic – for seaweeds, this means avoiding ocean outfalls and polluted waterways.

※ Check the regulations where you're going before you head off.

※ Take the freshest seaweed you can find – generally the lighter coloured and more unblemished the seaweed, the younger it is.

※ Storms dislodge seaweed, so a good time to go foraging is just after big seas (unless you have a wild coastline where the swells are always big).

※ Take a harvesting bag, basket or bucket with holes in it – taking seaweed home is great, but lugging extra sand and seawater is less so.

※ Stick to gathering seaweed well below the high-tide mark – the seaweed at or above the high-tide mark is generally colonised with all matter of critters, and is relied on by shorebirds for their lunch and performing important biosphere functions. Stick to the fresh stuff.

※ Forage lightly and mindfully – if we want vibrant ecosystems, it's up to all of us to take only our share.

Seaweed harvesting kit: a sturdy basket, a sharp folding knife, and a separate bowl for smaller species that you don't want tangled up with the big stuff.

OUR FAVOURITE SEAWEEDS

Where we live in Australia, two of the most common beach-cast seaweeds are *Phyllospora comosa*, a bladder wrack, and *Ecklonia radiata*, a type of spiky but tasty kelp. The precise species of your area may be different, but there are usually wracks and kelps about wherever you go.

According to all the seaweed scientists we've spoken to, a wrack is a wrack, and a kelp is a kelp, insofar as you can eat them all, and treat them in a similar way when it comes to cooking. The chemical and nutritional make-up of each kelp and wrack does vary, though, and some are better than others in terms of nutritional benefits.

Phyllospora comosa (Fucales): Crayweed

This brown wrack, found in the subtidal zone, is commonly called crayweed. As kids we called it 'wigweed' because it was the preferred seaweed for putting on your head and dancing around.

Across the world, various wild food companies, foragers and fertiliser companies collect and eat plenty of bladder wracks similar to crayweed. Bladder wracks generally contain iodine, iodide, algin, mucilage, bromine, sodium, potassium, lutein, zeaxanthin, chlorophyll, cellulose, mannitol, silicon, essential fatty acids, vitamin C, B vitamins, betacarotene, zinc, magnesium, selenium, manganese, iron, phosphorus, oleic acid, protein, fibre and polyphenols.

Crayweed – *Phyllospora comosa* (Fucales).

Ecklonia radiata (Laminaria): Golden kelp

Golden kelp is a particular favourite of ours. As you move towards the poles, the kelps begin – in the cold south it's bull kelp, in the cold north it's sugar kelp, bullwhip kelp and others. In temperate eastern Australia, golden kelp, a lighter, daintier kelp, is the best we have. And we love it.

Golden kelp is about 10 per cent protein and high in iodine and iron. It also has a large amount of antioxidants and for this reason it's used as a natural additive in food preservation.

Durvillaea potatorum (Laminaria): Bull kelp

Bull kelp is something you find as you move into southern Australia. With beautiful, huge leathery blades, bull kelp also has a large stipe. The plants are very heavy when harvested whole, but once dehydrated are a fraction of their raw weight. Found at the subtidal zone at the drop-off of rock shelves and also in great underwater forests, it makes an important habitat for many marine species.

We love gathering the freshly cast stipes for pickles, and the blades can be pickled fresh, or dried and then toasted and broken into pieces, although it's one of the tougher seaweeds so it's more suitable for using as pieces than as flakes. Traditionally, in both southern Australia and also in New Zealand, bull kelp was one of the kelps used to make baskets and bags because of its great strength when dried.

BELOW LEFT: Golden kelp – *Ecklonia radiata* (Laminaria).

BELOW: Bull kelp – *Durvillaea potatorum* (Laminaria).

PREPARING AND DRYING SEAWEED

If you're using your seaweed on your garden (see page 219), you don't need to wash or dry it before you use it. In fact, the trace elements found in the seawater that's still on the seaweed are of great benefit to your plants, and a bit of sand isn't a worry, either. If you've gathered your seaweed to eat, processing it sooner rather than later is a good idea. As soon as it's out of the water, seaweed starts degrading. If you can't process it for a few hours, leave it as is, in a container with a wet towel or sack over the top, to help keep it moist until you're ready.

First, wash your seaweed a few times in a big tub of fresh water or under a hose, to remove sand and any little critters that might be in there. Give each piece a once-over as it comes out of the tub. Anything that looks old, crusty or murky, or not like something you wish to eat, banish to the 'garden seaweed' pile. Once all your seaweed is washed and sorted, it's time either to cook it or dry it.

If you're cooking seaweed fresh, treat it as you would other greens – keep it somewhere cool and humid, but not too wet (in the bottom of the fridge wrapped in a paper bag is fine for kelps and wracks, or in some water, if it's a delicate sea lettuce type), and use it as soon as you can.

There are a few options for drying your seaweed, but sun-drying is our favourite method. It's free, it works perfectly and has a zero energy footprint. Sun-drying seaweed even has an added benefit – apparently, according to Ole G. Mouritsen in his book *Seaweeds: Edible, Available & Sustainable*, the UV light helps the polyphenols in seaweed break down into simple tannins, which makes them taste better.

For drying wracks and kelp, we use our washing line, which is perfect for the job. We lay the seaweed flat on top. If it has longer strands, it just hangs off the lines. You can use any kind of rack or line to dry your seaweed. In two to three sunny days' time, it should be crispy and dry. Depending on the type, it may have also turned from brown to dark green.

Other options for drying seaweed include using a dehydrator or, if the sun just ain't shining and the weather is wet, an undercover area with good airflow will work, too. You can dry smaller amounts in the oven on its lowest setting.

When drying more delicate seaweeds, such as sea lettuce, you can use any of the above methods, but lay them flat on a tray – and if you're drying them outside, watch out for wind! A sunny indoor spot will work too, although your house may smell slightly seaweedy while the seaweed is drying.

To sun-dry seaweed, first hose off the seaweed to remove any sand, then hang it on a sunny washing line for good airflow. The result – dried seaweed, covered in nutritious mannite (the white substance).

OPPOSITE: Seaweed hanging on the washing line, in the sun and the breeze. It's an easy, zero-energy way to dry. And surprisingly quick, too.

LEFT: Dried golden kelp is easy to snip into pieces with scissors, for an easy addition to soups and stews.

PROCESSING

Commercially speaking, everything but the highest-quality seaweed is reduced to a powder or flakes to increase palatability. For home use, it depends on what you like to do with your seaweed, and what sort you have collected.

Once the seaweed is dry, we chop our kelp into inch-long pieces with scissors. We chop bladder wrack into pieces, make sure it's crispy and dry and then use the food processor to chop it into flakes that are as small as possible. The wrack has a very strong taste, so it's used more as a flavouring sprinkle rather than as whole pieces.

Seal the processed seaweed in airtight containers and store it away from the light, and it will last you well. It's also an excellent barter material for trading with inland folks who have fabulous non-coastal foods, but need more seaweed in their lives.

The 'extra' dry for flakes and powders

If you're making flakes and seaweed powders, your seaweed needs to be very crisp and dry. Most seaweeds will need a little extra drying. The best way to do this is in the oven at about 100°C (200°F). The time will depend on the type and thickness of the seaweed. Once a corner snaps off easily (for thicker seaweeds) or crumbles when rubbed between your fingers (for more delicate seaweeds), it's ready.

SEAWEED IN THE KITCHEN

Seaweed is highly adaptable and can be eaten with just about anything. It enhances the taste of fish, meat and beans, and if it's used in small amounts, it won't taste 'seaweedy'. In its flaked form, seaweed adds umami as well as salt (and all those minerals and vitamins).

When you're using wracks and kelps that you have harvested yourself, there are certain methods that will work better than others. Here are some ideas to get you started.

※ Blanch young, fresh kelp, then slice if necessary and add it to a salad or vegetable dish.

※ Pulverise dried seaweed into flakes and make gomasio (see page 210) or seaweed sprinkles.

※ Add flakes or pieces of kelp when making sauerkraut or kimchi.

※ Add larger pieces of kelp to flavour soups, stews and bean dishes.

※ Make a seaweed pickle (see page 214) with fresh kelp stipes.

※ Add seaweed to your home-made sausages or meatballs for extra umami salty goodness.

※ Use carrageen or a similar species that is high in alginates to make a fruit jelly – it just needs to be lightly boiled to 'set' whatever fruity liquid it's in.

※ Bake seaweed flakes into a seaweed sourdough or other bread.

※ Make seaweed and olive oil crackers.

※ Slice fresh kelp super-thin and cook and use it as noodles.

※ If you can get your hands on some fresh laver/nori (*Porphyra* spp), cook up some traditional laverbread with onions, oats and bacon.

That's just the start of it. The options are endless, and only limited by your imagination. And all this from something that just washed up on the beach.

PREVIOUS PAGE: A simple seaweedy feast – slow-cooked kelp and lamb stew (page 216), boiled eggs sprinkled with gomasio (page 210) and bread with lashings of seaweed butter (page 214).

OPPOSITE: Seaweed butter on crusty bread, and boiled eggs sprinkled with gomasio. Deliciously simple.

This recipe, and the endless variations it inspires, is a great way to eat any foraged seaweed that is less than perfect in some way, as it's all crushed up. Perfect seaweed specimens also work fine, of course!

Gomasio is a westernisation of Gomashio, a traditional Japanese sesame salt. Traditional gomashio consists of roasted sesame seeds and salt that have been ground together with a mortar and pestle. It's made regularly in Japanese homes to sprinkle over rice. Gomasio is the western version that typically contains more sesame and less salt. Both gomashio and gomasio are delicious, and therefore could clearly only be improved with lashings of seaweed, and wild greens, like nettles!

There are nettles in the recipe below because they're one of our favourite super-nutritious weeds, and they often grow on farms near the ocean where we've lived. If you can't find nettles, go and pick some dandelions, dock, cleavers, shepherd's purse or any wild herb that isn't too strongly flavoured, as the seaweed and sesame are the stars here.

Make as much as you think you would use in a few weeks – the flavours degrade slightly with time, so you only want to make it in small batches for great flavour.

WEEDY GOMASIO

Dried seaweed (we use kelp tips, sea lettuce or wrack, or whatever's available)
Sesame seeds (preferably unhulled, if you can find them)
Dried nettle or other dried wild greens (see page 282 for drying tips)
The best-quality salt you can lay your hands on – flakes or fine salt (non-iodised)

Keep everything in separate bowls until you're ready to combine it all at the end.

Making sure that your seaweed and greens are super-crispy dry before you begin is key to a good result. Give them an extra dry on a tray in a low oven for 20 minutes if you think they could be drier.

1. Chop the seaweed into smallish pieces with scissors, then pulverise into small flakes in a food processor or with a mortar and pestle. A mortar and pestle will be fine for the more delicate seaweeds, but you might want to get out the food processor for wracks or tougher bits of kelp.

2. Lightly toast the sesame seeds in a hot pan, stirring constantly, until they are light brown – make sure you've got a bowl to tip them straight into once they're the right colour as they burn very quickly.

3. Chop the nettle or other greens up small as well, using whatever method suits – the nettle and seaweed pieces need to be about the same size.

4. Combine the ingredients in a bowl, in the following ratios: 4 parts sesame seeds, 2 parts flaked seaweed, 1 part flaked nettles or other greens, 1 part salt. Give the mixture an extra blend or grind at this stage to combine the flavours.

5. Transfer the gomasio to an airtight jar. It's amazing sprinkled on noodles, rice, vegies, fish, meat, eggs and… pretty much everything! You can also use it in a grinder if you prefer a finer finish.

TIP

Add a pinch of ground cumin, replace the sesame seeds with hemp seeds, linseeds (flaxseeds) or almonds, or swap the nettle with other dried herbs – the possibilities are as wide as the salty sea.

This recipe was shared with us by Stuart Whitelaw of Moruya, New South Wales. Stuart is a seaweed and compost whisperer, among many other things. He was given this recipe by a Japanese friend who came to visit. It's a lovely side dish with Japanese foods, and also fabulous in sushi rolls.

GINGER SEAWEED SALAD

1 large piece fresh golden kelp (or similar)
100 g (½ cup) julienned fresh ginger
1 tablespoon toasted sesame seeds

DRESSING
1 tablespoon mirin or dry sherry
Pinch of sugar
Pinch of salt
1 teaspoon sesame oil (or to taste)
2 teaspoons rice wine vinegar

1. Take the piece of golden kelp and cut off the side fronds (these are fine to set aside for other uses, like drying).

2. Immerse the trimmed piece of kelp in boiling salted water, at which point it will perform that magic seaweed trick of turning bright green! Boil the kelp until just tender – about 7–10 minutes, depending on the size. Drain and cool.

3. Thinly slice the kelp into strips, then add to a bowl with the ginger and toasted sesame seeds.

4. Combine the dressing ingredients, then mix with the salad and enjoy as a side dish.

We use bull kelp stipes for this recipe, but you could use any kelp with a hefty stipe. For thick-bladed kelps like bull kelp, you could also slice the blades and pickle those, too. These pickles are a truly unique taste and texture, and great with a cheese board for a taste of the seaside, wherever you are.

You will need clean jars with metal lids that have been heated in a low oven (see Tip on page 56).

PICKLED KELP STIPE

500 g (1 lb 2 oz) fresh kelp stipes, sliced into 1 cm (½ inch) rounds
250 ml (1 cup) water
250 ml (1 cup) apple cider vinegar
1 teaspoon salt
1 teaspoon sugar
1 teaspoon ground turmeric
Pepper, coriander seeds, mustard seeds
Fresh fennel or other herbs

1. Combine the kelp stipes, water and vinegar in a saucepan. Add the salt, sugar, turmeric and spices. Bring to a low simmer, then simmer for 10 minutes.

2. Take the jars out of the oven and place them on a tray. Add the herbs to the jars.

3. Scoop the kelp out of the pan and pack it into the jars, leaving 5 cm (2 inches) at the top free. Pour the hot vinegar mixture over the stipes, leaving the top 1 cm (½ inch) free. Screw on the lids and turn the jars upside down to cool. Store in a cool, dark place for a minimum of 4 weeks before opening.

This one is super-simple. And utterly delicious.

SEAWEED BUTTER

Fresh sea lettuce
Apple cider vinegar (optional)
Great-quality butter, softened

1. Gather a bowl of fresh sea lettuce (*Ulva lactuca*) and rinse well in cold water. Depending on where you harvest from, your sea lettuce may have tiny critters in it (amphipods – sea fleas). Don't worry, just make up a bowl of cold water with a splash of apple cider vinegar in it, and dump the sea lettuce in that for a moment, swirling it around. The amphipods should separate from the sea lettuce. Or you can just ignore them and carry on. Think of them as something like extremely small prawns (shrimp).

2. Once your sea lettuce is washed, spread it out on a baking tray and bake in a low oven (fan-forced is great) at about 100°C (200°F) for 10–20 minutes until the sea lettuce has dried out and turned super-crispy. Check it regularly.

3. Crush the sea lettuce into the softened butter and mix thoroughly. Serve on fresh bread, either with condiments, boiled eggs sprinkled with gomasio (see page 210) or just on its own.

This is a variation on our standard family stew, which is actually a lot more exciting than it sounds. It's hearty and warming and delicious, without being heavy. And it's great to put in a thermos and head for the beach or the mountains, or just out to the backyard to eat around a firepit with some crusty bread spread with seaweed butter (see page 214). It will serve about six people.

The lamb is optional. You could use any great-quality, ethically sourced meat for this stew, and tempeh works beautifully too.

SLOW-COOKED KELP, BEAN, LAMB AND WILD GREENS STEW

2 onions, sliced

Olive oil

4 garlic cloves, crushed

1 tablespoon cumin seeds

About 1 kg (2 lb 4 oz) lamb (stewing chops with the bones in are most delicious, but diced lamb is fine too)

190 g (1 cup) dried kidney beans, soaked in water for 24 hours (they'll swell to about double the volume after soaking)

400 g (2 cups) chopped tomatoes (or tomato passata, see page 52)

6 good bits of dried or fresh kelp, chopped into small pieces (about 50 g/1 cup)

100 g (2 cups) roughly chopped wild greens or English spinach

Salt and pepper, to taste

1. Fry your onions with a big lug of olive oil in a heavy-based pot for about 5 minutes over medium heat. Then add the garlic, cumin seeds and lamb. Stir around until the lamb is a bit browned and the cumin seeds smell amazing.

2. Add the drained kidney beans, tomatoes, kelp and enough water to cover everything well. Bring to a gentle boil and give it all a stir, then turn the heat right down to low, put the lid on and go and do something else for a few hours.

3. During this slow-cooking phase (we often do this bit in the oven, at about 150°C/300°F), check every hour or so how the beans are going, as they are the important bit – everything else will just happily cook away, getting better and better. When the beans are soft but not too mushy (about 2 hours, but this varies), turn off the heat. Stir in the wild greens or spinach, season to taste and let stand for 5 minutes to wilt the greens. Serve in bowls with some crusty bread and seaweed butter.

SEAWEED IN THE GARDEN

Seaweed can be a fantastic resource for fertilising your garden. There are lots of easy ways to use it to increase the health of your soil, as well as your vegies and flowers.

As mentioned previously, seaweed contains many of the elements that are identified on the periodic table, though most of these are only found in trace amounts. It does, however, typically contain useful amounts of iodine, copper, iron, potassium, manganese, phosphorus and zinc. You can use it on your garden as a mulch, add it to your compost or brew it into a seaweed tea (see pages 221–223). Whichever form you use, seaweed is a great soil conditioner that helps to build a healthy soil food web in your garden. In its liquid form, it's also used as a foliar spray for both ornamental and edible gardens.

SEAWEED MULCH

You can use seaweed to mulch around and underneath your plants straight up. It will decompose faster if it is underneath another layer of mulch, or go dry and crinkly and decompose slower if it's on the top.

There are so many benefits of mulching with seaweed.

* It's an instant organic fertiliser – lay it down, and you're done!

* It's a great broad-spectrum, slow-release fertiliser for plants.

* As a dried-out spiky top layer, it's helpful for deterring snails, slugs and some household pets.

* As a faster-decomposing under layer, it's also great for slug control, as the slugs dislike the small amount of salt.

* Seaweed is a weed-free mulch – unlike many straw mulches, there are no embedded weed seeds.

* It doesn't blow away in the wind like some mulches can.

* It's organic – if it's gathered from clean waters and not near ocean outfalls, your seaweed should be a healthy addition to your garden.

* In sandy soils, the alginates in the seaweed (particularly bladder wracks) can really help as an additional wetting agent.

ABOVE: Foraged seaweed used as top-mulch (you can tuck it under existing mulch, too).

OPPOSITE: As it's weed-seed-free (land weeds, that is), seaweed makes a great and versatile mulch for gardens that breaks down slowly.

SEAWEED FERTILISER TEA

Home-made seaweed tea is a great addition to any garden. It's packed with plant-friendly nutrients. We love it because it can be made seasonally when the seaweed shows up, and then used throughout the year.

Seaweed tea is great for starting strong seedlings, as it contains some natural hormones that aid plant growth. We use it frequently as the liquid in our seedling mixes, as well as in seed balls. It's known for producing resilient vegetables (it's a huge help against marginal frosts), as well as improving their transport and shelf-life. You can also use it as a foliar spray for plant leaves. It can be a helpful anti-fungicide against powdery mildew and some other fungal diseases. As we all know, super-healthy plants mean fewer pest problems, longer fruiting periods and general garden goodness.

You can make a single-ingredient seaweed tea or combine it, as we do, with other nutrient- and mineral-packed plants for an all-round liquid fertiliser. We add comfrey and borage for extra potassium, nitrogen and phosphorus, as well as nettle for extra nitrogen and trace minerals. With or without the extra ingredients, the process is basically the same.

CAUTION!

Handling seaweed tea, especially during the anaerobic stage, may not be a good idea if you're immuno-compromised or pregnant. And, as with any natural brew, use common sense and high-quality ingredients. If it smells bad at the end of brewing (when it should smell great), discard it.

OPPOSITE: Borage is a fast-growing, mineral-rich dynamic accumulator. It makes a perfect addition to your seaweed fertiliser tea.

BELOW: Seaweed fertiliser ingredients: seaweed, comfrey, nettle and borage.

SEAWEED TEA WITH COMFREY, BORAGE AND NETTLE

You will need:

- ☀ A bucket or barrel with a lid
- ☀ As much seaweed as will fit in your bucket
- ☀ Comfrey, borage and nettle leaves
- ☀ Unchlorinated water (rainwater is great – go and catch some!)
- ☀ A stick for stirring
- ☀ A shady spot to stash your bucket while the tea is brewing

1. Fill your bucket with lightly washed seaweed, add your herbs and other leaves and then fill it to the top with unchlorinated water. Place the bucket somewhere out of the sun (maybe not next to the front door, as it will smell bad at certain stages of brewing) with the lid on lightly, but not tight.

2. Stir the brew with your stick each day for a week or so if you remember. Then wait for about 3 months. During this time, the tea mix will start off aerobic, which smells fine, then it will slowly turn anaerobic, which is the stinky stage. Fear not – leave it alone.

3. After a few months or so (the timing depends a lot on your ambient temperature – it will progress faster in summer than in winter), the anaerobic stage will give way to a second aerobic stage (as more good bacteria have moved in), at which point your seaweed tea will smell good again. And now it's ready to use!

4. Dilute your concentrated seaweed tea 1 part tea to 10 parts water, and apply it weekly to plants or seedlings.

BREWING TIPS

The recipe can be scaled down to a small bucket, or up to a 100 litre (26 gallon) barrel. The size of your brew is only limited by the ingredients you can source and the size of your vessel.

If you can get your hands on unchlorinated water for this tea, you should get a better result as the water will be more able to support microbiology, which you want to encourage. So rainwater or filtered water is best, if you can manage it. If that's not possible, fill some buckets with chlorinated water and leave them out in the open for 24 hours. Most of the chlorine will evaporate during this time.

Once the tea is brewed, you'll probably find that most (if not all) of the seaweed and leaves have broken down entirely, or there may be some sludge at the top or bottom of your bucket. While this sludge is like liquid gold, it's best put in your compost pile rather than straight onto your plants, as its concentrated goodness might be a bit much for them. You can pour the liquid off into another vessel from the sludge for applying to plants, or leave it in the same vessel – it's up to you.

You can aerate the seaweed tea throughout the brewing process with a small aquarium oxygenator or a compost tea brewer. This will dramatically shorten the brewing time and cut out the stinky stage, but obviously it requires more energy input.

You can also add microbial inoculants to your seaweed tea to increase microbial activity and speed up the process, as well as possibly enhancing the result – these can be found at some garden stores or online.

If you live somewhere where seaweed harvesting is not possible, you can buy dried kelp from most rural supplies stores, where it's sold as an animal feed supplement. It will work just fine in the seaweed tea.

WILD FOOD

THE WILD FOOD IS ALL AROUND US

The food is all around us. It's under our feet, along the path edges and next to the highway. It's in the sand dunes, all over our favourite park and down nearly every back lane. There's food out the back of the doctor's surgery, hanging over the fence. It's even between the cracks in the bricks of our patio. We just need to learn how to see it.

Foraging for weeds, wild food and feral fruit is a simple art and a pleasure that's available to absolutely anyone. You don't need a backyard, or a garden, or a farm – you can live in a high-rise apartment and still become a competent forager. All you need is a willingness to learn, good information and the eyes to see.

Foraging connects us with the world, and with each other, in many different ways. Pattern recognition takes up a large part of the human brain. Traditionally, learning and knowing the patterns of which leaves and berries to eat and which ones to leave alone was central to life (quite literally).

Once you know what you're doing, thanks to our capacity for recognising and remembering patterns, telling the difference between nettle and fat hen, or spotting a plum tree at a distance becomes as obvious as looking at a tomato. *That is clearly a tomato,* we think. *I know it has no poisonous close lookalikes, so I can happily eat this tomato without asking or checking with anyone, for I know that it is a tomato.* It's the same with foraging, once you get the hang of it.

Children are pattern engines of the most focused kind: this is different from that; this goes with this one, not with that one. As parents and carers, we have a huge influence on what patterns children learn from an early age. Foraging as a family gives kids the chance to use their clear-eyed abilities for pattern recognition to build life-long skills – this is a nettle; that is a dock leaf; that tree is a plum, this one is not. These skills will help nourish them in a very different way to learning the faces of Thomas the Tank Engine and all his friends. Take your kids with you when you go foraging and learn to see your local 'hood differently, together.

Kirsten's family spent many summers in the back gullies of the Lithgow valley, where Kirsten's mum was raised. Ruins of old shacks and houses from the early coalmining days are everywhere, now slowly being reclaimed by the Australian bush. These gullies were (and still are) peppered with feral fruit trees of European origin, both old and new. Some mark where a small home once stood and some are the result of birds dropping seeds.

'The bounty of these gullies can be immense, so each summer and autumn we'd load up the car with buckets, baskets and bags, and go out hunting. We had staked out the trees by noticing their blossoms in the spring, as Mum knew (mostly) by the flowers which were apples, plums, pears and all the rest. We'd make a note and then check back in late summer. Sometimes the harvest was small and sometimes it was huge. Pears and nectarines and apples for days – so much preserving! It was free feral fruiting, a family exercise that meant we spent a bunch of time helping and talking to each other as we picked.'

Foraging around where you live, or in a place that you visit often, also embeds you in a place like few other activities can. A map grows in your head of your local park, gully, headland or railway easement, with points

ABOVE AND OPPOSITE: Visiting our favourite mulberry tree, down the road at an abandoned farmstead. Many an evening has been spent filling baskets with sweet berries in these branches!

TOP: A bowl of bitter wild greens ready to be cooked and eaten.

ABOVE: Gathering turkey tail mushrooms from fallen logs down the gully.

OPPOSITE: Taking kids foraging is a gentle yet powerful way to let them learn the patterns and tastes of the landscape they live in.

of reference that are different from how you would usually see the local environment. The patch of wild fennel, the boggy ground where the dock grows, the salty soak where there's always some samphire, that plum tree down near the bridge by the railway that fruits just before midsummer. It's a map of belonging, drawn with lines of food, seasonality and small discoveries of knowledge, collected over time. Foraging is a connection to land of the first, and possibly best, kind.

Foraging also connects our palates with our local terroir like few other foods we have access to. It allows us to source local, seasonal food with zero food miles and removes many of the unknowns about how that food was produced. We know what we're eating and what it took to get these greens, these apples, this fennel from where they grew and into our kitchen. And that is a very good thing.

So foraging is the story of us, as a people, as a species. Long before we cultivated land and kept animals, we foraged. And still, up until the last generations, we continued to forage, regardless of what was growing in our fields, because wild food is always different and it's vital. Different soil, different nutrients, different medicine – all good things to bring into our homes. Our ancestors knew this, and we can learn to remember.

A word about weeds vs indigenous plants

A weed can be defined as 'a plant out of place' – which is a pretty wide definition. Even native species can be classified as weeds if they grow vigorously in the 'wrong' spot. The word weed is highly subjective and often fraught with agendas. Most of the species that we forage for in Australia are 'weeds' – introduced species that have gone feral – from plum trees to dandelion. With a few exceptions (samphire, pigface and warrigal greens), all the plants outlined in this chapter originated on other continents and were brought here, intentionally or not, following the arrival of the British in Australia.

Australia has its own cornucopia of indigenous wild foods and cultivated crops that have been gathered and grown here for over 40,000 years. But most of these species are bound up with traditional knowledge, practice and heritage, which is for others to share. See the Resources section on page 293 if you'd like to learn more about Australia's long food history.

As permaculturists, we are careful not to view weeds as the random and recently introduced demon plants of doom that some people think many common weeds are. Weeds are plants. Many of them are useful – either to us or to the ecologies in which they root themselves. We prefer to look at plants for what they can give, and make the most of them. Foraging what we can – to eat now and also store for later – means less reliance on faraway food systems. It also allows us to adapt to foods that are immediately available to us, wherever we are, which is a useful skill.

RULES OF ENGAGEMENT

THE RIGHT TO ROAM (OR NOT)

In some countries, the importance of, and therefore the right for, all to forage are enshrined in law. Sweden has *Allemansrätten* – the right of public access – which allows anyone to collect wild food and flowers from the forest (excluding any protected species), regardless of who technically owns that forest. Scotland has the 'right to roam' law, which allows anyone to use land, public or private, for recreation or to gather wild foods for personal use. Both laws require foragers to not destroy or disrupt any vegetation in the process.

In some other countries, the laws are the opposite. It depends where you live, as well as where and what you're hunting for. Sometimes it's considered trespassing, sometimes it's not. In Australia, it depends where you go – foraging in national parks is not allowed, foraging for pine mushrooms in state-owned pine plantations is fine, and gathering mushrooms in privately owned pine plantations is not.

In Australia, there are also 'threatened ecological communities', which are groupings of native plants that are protected by default, if they're found growing together, no matter where they're growing. The saltmarsh ecological community, which tasty samphire is a part of, is one example. However, if you find samphire growing on an urban coastal headland, just between where the backyards end and the rockshelf begins, and without any other significant plants around it, judicious harvesting is possible.

And then there are all the other spaces – the nectarine tree growing by the railway siding, the dandelion in the spare lot by the bus stop, the fruit trees down the gully, the fennel by the highway. Use your head and your common sense. Be safe, be careful and find out what you need to know about where you want to look. Always keep your eyes sharp for new plants, wherever you are. You'll be amazed at what you'll find.

BASIC FORAGING GUIDELINES

No matter what you're gathering and where you're gathering it from, ethical foraging comes with certain responsibilities and considerations.

Harvest leaf and fruit, not the whole plant

Being careful not to damage the plant you're foraging from is paramount. This ensures it's a resource for those who come after you, as well as ensuring that the plant continues to be healthy for whatever purpose it's growing there.

Observe and interact

As well as being a core permaculture principle, 'observe and interact' is good advice for foragers. Do you definitely know what species it is? Does the plant look healthy? Is it in an area that's likely to be sprayed by the council? If urban, is it in a heavy foot traffic and dog-walking (and therefore dog-pooing) area? These are all good questions to ask.

Roadside verges can be the perfect space to harvest all sorts of things, like this flowering fennel.

Consider the inputs around the plant

Many councils spray their roadside and parkland weeds and unwanted plants with herbicides to control their growth, despite the damage these chemicals do to many parts of the ecosystem. You can usually find out where and when this has occurred from your local council, and it's a good thing to consider before you go foraging. Streams are also worth looking into – if there's heavy industry upstream, which might contribute to significant heavy metal loadings in vegetation, it's best not to eat the greens that you find there.

Likewise, in country areas, try to find out what went on in the past. Most times it will be completely fine, but occasionally it won't be. We once found a great crop of nettles down by the woolshed and were happily eating them until someone mentioned that was right where the old sheep dip used to be, where the sheep were dunked in chemicals twice a year, meaning a very nasty toxin loading in the soil around that area. We stopped eating them and found another good patch of nettles in an open paddock up the hill.

As wild food lovers, we're happy to take our educated chances on eating what we find – you soon get to know what kind of areas are likely to be clean. The alternative is often eating fruit and vegetables that have been grown far away and had questionable inputs applied during growing or harvesting to prevent spoilage. We'll take the weeds and random feral fruit, thanks!

Tasty samphire to be made into pickles, from a local rock shelf. Always harvest lightly, no matter where you go.

FORAGING TOOLKIT

There are many plants that can be harvested easily and gently with a small sharp knife, but without one are nearly impossible to harvest without ruining the plant. Always take a pocket knife and a bag.

- A food map and a pen
- Gumboots (excellent for clomping over spiky blackberries and through long grass, especially in summer)

- Baskets, buckets or bags
- A pocket knife
- A bottle of water
- Small containers with lids

Public vs private land

Going into someone's yard or farm to pick fruit or anything else without asking is not okay, of course. But a fruit tree branch overhanging a public laneway is generally considered (by us and many others) to be fair game. Public parks and gullies offer little problems for foraging, as do headlands, public reserves and roadsides.

The art of asking

If you've found an amazing lemon, apple or persimmon tree that's technically on someone's block but seems to not be being picked, go and ask if you may. You'll be surprised how often you get permission. A big jar of home-made jam or preserves, returned to the owner, often seals the deal for next year's access – be brave!

Sometimes it's a case of being prepared to ask forgiveness rather than permission, such as in the case of crown land, like in the gullies of Lithgow. Or at an abandoned farmhouse that has a beautiful big mulberry tree alongside, with no one around to ask permission. If you're respectful in your attitude and in your harvesting, leaving everything as it was except for the fruit now in your basket, sometimes that's the best you can do.

If in doubt, go without

For fruits like apples and plums, there may be little doubt with identification – we're so familiar with these plants from the supermarket, media and our own backyards. However, for some wild plants and fungi, the forms of branch, leaf, fruit and berry may not be so recognisable.

If you find something that you 'think you've been told is edible but can't remember if this is the one', it's a good idea to pick a bit, take it home (uneaten) and do your research with the plant or fruit beside you. If you were right, oh, happy day. If you were wrong, it's just as happy a day that you didn't eat it.

There are some great pocket reference guides for weeds and wild food, so find one that covers the species you're likely to find. If you live in Australia, take particular note that many of our indigenous fungi are not well researched when it comes to edibility. Species can look like a common edible European mushroom when they are not. Go gently, take care, observe, test, confirm, and only then, taste.

Only take what you need

If the plum tree you've found down the gully is full of ripe plums, it doesn't mean you need to harvest 12 buckets if you will, in fact, only use three. Harvest three buckets instead and tell your friends where the tree is. Consider also that you may not be the only forager of this tree. Resources held in common good on common ground should be treated as just that – a common resource, not just for you.

Leaving plums on the tree is not wasting them. It's allowing for other possibilities, outside your small reckoning. Use what you harvest and use every bit. This is gratitude, and ethical foraging.

Mandarins overhanging a fence onto the street are fair game for gentle harvesting in our books, as are wild plums, self-seeded down the gullies where we live.

WILD FOOD MAPPING

In early spring, many fruit trees are a mass of flowers and easy to spot from a distance. It's a perfect opportunity to start plotting where the public food, feral fruit and other accessible delights of your area are situated. All you need is a map of your local area and a pen, or even just a notebook and pen.

You can add to this map all year round to create a valuable household resource, or even a community resource if you choose to share it. There has been an emergence of apps and websites doing just this in recent years – plotting public food and sometimes available excess from backyards and such.

We go walking in spring with a map of our local area and plot on our map the species (or our best guess) that we find. We also add any significant patches of other wild-ish foods we find, such as asparagus, olive trees or wild garlic. Then, as the seasons turn, if we don't have enough food with what we've grown ourselves, we head out and about, collecting. We quickly learn what

time of year the plums will be ready, or the mulberries. And when it's olive season, we go around and check the wild or public trees that we know of. Sometimes they're laden with fruit. Sometimes they're bare. That's the trade-off with wild food – in return for not needing to care for the tree or plant, you receive only a possible harvest. But with a good map, either in your hand or your head, there are usually other options around. Roll with the seasons, always be prepared and you will harvest much deliciousness here and there.

Once you've found and mapped all the feral fruit trees, likely mushroom haunts, and brambles, greens and berries, it's often a waiting game until they're at their best. Then they seem to come all at once and the business of harvesting, storing and preserving rolls into action as you make the most of these short windows of plenty. The following pages contain some ideas for making the most of what you find.

FERAL FRUIT TREES AND WILD BERRIES

APPLES

Apples belong to the *Rosaceae* family, along with pears, blackberries, roses and hawthorn. Like their cousins, once apples grow wild they're tough and hardy customers, often thriving in gullies and on a range of soils. Originating from Central Asia, apples grow wild wherever the climate and soil will allow. We find them most often near the ruins of old homesteads, and in deep gullies where the soil moisture can withstand drought years.

Unripe apples for pectin

Unripe apples are an excellent source of pectin, which is used for setting jams and jellies. Pick some unripe apples and freeze them whole, adding them at the beginning stages when you're making batches of jam. Alternatively, you can use unripe apples to make a 'pectin stock', which you can add to other fruit to make a quicker jam that doesn't require boiling all the fruit for hours.

Apple pectin stock

Take as many green apples as you like, remove any bad bits and then cut the apples into quarters. Put them in a pot and add enough water to just cover them. Bring to the boil, then reduce the heat and simmer for an hour or until the apples disintegrate.

Strain the broth through a piece of muslin (cheesecloth). If you want clear pectin stock, don't squeeze the solids; if you don't mind cloudy stock, squeeze away. Pour the stock into a clean pot and bring to the boil, then reduce the heat and simmer until it has reduced by half (or by two-thirds if you want a really thick set).

You can either freeze the pectin stock in airtight containers or preserve it in jars using the water-bath technique (see the passata recipe on page 52).

Use the pectin stock in jams when recipes call for pectin. To avoid adding too much at once, add 125 ml (½ cup) at a time, and test the jam as you go.

Dried apples

Oh, how we love to dry apples! Some folks dip each slice in lemon juice as they go, but we never bother. We slice them whole with the seed-star inside. If they're big apples, we use the 'apple slinky', an ingenious hand-cranked peeling and coring machine that's readily available in kitchen stores.

Once the apples are sliced, it's time to dry them. We make the most of every possible source of drying we can think of. An electric dehydrator in the greenhouse (for extra warmth) on hot, sunny days works well and takes no more than a day. Sun-drying slices on recycled flyscreen frames or shadecloth stretched over wooden frames on the trampoline, on the water tank or on the verandah roof takes two days.

ABOVE: Dehydrating apples in slices is a great way to quickly process large harvests – they will take only a day in a dehydrator. Don't forget to store them in airtight containers.

OPPOSITE: Having a bag or basket on hand whenever you go out adventuring means you're much more likely to return with an opportunistic harvest!

Green wild apples on the tree – these aren't quite ready. If you need to pick them early, they can still be used for apple pectin stock (see page 239).

Stewed apples

Stewed apples are simple, preserved deliciousness for cold winter nights, eaten with yoghurt or pudding, or with porridge in the morning. We stew up the odd bits and the gluts of wild apples with a little water and some ground star anise, cloves and cardamom, and sometimes add whatever other fruit is 'happening' just then – blackberries, feijoa or mulberries.

Just put the apples in a big pot with a handful of sugar or a slop of honey per 1 kg (2 lb 4 oz) of apples and bring to the boil. Decant the hot mixture into clean jars, screw the lids on tight and preserve using the water-bath technique (see the passata recipe on page 52) for 10 minutes.

Apple scrap vinegar

Apple scrap vinegar is super-easy to make and it can be used in the same ways as apple cider vinegar. It's not as strong as apple cider vinegar, unless you leave it for a long while before decanting. You can also use it for household cleaning.

Gather all the cores and skins of apples that you're processing (or eating) and add them to a clean jar. Cover with filtered water and add about 3 tablespoons of sugar per 1 kg (2 lb 4 oz) of apple scraps. Weigh the solids down with a small plate, a clean stone or similar to keep them under the water level. Cover lightly to allow air out but no bugs in and leave on a windowsill.

Over the next few weeks, the mixture will ferment, thanks to the sugars in the apples, the extra sugar you've added and the natural yeasts on the apple skins. It will form a foamy layer on top, and then, after 1 to 4 weeks (depending on how much apple is in the jar), the bubbling will calm down. Give it a taste – if it tastes nice and vinegary, it's done. If it's still a bit sweet, leave it for longer. Once you're happy with the taste, strain off the solids and bottle the vinegar.

Simple wild-fermented cider

All hail the wild apple cider! It's possibly one of the easiest drinks to make, ever. Juice your apples, however you want to do that, and add the juice to a clean vessel, jar or jug that has an airlock for a top. Leave the vessel sitting uncapped, covered with a piece of muslin (cheesecloth), for a few days until you see bubbles start to form, indicating that fermentation is starting. At this point, add the airlock on top and leave the cider somewhere visible for 2 to 4 weeks, until the airlock stops bubbling at a cheerful rate. At this point, you will have young wild-fermented cider that can be siphoned off and bottled, ready to drink.

You can also do a secondary fermentation, to make the cider stronger and the flavours more complex. There are lots of good cider-making resources around if you want to investigate further (see page 293). Worst case scenario: if you get it all wrong, you'll end up with apple cider vinegar, which is also excellent to have around. Experiment, and enjoy.

The wild plums of plenty. We call these 'chums' – short for cherry plum. Small but delicious.

WILD PLUMS

The *Prunus* genus are in the *Rosaceae* family, too. They originally hail from eastern Europe and Asia, and are thought to be one of the earliest domesticated plants, along with olives, grapes and figs.

When wild plums come into season, they are the most abundant thing we gather. From roadside trees, down the gully, up the hill… the small, wild-seeded cherry-sized plums (which we call chums) are everywhere. We frequently find wild plums along roadsides in country areas, hiding in between willow trees along streams, and often in abandoned goldmining country.

Usually there are quite a few trees to choose from, so we try a few from each before making a decision about which plums to pick. Super-sweet ones are picked for juice. Tart-but-awesome plums, with the more solid flesh, are picked for sauce, drying and jam. Watery, not-that-interesting ones we leave for the birds, unless there are no other plums available.

Dried plums

If the plum seeds are small enough, we remove them with a cherry pitter and dry the plums whole. If the seeds are too big for pitting, we slice off the sides of the plums and dry those, keeping the middle sections with the seeds for making jam, juice or jelly.

Harvesting cherry plums. Always taste each tree's fruit for deliciousness before proceeding with a large pick!

We dry the plums with all the same drying techniques as for apples. Dried plums are little sour–sweet powerhouses that are great for lunch boxes or rehydrating as part of a fruit compote.

Plum jam

We don't make much jam at our house, but plum jam is a big favourite, so we make the effort when we have a huge amount of plums.

The one big rule when making plum jam is this: count your plums as they go into the pot. Once the jam is all boiled down, you'll be needing to take those seeds out again. You really don't want to leave a single one behind, to be found later during an enthusiastic bite of toast. Ouch.

Add the whole plums to a pot, counting as you go. Then add a cup or so of water, just enough to ensure the plums don't stick when you heat them. Simmer and stir until all the plums are dissolved and the seeds have separated from the flesh, then take off the heat. Carefully pour the mixture through a colander, reserving the liquid, and let it cool for a while – overnight is fine.

The next day, wash your hands, get in there and find *all* those plum seeds in the colander. Once you've done this, tip the colander mush back into the pot of plum liquid. Return the pot to the stove to simmer for longer. At this point, follow whatever jam recipe you like to use, adding sugar, spices and pectin as needed.

The method for preparing wild plums for jam making can also be used to start off a truly great plum sauce. It's so good that it may soon rival tomato sauce (ketchup) at your house. We received the recipe from Oliver Brown, a forager and archaeologist who's based in Sydney. Oliver travels a lot for work and when he sees roadside cherry plums, he's there at the ready with buckets and bags. This terrific sauce is based on a Stephanie Alexander recipe and we use it for everything

from marinating ribs to ramen soups to sausages. It makes about 4 litres (3½ quarts) and will keep, unopened, for up to a year.

PLUM SAUCE

4 kg (9 lb) plums
1.5 litres (6 cups) apple cider vinegar
    or apple scrap vinegar (page 240)
2 teaspoons ground cloves
1 teaspoon ground cardamom
2 teaspoons ground black pepper
2 tablespoons grated fresh ginger
1 tablespoon salt
440 g (2 cups) sugar

1. Put the plums in a large pot – don't forget to count how many there are! Add the vinegar, spices, grated ginger and salt. Bring to the boil, then reduce the heat and simmer until the plums fall apart completely. Strain through a colander into another pot and leave to drip overnight.

2. Take out all of the plum seeds (you counted them, right?) and tip the rest of the mush back into the pot with the liquid. Add the sugar and bring to a simmer, then cook until the mixture has reduced and thickened. Taste the sauce, adding more sugar if it's too sour. When the sauce is as thick as you imagine warm tomato sauce might be, take it off the heat. If you prefer a super-smooth sauce, use a stick blender to break up any remaining plum skins. Carefully pour the sauce into hot, sterilised bottles with good lids (see Tip on page 56; we re-use red wine bottles with screw-top lids). Seal, label and date.

ABOVE: Picking wild blackberries on the roadside, from an area that we are sure has not been sprayed.

OPPOSITE: Sweet, sweet blackberries! This handful probably won't make it home. Oh well.

BLACKBERRIES

Blackberries (*Rubus fruticosus*) are native to Europe but are very adaptable to whatever location they find themselves rooted in. They are a thorny, trailing perennial cane that loses its leaves over winter in cold climates, and are also part of the rose family. There are other *Rubus* species, too, in parts of the northern hemisphere.

As anyone who has blackberries growing nearby knows, blackberries are tough customers. Considered a noxious weed in Australia, they also hold together eroded soil, provide habitat, and can be grazed down effectively (and organically) by goats. The berries are delicious as well as having medicinal properties. The leaves are medicinal, too.

Ripe berries

Kirsten's mum always took a long board when going blackberry picking. The board gets laid down on top of the brambles, allowing you to 'walk the plank' to pick deeper into the patch on each side. You can just pick from the sides of a patch if you're plank-less. Pick enthusiastically and use the berries in sauces, preserves and jams. Add them to whatever other fruit you're stewing – blackberries make everything better.

In our opinion, dehydrating blackberries by themselves isn't a good idea (apart from medicinal uses, perhaps) as you end up with a small, very seedy rock. Dried berries on the vine are worth tasting, though.

Dried leaves

Blackberry leaves have been used medicinally since ancient times in Europe and north America. They're packed with tannins and very high in vitamin C. Dried and then steeped, the leaves make a useful tea for sore throats, colds and flu, inflammations of the mouth, cystitis, and also diarrhoea.

Fermented leaves

You can also ferment blackberry leaves, which apparently increases their medicinal qualities. Fermenting makes the leaves smell wonderful and taste a lot more earthy, quite like black tea (which makes sense, as black tea is also fermented).

To ferment blackberry leaves, pick them fresh and then bruise the leaves somehow. You can do this by scrunching them with your hands, bashing them with a kitchen mallet, rolling them through a pasta machine or any other way you can think of.

Tightly pack the bruised leaves into a jar, screw on the lid and leave the jar in a warm spot for a few weeks – the kitchen, inside your car or wherever is warm. Check the leaves after 2 weeks, at which point they should look blackened and smell floral. Spread out the leaves on a rack to dry. Once the leaves are dry, store them as you would herbal tea and drink them for taste or medicine as needed.

We were introduced to the simplicity and deliciousness of country wine making by Sandor Katz, a fermentation revivalist who we enticed to Australia some years back to get more folks excited about DIY fermentation. (It worked!)

Country wine is made using just fresh fruit, water and wild fermentation. And a bit of sugar or honey to boost things along, if you like. The fermentation comes from the wild yeasts on the surface of the fruit, and also from the honey, if you use it.

BLACKBERRY WILD-FERMENTED YOUNG COUNTRY WINE

2 litres (8 cups) unchlorinated water
250 g (about 2 cups) unrefined sugar or 250 g
    (about ¾ cup) raw cold-pressed honey
1 kg (2 lb 4 oz) whole blackberries (or whatever
    fruit is available)

1. Add the water to a 4 litre (3½ quart) jar along with the sugar or honey, and stir to dissolve. Add the blackberries, stir, stir and stir again!

2. Put the uncapped jar on the kitchen bench and cover with a cloth to keep out bugs. Stir multiple times a day to submerge the fruit.

3. After a few days (depending on variables like the temperature of your kitchen and the natural yeasts on your fruit), the liquid will start to bubble. Wait until the bubbling has peaked and begun to subside (but hasn't disappeared entirely). This stage will take somewhere between a day and a few days, depending on the brew. Remove the fruit (which will be strangely tasteless), pour the wine into bottles, refrigerate and enjoy. The finished brew will be mildly alcoholic, sweet and delicious.

4. If you want to ferment the wine further, transfer it to a vessel with an airlock. The flavours will mellow and the alcohol content will increase slightly over time.

ABOVE: Adding blackberries to the dissolved sweetness and water.

OPPOSITE: The result! A delicious and highly variable young wine or melomel – add some ice and a twist of citrus, and away you go.

TIPS

Stirring multiple times a day is central to the success of this ferment. Every time you stir, you are doing a number of things: drowning any moulds that might be starting to grow on the surface, adding air to the brew and agitating the overall ferment (in a good way).

Wild fermentation can be highly variable according to the type of fruit used, its inherent sugars and the wildness of the yeasts – so taste as you go and watch closely! If the fermentation goes too far, you will have a sour blackberry vinegar/shrub on your hands, which is still delicious and useful. As with any home ferment, if it doesn't smell or taste good, compost it.

If you use honey for this brew, you are technically making a fruit mead or 'melomel', which makes the whole situation even better, in our opinion. Cheers!

ELDER

Native to most of Europe and north America, elder (*Sambucus nigra*) is a spindly stemmed, fast-growing deciduous shrub that flowers wildly in spring, followed by deep black clusters of berries. It requires fertile soils, but will grow in either wet or dry conditions. There are many other *Sambucus* species that are also known as elderberries, but *Sambucus nigra* is the one that is most commonly eaten and used for medicinal purposes.

The elder is another old medicinal and beloved plant that has naturalised far beyond its native lands. It is a powerful plant that should be approached with caution as some parts of it can be toxic, particularly its larger stems, leaves and unripe berries, as well as its bark. The elder flowers and ripe berries can be gathered safely, however, and have such a special taste and beneficial attributes that learning how to deal with this lovely weed is entirely worthwhile.

Elderflowers

Gather a big batch of the flowers in spring and remove them from their larger stems, then proceed into elderflower everything. You can dry the elderflowers on paper or on a fine mesh rack, to use in drinks and herbal teas, and to sprinkle on salads and cakes. Elderflowers also make an amazing cordial that is fantastic on a hot day, diluted with mineral water and served with fresh mint. You can never make too much of this!

LEFT AND OPPOSITE: Elderflowers bloom in spring; where we live they can often be seen as a tall shrub with a dusting of white, here and there in gullies, forests and verges. We gather as much as we can.

This is a spring recipe that we love. It's family-friendly and entirely delicious as an afternoon treat. The fizz comes from whey and the copious yeasts in the elderflower pollen. Because there is so much fermentation potential in this recipe in the form of pollen yeasts, it ferments very quickly, before all the sugars are consumed and the alcohol content rises. This means everyone can drink it, not just the big people in your household.

WILD FERMENTED ELDERFLOWER SODA

2–3 elderflower floret heads
1.5 litres (6 cups) unchlorinated water
1 heaped tablespoon light, raw honey
3 tablespoons whey (the clear liquid sitting
   on the top of plain yoghurt will do)

1. Remove the large stems from the elderflower heads with scissors. Some people remove all the stems, but we don't bother, and have happily consumed this drink for years.

2. Fill a 2 litre (8 cup) jar three-quarters full with the water and add the honey, stirring to dissolve. Add the whey and then the elderflowers, stirring them all around.

3. Place the uncapped jar somewhere warm, where you will pass it multiple times a day. Lightly cover the top with a cloth to prevent critters getting in. Whenever you pass the jar, give it a stir to submerge the elderflowers – they will whirl around and then rise back to the top.

4. Within 2–6 days, depending on room temperature and the wild yeasts in the elderflower, the mixture will start to bubble. Taste it and see if it's fizzy yet. If yes, ta da – you've made elderflower soda. If no, leave it a little longer. Once it's done, strain off the solids.

5. Now you have a decision to make. You can bottle and chill the soda, which will have a very light fizz, or you can bottle it in swing-top glass bottles or plastic bottles and leave them on your kitchen bench to let the fizz build for a day or two. The pressure will build up, so be careful when you open the bottles. When it's as fizzy as you like it, chill the soda to halt fermentation and drink it within a day or so.

TIPS

The longer you leave the soda to ferment, the drier it will taste as the yeasts eat all the sugars. It will also become more fizzy, slightly alchoholic and potentially explosive when opened, so be careful.

We prefer to make this soda fresh in small batches, and drink it with a light fizz. If you'd like to add a little fresh mint or lemon balm at the bottling stage, go for it.

This basic recipe can be used to make all kinds of wild fermented fruit sodas. We've made blackberry, rhubarb, peach, nectarine, apple and more. You can also 'backslop' some liquid from one batch to the next to help get the fermentation started. There's a whole world of sweet, fizzy DIY sodas to discover – experiment and enjoy.

If you can't get hold of whey, a tiny pinch of champagne yeast or normal bakers' yeast will have a similar effect. Or you can leave it out – the elderflowers and the honey will create their own ferment in time, it will just take a little longer and possibly be a bit more alcoholic.

ABOVE: Elderberries, ready for drying or using straight up, once we've removed their stems.

OPPOSITE: Elderberries are best harvested with a knife or scissors. If you pull off the berry clusters, you may end up in an elderberry shower.

Elderberries

Elderberries should only be picked when they are fully ripe. Since there are many species of elder around, do look up the one that you have nearby and check what constitutes 'ripe' for that species. Down the creeks of our area we have feral *Sambucus nigra* – the European or black elderberry – whose fruit is glossy black when fully ripe. We gather the berries in summer along the creek and its hollows, returning bumped and scraped and smiling with great baskets and bags of berries.

Elderberries can be consumed in many different ways. They have been used in folk remedies as an immune booster since ancient times, and contain powerful antioxidants that aid recovery from colds and flu. Some people caution against eating the berries raw as it's possible to have a reaction to them, however this is nullified when the berries are cooked or dried.

Removing the ripe berries from the stems can be a long-winded job, but there are workarounds. If you have a flat garden sieve with a gauge of 7 mm (¼ inch) or so, you can rub the heads through it, collecting the berries in a bowl below. Some people freeze the heads to make the berries easier to detach. Some just use their hands to shuck the berries from their stems.

Note that elderberries make an excellent and quite permanent dye, to which the earthen floor in our home can attest – in large, permanent purple blobs. The elderberries will always be with us.

Dried berries

Drying elderberries on trays or baskets, stirred daily until they're all dry, will yield shelf-stable dried berries that can be bottled and used in teas and also in medicinal tinctures. There's a tincture recipe on page 286 that can also be used for elderberry.

We throw a pinch of dried elderberries in pots of herbal tea – if steeped for a while, they give the tea a purple hue and a bonus immunity kick to whoever drinks it.

Throwing all your harvested berries into a big pot and making elderberry syrup is a great way to make the most of a large harvest, either for medicinal or culinary use. We make a medicinal syrup each year that goes away into the cupboard until winter, then comes out to treat colds and flu, with big and small bottles being distributed throughout our community as needed. It's not actually a syrup in the super-thick, super-sweet sense of the word, but that's what everyone calls this medicine. And if the name makes it more palatable to cranky sick people (both big and small), then we're all for it. Dosage is commonly a few teaspoons, a few times a day either as a preventative when cold-weather sickness feels like it's coming on, or to aid recovery.

ELDERBERRY SYRUP

900 g (4 packed cups) fresh elderberries
2 teaspoons ground cinnamon
1 teaspoon ground cloves
6 litres (about 1.5 gallons) filtered water
2.5 cm (1 inch) piece of fresh ginger, grated
350 g (1 cup) honey
250 ml (1 cup) apple cider vinegar

1. Put the elderberries, cinnamon and cloves in a large pot. Cover with the water, then bring to the boil. Take off the heat, put the lid on the pot and leave the berries to steep overnight.

2. The next day, return the pot to the stove and add the ginger. Bring to the boil, then reduce the heat and simmer for 30 minutes.

3. Line a colander with a clean tea towel. Pour the mixture through the colander and into another pot. Squeeze the elderberries in the tea towel to extract all the liquid. (Your tea towel will be purple for a month or so after this operation, but it will wash out eventually.) Give the elderberry mush to your chickens or add it to your compost.

4. Bring the liquid to a simmer, then add the honey and apple cider vinegar and stir to combine. At this point, taste the mixture. If it tastes like your family will slurp it up in spoonfuls, you're done. If not, adjust the sweetness accordingly.

5. Pour the hot syrup into sterilised bottles (see Tip on page 56). Seal, label and store in a dark place. We store the syrup in re-used red wine bottles somewhere cool and dark, and keep any opened bottles in the fridge.

TIPS

You can preserve the bottles of syrup using the water-bath technique (see the passata recipe on page 52).

It might seem silly to boil up that honey goodness and negate the antibacterial compounds of the honey, but if the syrup is made using raw, unheated honey and then stored, it may ferment and explode. If you like, you can leave out the honey and, when administering the syrup, mix it with a little honey so you get a tasty result and all the benefits of raw honey. Or you could just eat lots of honey, as well as this syrup, which is our preferred option.

Wild liqueur

The process of making wild liqueur is worth mentioning, as it's a simple and delicious thing to have in your pantry. It makes an excellent addition to any celebration, whether warmed and sipped in small glasses on a cold winter's night, or poured over ice in a tall glass and served with sparkling mineral water in summer.

The shortest version is made by filling a clean jar with strong-flavoured fruits or berries – we use everything from plums to elderberries to mulberries to blackberries. Add some spices (cinnamon, star anise and pepper are our favourites) and sugar or honey if you like things sweet – 1 tablespoon of sugar per 1 litre (4 cup) jar is a good guide. Finally, pour over enough spirits to cover the fruit. We usually go for the cheapest vodka we can find, but some people use gin. Seal and store the jar in a dark place for up to 6 months or so, then strain out the fruit. At this point, either drink the liqueur or continue to store it – the flavours will continue to develop and change over time.

The flavour combinations you can add to wild liqueurs are endless. Try dandelion flower, elderflower and mint; or dandelion root, turkey tail mushrooms and blackberry.

ABOVE: Wild plum liqueur.

BELOW: Harvesting hawthorn.

ABOVE LEFT: The bright red haws of hawthorn can be dried simply by being left in open baskets.

ABOVE: Hawthorn buds, flowers and young leaves – all edible and medicinal.

HAWTHORN

Hawthorn is the name commonly applied to the plants in the *Crataegus* genus, which are indigenous to many parts of the northern hemisphere and also to central America. Hawthorn has a long history of being a beloved plant in its native countries. Its young leaves and flower buds, as well as its bright red berries, have been important food and also medicine, especially for lowering blood pressure. Hawthorn wood is very hard and valued for tool handles, and it provides an excellent rootstock to graft some other *pome* fruit onto, particularly medlars and pears.

In southern Australia, hawthorn is considered a weed, however it still retains all its useful properties, as well as being an important habitat for native fauna, especially small birds and ringtail possums, who build their nests and dreys in its sheltering thorns.

Ripe berries

Hawthorn's ripe red berries are hugely abundant in autumn, and they're worth seeking out. The raw berries taste a bit like apple and are very high in vitamin C. The ripe berries are also very high in pectin, especially earlier in the season, which makes them perfect to use in wild apple or plum jam. They can also be squashed, sieved and combined with other fruit flavours to make delicious fruit leathers (see page 258). The berries can be eaten just as they are, but they're more of a novelty than a taste sensation.

Dried berries, flowers and leaves

If you do nothing else with hawthorn berries, dry them to add to herbal teas. Just harvest a basketful and dry the bright red ripe berries, along with the flowers and leaf tips, out in the sun. The ripe berry (which can be bought as a powdered herbal supplement) is a powerful antioxidant used as a tea to promote cardiovascular health and lower stress, and as a digestive aid.

Our neighbours Meg, Patrick and Woody are a family of dedicated foragers who grow, scavenge, swap and hunt for nearly everything they need. This is their recipe for delicious wild fruit leathers. We actually have to hide these at our house, otherwise they're all eaten rather quickly. With the bite of hawthorn and the sweetness of apple, the leathers are fantastic as trail and travel food, or whenever you need a sweet, chewy hit of vitamin-rich goodness.

You'll need to harvest a bowl of ripe hawthorn berries without the leaves and stems. The fastest way to do this is to strip a branch by clenching your fingers around it and pulling down hard. If you have sensitive hands you may want to use gloves.

SPICED HAWTHORN AND APPLE FRUIT LEATHERS

800 g (4 cups) ripe hawthorn berries
6 wild apples, peeled, cored and sliced
Spices, to taste, such as ground cinnamon,
    cardamom, ginger, pepper or ground dried
    orange zest

1. Start by mashing the hawthorn berries. If it's been a wet year, the berries will be juicy; if it's been dry, you'll need to add some water. Start by adding a little water, then mash the berries with your hands or a potato masher. The consistency you're looking for is a thick paste. If the mixture is still too dry, add a splash more water.

2. Place a cup of the berry paste into a fine sieve over a clean bowl and use a spoon or a potato masher to push the berries through the sieve. Scrape the gel that forms on the underside of the sieve into the bowl (the gel is full of pectin, especially earlier in the fruiting season). Keep pushing the berry paste through the sieve until only the pips and skin are left inside the sieve – these can go to your chickens or compost. Repeat with the remaining berry paste. You've now done the most difficult part of the recipe.

3. While all this sieving is going on, gently stew the apples with a splash of water until they're soft.

4. Mash the stewed apples and add them to the hawthorn gel, which will have started to set to a thick jelly. Mix thoroughly, adding whatever spices take your fancy (sugar is not needed).

5. Spread the fruit mixture evenly over a sheet of baking paper or a silicone mat until about 4 mm (¼ inch) thick. Set it aside to dry in a warm place or a dehydrator, turning so both sides dry. Once the fruit leather is completely dry (this will take 1–2 hot days), cut it into strips or pieces and store in a jar in a cool place.

WILD GREENS

FENNEL

Fennel (*Foeniculum vulgare*) is native to the Mediterranean but naturalised on many continents, including Australia, where it can be found along disturbed land, railway tracks and highways. Beloved by pollinating insects, it's a great weed to have in your local ecosystem.

Fennel is a perennial, hardy herb with yellow florets and feathery green leaves. When it's grown like an annual in a well-prepared garden bed with consistent moisture, its bottom section swells up into a bulb and is harvested and eaten before the first florets shoot upwards. Feral or wild fennel, tall and spindly, is usually harvested for its flowers, stems, leaves and seeds.

Flowers

Wild fennel flowers are a fantastic addition to drinks and ferments you're making – from pickles to sauerkraut to fizzy sodas (see Wild fermented elderflower soda on page 250). Snip off the flowers and add them to salads and stews. Or dip the flowerheads in batter and fry them. A bunch of fennel flowers also looks beautiful in a big vase.

Pollen

If you're super-keen, you can harvest the fennel pollen from recently opened flowers by rubbing the flowerheads through a fine sieve. The pollen is used to enhance flavour, adding a delicious note to dishes just before serving – from fresh pasta to vegetable and meat dishes, and also cakes and muffins. Use it very sparingly.

Fresh stems

The fresh stems of wild fennel, which shoot from the base of the plant each spring, are juicy goodness with an aniseed tang. Thinly slice them and use in salads or stews. You can pickle them, too.

Seeds

Fennel seeds are great in soups and stews, and also in tea. Harvest the seed heads when they are full of fat green seeds and use them immediately in cooking, or dry the heads in a paper bag and store the dried seeds to use in cooking or to add a lovely aniseed tang to your tea. Fennel tea is great for sore throats and improving appetite.

LOOKALIKE WARNING

Fennel sometimes grows near hemlock, which is poisonous in large quantities. While the distinctive wide, carrot-like leaves of hemlock are easy to avoid, the seed heads look very similar to fennel. In cold areas, once the greens have died back and only the seed heads remain, it can be hard to be sure what you're harvesting. Test by looking for foliage at the base of the stems and identifying the leaf, or by smelling the seeds – fennel seeds smell like aniseed, whereas hemlock seeds have no smell. Remember, if in doubt, go without.

ABOVE: Harvesting wild fennel flowers for pickling and drying. Always remember your pocket knife!

OPPOSITE: Fennel growing wild along a headland path. Always double-check you're harvesting fennel, not hemlock. Once you know the signs to look for, all will be well.

ABOVE: Harvesting pigface fruits in the sand dunes – the ultimate beach snack.

OPPOSITE: Look for the ruby-red signs of ripeness, and pinch the fruit off at the base.

PIGFACE

Pigface (*Carpobrotus* spp) is a trailing, vine-like succulent that is native to salty country – the sand dunes, coastal cliffs and foreshores of southern Australia, Africa and South America. The variety we most often come across is *Carpobrotus glaucescens*, which is commonly considered the most edible. Inland versions of pigface also exist.

In Dharawal country on the south coast of New South Wales, where Kirsten grew up eating this tasty treat, pigface is known as kupburril or korowal. Other names include ice plant, karkalla and coastal fig.

Every part of this unassumingly awesome plant is edible and useful. As with any native plant, make sure you're not in a protected area before harvesting, and also harvest mindfully, to ensure there's enough for the plant to stay healthy and regenerate itself.

Leaves

Pigface leaves are edible and can be sautéed or eaten raw (they're quite salty and astringent). Leaves from a commercially bred version are sold in Australia as 'sea bananas'. The juice from the leaves can be used to soothe sandfly bites, sunburn and cuts.

Fruit

The purple–pink flowers of pigface are followed by purple fruit, which can be twisted off and eaten whole, including the purple outer cover, or sucked out of their skins. You can make a basic jam from the fruit (see right), or just eat them all in the sand dunes. When fully ripe, they taste like a salty strawberry crossed with a fig. If you're lucky enough to find dried ripe fruit on the plant, you're in for a treat – delicious crystallised salty–sweet fig bites for you!

Pigface jam looks quite figgy, with lots of small seeds, and it's probably where the common name 'coastal fig' came from. The taste is strawberry-meets-guava-meets-fig, and the texture is unlike any other jam we know – gloriously gloopy. It's great on fresh bread.

PIGFACE JAM

400 g (2 cups) pigface fruit
750 ml (3 cups) water
2 lemons
525 g (1½ cups) honey
Pinch of ground cinnamon and cloves,
    or a little grated fresh ginger, if you like

1. Prepare the pigface fruit. You can peel them, slice them or use them whole (which will make for a ruby-red jam with a salty–sweet taste and more solid bits). Put the fruit in a heavy-based pot and pour in the water to cover it. Squeeze the lemon juice into the pot and add the skins, then add the honey and any spices you're using.

2. Cook, stirring, until the mixture comes to the boil, the fruit has softened and the honey has dissolved. Reduce the heat and simmer gently until the mixture has reduced to a consistency that you're happy with. Remove the lemon skins.

3. Ladle the jam into hot, sterilised jars (see Tip on page 56), then seal, label and store for up to a year.

SAMPHIRE

Samphire (*Tecticornia* spp) is an edible succulent that grows in salty marshes and sometimes where soil meets sand, along coastlines and also salty inland regions of southern Australia. It's also known as 'glasswort' and 'sea asparagus'. There are many other species of coastal samphire worldwide (the European ones are in the genus *Salicornia*). Historically, samphire has been an important food source for coastal people, as well as providing an ash that has been used to make soap and glass. The Wangkatha people of inland Western Australia have gathered the seeds of *Tecticornia* to make into a cake (karumi) for many thousands of years, sprinkling some seeds back into cracks of the claypan to ensure regeneration of the plants.

In Australia, samphire is identified as being part of a threatened saltmarsh ecological community. That means that if it's found growing with the other plants of this community, it should not be harvested. We tend to find patches of samphire on headlands where soil meets salt, and sometimes on rock shelves. If you come across a suitable patch, harvest it responsibly.

Green shoots

The green shoots of samphire can be harvested and eaten raw, but they're pretty salty. They're often blanched in boiling water for 20 seconds or soaked in cold water for a few hours before using. Samphire shoots are paired with fish and used almost like a seasoning, and they can also be pickled in the same way as asparagus.

Across the Mediterranean and the British isles, samphire pickle can be found as a condiment. If you can forage enough samphire, make the pickle by pouring a basic hot water/pickle mix (see the recipe for Vinegar-pickled mushrooms on page 115) over fresh samphire, with some added spices.

OPPOSITE: Harvesting samphire where basalt rock shelf meets sandy soil.

BELOW: Harvesting just the tips of samphire has an added benefit: less sand in your foraging bowl!

The distinctive leaves and low growth habit help identify warrigal greens. You'll find them from the back of the sand dunes through to the first stand of coastal brush.

WARRIGAL GREENS

Native to Australia, New Zealand, Chile, Argentina and Japan, warrigal greens (*Tetragonia tetragonioides*) grow in sandy, salty, marginal soils, both inland and on the coast. Other names include Botany Bay spinach, indigenous spinach, New Zealand spinach and kōkihi (in Māori).

We most often find warrigal greens along the coast, underneath the scrub trees just behind the sand dunes. Few insects or pests like them, so there's often a lush carpet of green, waiting to come home for our dinner.

Green leaves

The green leaves of warrigal greens can be harvested and used along with their stems. You'll find seeds along the stems as well, but these are a bit hard for eating, so remove them before you prepare the greens. It's important to blanch the leaves and stems in boiling water for a minute or two to remove their high levels of oxalic acid.

Warrigal greens are delicious in anything that calls for cooked English spinach – in dumplings, soups, or even a pie with ricotta. Warrigal greens pesto is fantastic, as are warrigal greens fritters and pasta. We love them in cannelloni with home-made ricotta cheese and tomato passata – great comfort food on winter evenings. Simply follow a basic spinach and ricotta cannelloni recipe, and substitute the spinach with warrigal greens.

Dandelions with their distinctive sawtooth leaves – often found at the margins of gardens, roads and fences.

DANDELION

Strong medicine and entirely edible, dandelions (*Taraxacum officinale*) originate from temperate regions of Europe and Asia, and have spread across the world as a medicine and wildflower. Since they're considered a weed by those who like perfect lawns, dandelions should only be gathered from areas that you know have not been spot-sprayed.

The dandelion has a short-lived perennial root with annual leaves. In cold areas, they will die back over winter and emerge with new shoots each spring. If you're after the greens, the new spring growth is the tastiest.

Roots

Since the root is the perennial part of the dandelion plant, it just gets bigger and better over time. Harvesting should be done carefully – it's a central taproot, a bit like a carrot, and is best harvested after rain when the ground is soft. The dandelion forks you can buy are for harvesting the top, snapping it off from the root, so get yourself a long, thin trowel to harvest the roots successfully.

The roots are fattest in autumn and they can be eaten like a root vegetable, or dehydrated or roasted to make dandelion tea or coffee. Dandelion tea is considered a diuretic and a powerful liver cleanser. If you're using dandelion root as a medicinal, dehydrating it is the best method to use as more properties will be retained. Simply cut the washed roots into small pieces and dehydrate them, then store the dried pieces in an airtight jar.

To roast the dandelion roots, cut the washed roots into small bits, then roast at 170°C (340°F) for 45 minutes or so, checking every 10 minutes to make sure they don't burn. The smell in your kitchen will be amazing. Once the pieces are nicely brown and crisp, cool them and store in a jar. Grind the roasted roots and use them to make coffee in a stovetop espresso pot. To make tea, steep the roasted root pieces in hot water. The longer you steep them, the more bitter the result. For a sweeter tea, grind the roasted pieces like coffee grinds (we do this bit by bit, as we need it) and steep them for a shorter time.

Leaves

The young dandelion leaves (in the middle of the floret) are the tastiest, especially if they're picked before the flower buds open. After that they're still edible, but more bitter. The leaves can be used raw in salads, blanched or briefly cooked as you would for spinach. We love them raw, drizzled with a bit of olive oil, lemon juice and cracked pepper.

A fabulous pesto can be made from dandelion leaves if you have enough – just replace the basil leaves with dandelion leaves in a basil pesto recipe.

Flowers

Dandelion flowers are bright yellow and are what gave the plant its common name – the French '*dent de lion*', meaning 'lion's tooth'. They are most abundant in spring, but can be picked at any time of year that they appear. Dandelion flowers close up each night on the plant and they may do this in your kitchen, too, so it's best to process them the same day as you pick them. The flowers can be used whole in tea for their chamomile-like properties, or made into syrup or cordial.

The whole flowers can be dipped in egg, rolled in breadcrumbs and then fried to make fritters – yum. And there's also dandelion wine, which can be made using a basic country wine recipe, often with lemon added (you can use the Blackberry wild-fermented young country wine recipe on page 246, adding extra sugar or honey, to taste).

Plucked or cut off the flower head, the petals can be added to risotto for a gorgeous yellow hue, or added to salads, fritters or whatever else you're making.

BELOW LEFT: Dandelion roots, scrubbed and ready to be roasted.

BELOW: The whole dandelion plant, showing its single taproot. And it's all useful!

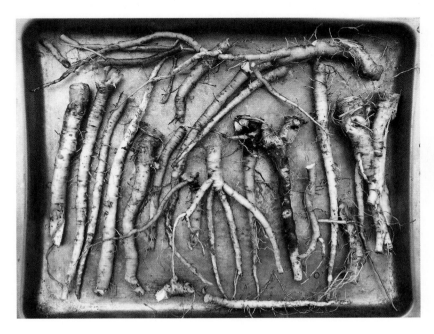

OTHER WILD GREENS

It's worth mentioning a few other common wild greens that are good for eating and packed with nutrients. They can be blanched and added to dishes as a wild greens mix, and most can be picked young and eaten raw. All these greens are native to the northern hemisphere, but they've naturalised in Australia and some other southern hemisphere countries.

Nettle (*Urtica dioica*) is found where there are high nutrient loadings in the soil, often around abandoned houses or sheep and cattle yards. It's high in minerals and delicious eating, but pick this one with gloves as the leaves are covered in stinging hairs (which won't sting once the leaves have been plunged into boiling water). Nettle makes great pesto and is good in our Weedy gomasio (see page 210). The leaves can be dried to make a tea that is useful for relieving hayfever (nettle is a great anti-inflammatory), and also as a diuretic.

Dock (*Rumex* spp) is a broad-leaved plant that is found in disturbed ground. The broad-leaf species is also known as 'butter dock' as it was historically used to wrap portions of butter for transport. Dock often grows near nettles and it's a great remedy for nettle stings – mash up a leaf and apply it directly. Young leaves are tasty raw or cooked.

Chickweed (*Stellaria media*) is a soft little cool-season herb that's found in disturbed ground and common in gardens. It's excellent picked and eaten raw in salads, and is very high in iron and vitamin C. Chickweed is dried to make a tea that aids arthritis and period pain, and is also applied topically to treat itchy skin and mange.

Mallow (*Malva* spp) has stiff, star-like leaves that identify this family of edible herbs. The leaves, flowers and the green seed pods (called cheeses) are all edible and highly nutritious. When cooked, the leaves have a slightly gooey consistency, great for thickening soups. The leaves and flowers are dried for a medicinal tea to treat coughs and hoarseness, as well as promote kidney and urinary tract health.

Cleavers (*Galium aparine*) is sometimes known as 'sticky weed' as the little leaves attach to clothes like velcro. It's found in disturbed soils and must be cooked or dried to be eaten – it's a great addition to cooked wild greens. Dried and then steeped as a tea, cleavers is considered a powerful medicine, being an effective diuretic and offering great lymph support. Topically, the tea is used for treating persistent skin conditions, such as eczema, and also sunburn.

Sow thistle (*Sonchus oleraceus*) has wide, smooth and spike-edged thistle-like leaves when young. The young leaves are bitter and super-tasty, but the bitterness can be negated by blanching. Sow thistle is traditionally used as a salad green and the leaves are very high in vitamin C. It's found in disturbed soils and is a member of the dandelion tribe, but it has a taller habit than the dandelion.

Gather too many? Wild herbs can be easily dried in bunches tied with string and strung up in an airy space. They'll take a few days to dry, at most.

OPPOSITE, CLOCKWISE FROM TOP LEFT: Nettle, mallow, dock and cleavers.

This stock powder is a simple and nourishing way to take the wilds with you, no matter where you go. It can be stored in an airtight jar to make a simple and tasty soup, or to use in place of commercial stock in cooking. Alternatively, you can make the powder into balls and dry them, ready to take with you when camping or travelling. A stock ball dropped into a thermos of boiling water will yield a light, nutrient-packed soup in just 15 minutes. These stock balls were originally inspired by Pascal Baudar's *The New Wildcrafted Cuisine*.

WILD STOCK POWDER

To make this mixture, you will be aiming to dry enough ingredients to end up with:

6 tablespoons powdered nettle
1 teaspoon powdered dandelion greens
1 teaspoon powdered cleavers
1 teaspoon powdered parsley
3 teaspoons powdered garlic
3 teaspoons powdered potato (or brown rice flour)
½ teaspoon good-quality fine salt (or gomasio or shiitake salt)
½ teaspoon finely ground black pepper

1. The first step is the drying stage. Dry all of the ingredients by hanging them in bunches or placing them on trays (cut the garlic and potato into thin slices first).

2. Once everything is completely dry, it's time to make the ingredients into powders. The method you use depends on your available kitchen technology. If you have a super-duper something that can take dried leaves through to powder, go for it. If not, make sure that everything is crispy dry – this will help a lot – by putting the ingredients on a tray in a low oven for 10 minutes before beginning. We usually finely chop each ingredient in a food processor, then grind them into a powder using either a mortar and pestle or our trusty hand-cranked coffee grinder.

3. Combine all of the powdered ingredients in the proportions listed and mix well. If you're just making the wild stock powder, hurrah – you're done. Transfer it to an airtight jar, label and store it somewhere cool and out of the sunlight. Use the powder within the next few months.

4. If you're making wild stock balls, put the well-mixed stock powder in a big bowl. Slowly add water, bit by bit, until the mixture reaches the consistency of a stiff dough. Stir with a fork until it's stiff but not sloppy, then let it rest for an hour if you have the time (this helps the final mixture to stick together). Form the mixture into cherry-sized balls, cubes or whatever shape you like – we make balls because they're fun, but do whatever works and is quickest for you.

5. Now it's time to dry the stock balls. Use a dehydrator or a rack over a wood fire, or put them in your oven on its lowest setting, or in the back seat of your car – use whatever works for you. Keep them out of direct sunlight if you can to help protect the goodness inside.

6. Once the stock balls are completely dry, store them in an airtight container and pull out a few whenever you're going off adventuring. A small jar or container is useful to ensure they stay dry. Simmer the balls in a pan of boiling water for 5 minutes, or add one to a thermos of boiling water and wait about 15 minutes before drinking.

TIPS

There are endless combinations for this recipe – add a little sea lettuce, kelp, mushrooms, you name it. You can also add miso paste instead of water to the balling stage to make miso stock balls. These will take a little longer to dry but are extremely delicious.

We prefer to make all our powdered ingredients from scratch if we can, but if you need to substitute one or more fresh ingredients with shop-bought powdered versions, go right ahead.

If you're using the mixture as a powder, rather than as balls, you can use slightly larger pieces of the dried ingredients if you need or want to, rather than grinding everything all the way to powder.

The stock powder makes a wonderful dusting for home-made popcorn. Eat your weeds, kids!

For us, this is winter food, when all the garden is sleeping and the wild greens make up a larger part of our diet. But it can also be a summer food, and it's perfect for picnics. Use whatever wild greens you have growing around you. Assuming you're using whole-grain flour, you can rest easy with this pie crust. Unlike crusts made with white flour and butter, which go wrong if overworked, this crust is pretty stable – bombproof, even!

WILD GREENS GALETTE

SOURDOUGH PIE CRUST
300 g (2 cups) spelt flour
150 g (½ cup) sourdough starter
½ teaspoon salt
4 tablespoons olive oil
1 tablespoon apple cider vinegar or apple scrap
    vinegar (page 240)
Splash of water

FILLING
4 garlic cloves, crushed
100 g (1 cup) wild greens, blanched and chopped
1 small potato, cubed and parboiled
200 g (7 oz) feta cheese (other firm cheeses work
    well too), chopped
Drizzle of olive oil
Salt and pepper, to taste
Pinch of ground nutmeg
Grated parmesan cheese, to sprinkle (optional)

1. To make the sourdough pie crust, combine the flour, sourdough starter, salt, olive oil and vinegar in a large bowl. Mix well with your hands until you have a firm dough. If it's too wet, add a little more flour. If it's too dry, add a splash of water. Tip the dough out onto a floured board and form it into a fat disc. Wrap it in a large beeswax wrap (see page 166) or waxed paper and leave it in a cool place for at least 2 hours or overnight.

2. Once the dough is rested, turn it out onto a floured board again and give the centre a few whacks with the side of a rolling pin to loosen up the dough. Roll the dough into a 30 cm (12 inch) circle, rotating the board as you go to make this easier. Carefully transfer the dough to a well-greased baking tray. Preheat the oven to 200°C (400°F).

3. Combine all of the filling ingredients in a bowl and mix well. Taste for seasoning and adjust if needed. Carefully spoon the filling into the middle of the pastry and spread it out to the edge, leaving a 5 cm (2 inch) border. Fold in the side of the pastry over the top of the filling, bit by bit. Top with the grated parmesan, if using.

4. Bake the galette for 30–40 minutes until the crust is brown and the filling is bubbling. Drizzle with olive oil and serve with a fresh salad, wild fruit leathers (page 258), dandelion coffee (page 268) and good friends.

TIPS

We use spelt flour as it's available locally, but you can use whatever flour you like – you'll just need to watch as you're adding the liquid to make sure you get the right consistency for the dough.

If you don't have a sourdough starter, you can replace it with the same volume of yoghurt. Alternatively, you can replace it with the same volume of flour, but your mixture may need a little more water.

WILD FUNGI

Each year, as the weather gets colder in the forests and anywhere wooded and wet, fungi of all kinds appear. Mushrooms are the fruiting bodies of mycelium, and designed to be eaten – if not by you, then by whatever species finds them first. Doing your best to pick fresh ones is ideal, as older specimens will have critters and possibly larvae lodged in them, which don't affect their edibility but make the mushrooms harder to clean and generally less exciting. Early or midmorning is the best time to pick each day's crop, as the mushrooms emerge from the forest floor.

Always cook wild mushrooms well before eating them, to protect against critters and also to ensure their digestibility. Wild food is strong food and it needs to be treated well to make the most of it.

COMMON PINE MUSHROOMS

If you're after pine mushrooms, you'll first need to find a pine forest or a few established pine trees. The pine mushrooms that grow below the trees are mycorrhizal. This means they have a direct relationship with their host tree, which must be a conifer.

It's best to hunt for pine mushrooms after the weather turns cold and there's been some rain – in mid to late autumn. Take a sharp knife to harvest and a little brush to clean the mushroom tops before harvesting. This makes for much less washing and getting grit out of gills at the other end. If you can get the mushrooms clean enough to avoid having to wash them, that's even better.

Also take a basket for your mushroom harvest if you can, rather than a bag or a bucket. As you wander through the forest, you'll scatter the spores from your harvested mushrooms back across the forest floor through the wickerwork of the basket's base. Net or string bags work well too. It's a simple way to return the surplus of your harvest, leading to more abundance for the next year.

As with any wild food, don't pick a mushroom if you're not sure what it is. Familiarise yourself with any inedible lookalikes to pine mushrooms in your area, and build up your knowledge so that you can confidently make the most of this amazing food.

Saffron milkcap (*Lactarius deliciosus*)

Saffron milkcaps are native to Europe, but they are found in many countries under introduced pine trees. The mushroom has an orange cap, which develops a dent in the middle as it grows. The gills underneath are also orange, and the stem is often hollow. Saffron milkcaps exude a milky sap when cut fresh (hence their name) and stain dark green with bruising and handling, although this doesn't affect their edibility.

Delicious sliced and fried with butter and herbs, saffron milkcaps are meaty mushrooms that hold their shape and texture through cooking. They're great in pies, roasted or in soups and they can be dried in slices, ready to add to stews. They also make a great pickled mushroom (see Vinegar-pickled mushrooms on page 115).

WHAT'S SAFE?

In Australia, our indigenous fungi is far from being well documented. Learning what can safely be eaten, and what to leave alone, can be difficult unless you go hunting with a local expert who knows their mushrooms well. So we've mostly dealt with introduced pine mushrooms here, ones that grow near introduced pine species (or native pine species, depending where in the world you live). We've also included a few of our favourite, easily identifiable native edible mushrooms that grow where we live.

Familiarise yourself with any inedible or poisonous lookalikes to the edible mushrooms in your area. A guide book for your region is super-helpful.

WHAT'S TOXIC?

It's quite common to find *Amanita muscaria*, the red-and-white capped fairy mushrooms, growing near saffron milkcaps. Often you'll see the amanitas first, but don't pick them! Amanitas are toxic unless prepared properly (which is complicated) and not for beginners. They are very pretty, though, and a helpful 'over here!' signal for foragers on the hunt for saffron milkcaps.

Foraging for saffron milkcaps and slippery jacks in our local state pine forest. Taking a big basket is a good idea, though Ashar hasn't quite filled his yet.

Slippery jack (*Suillus luteus*)

Native to extensive parts of the northern hemisphere, you'll often find slippery jacks growing near saffron milkcaps. These, though, are a boletus fungus. Their cap is brown and often slippery if the weather is wet, coated with a gooey substance. The underside looks like a yellow sponge with tiny, tiny pores, hidden when young behind a 'veil' that remains on the stem after the mushroom has grown.

To eat slippery jacks, we peel off the slimy cap, which is easy to do if you do it the same day as harvesting. We also remove the yellow spongey underside, leaving the thick, creamy centre part that makes great eating. We do this as some people's tummies react to the cap and the sponge layer. The large, fleshy, whitish cap that remains is great fried or dried in slices for adding to winter stews. It's one of our favourite dried mushrooms.

COMMON NON-PINE MUSHROOMS

Field mushroom (*Agaricus campestris*)

Field mushrooms are a close relative of the button, brown or Swiss brown mushrooms that are often available in supermarkets. They have a smooth white cap with pink gills (never white) that darken to brown with age. The stem has a single ring on it, and the flesh of the mushroom stains to red or brown if broken. Found in fields and grassy paddocks, field mushrooms also pop up in lawns after rain, all year round, so assess for possible herbicide loading if this is where you find them.

In Australia, there's a non-edible lookalike that you will occasionally see – 'yellow stainers' (*A. xanthodermus*). These look very similar to a field mushroom but their flesh stains yellow when cut or broken, sometimes after a few minutes. Avoid these mushrooms – some people can eat them cooked without stomach complaint, but many people can't.

Happily, the mycelium of field mushrooms grows slowly, so if you find a good patch, the chances of there being more field mushrooms near that same spot next year are high.

Turkey tail (*Trametes versicolor*)

Turkey tails are a multi-coloured polypore fungus that eats dead and decaying wood. They're indigenous to all continents except Antarctica. You'll find them in the forest on fallen trees and stumps, and potentially anywhere there's dead wood and the moisture to support their growth. They're identifiable by a multi-coloured, velvety, banded cap and a white pore surface underneath, with two to eight tiny pores per millimetre. Turkey tails stay thin as they grow – the thickness of thin cardboard – and don't increase in depth at their base. They are flexible when fresh.

Turkey tails typically grow over the course of one season. After that they will dry off, getting eaten by critters and sometimes turning green with mould. They can be harvested with a sharp knife. Once you have them home and have checked them against your local fungi guide, turkey tails are often dried as whole mushrooms, then boiled for medicinal tea or ground to a powder to be taken in liquid or in a tincture.

OPPOSITE, CLOCKWISE FROM TOP LEFT: Saffron milkcaps, slippery jacks, turkey tail and field mushrooms.

FOLLOWING SPREAD: Woody brushing off a saffron milkcap he found. Back at home, he can cut it up, too – mushrooms are great for kids to practise knife skills.

ALL HAIL TURKEY TAIL

Turkey tails have been used medicinally for many hundreds of years. Recently they have been shown to be potent in clinical trials of anti-viral and cancer recovery treatments. They're a very good forest friend to have in your medicine chest and tea cupboard. There's a recipe for making them into a tincture on page 286.

DEHYDRATING WILD FOOD

Drying your bounty is a great way to deal with a large harvest of just about anything, especially if done properly. It's the preferred option for wild plants that you want to store for tea. Drying provides shelf-stable and zero energy storage once complete, so it's an energy-efficient way of preserving harvests that may have multiple future uses. Once dried, fruits, herbs and mushrooms are best stored somewhere cool and dark, in a sealed container.

We use large, well-sealing buckets in the pantry for storing our dried food. We then pull out small amounts for storage in kitchen jars, maximising both shelf-life and convenience, while minimising the number of times that the main supply is opened. This prevents critters and moisture from entering our main stores.

Getting the slices the right thickness is important for successful dehydrating. Too thick, and they'll take ages to dry and may go bad before they manage to dry out, especially in cooler weather. Too thin, and they will turn into chips (which is not necessarily a bad thing, but not always ideal). We stick to slices between 5 and 10 mm (¼ and ½ inch) thick, depending on how dense and juicy the substance is. The more dense it is, the thinner we slice.

One option for drying everything is to use an electric dehydrator. These can be used at any time as they aren't weather dependent. We use an electric dehydrator in our off-grid solar household, running the dehydrator in our passive solar greenhouse during sunny days to maximise heat and minimise energy loadings. If you're running off a centralised energy service and want to dehydrate in ways other than using electricity, there are lots of other ways to dry your food, especially with large harvests.

RIGHT: Dried apple slices and plums – treats for winter and spring lunch boxes and snacks.

OPPOSITE: Dehydrating everything we can, for low-energy storage – saffron milkcaps, wild apples and wild plums all dry really well.

Sun-drying

Some foods are suited to sun-drying, particularly fruit and mushrooms. If you've got a few sunny days, use them well. Successful sun-drying depends on two factors: airflow and sunshine. Figure out how to maximise both of these factors in your situation.

Sun-drying can be done on recycled flyscreen frames (check your local tip shop) or home-made frames made by stretching shadecloth, flyscreen wire or a similar screening material over a simple wooden frame. Airflow is very important, so find a spot that ensures good airflow both above and below the drying food. Smaller loads can be spread on wire cake racks with a baking tray underneath and left somewhere that gets full sun all day. Trampolines, dragged into full sun, are excellent places to put many racks, as are accessible roofs and the tops of water tanks.

Ensure you bring everything in undercover overnight so the food doesn't absorb moisture from dew and rehydrate. If you're not expecting rain and don't have rodent problems, throwing a plastic sheet over your trays in situ can be a good solution.

'But what about birds? They might steal them or poop on the food!' We get asked this question frequently. And the answer is... see how you go and adjust your strategies if needed. We find that the local birds have much better things to do than eat our few little fruit slices, particularly in high fruit season. And if one slice does get some poo on it, we don't eat it! Problem solved.

There are lots of DIY solar dryer plans available if you need higher heat (for things like figs) or insect-/rodent-proof solar drying space (see page 293).

Bunches and bags

Some foods are suited to shady drying. For example, if you're drying herbs or mushrooms for medicine, it's important to retain all their properties and not lose any via UV exposure.

If it's possible to gather the substance together into a bunch, such as with cleavers or nettle, do that first. Then place a paper bag over the bunch, tie it off like a hidden bouquet, label the bag and hang it somewhere shady, dry and breezy. Medicinal turkey tail mushrooms and fennel seeds can be dried like this, too. Just put them in a labelled bag and hang it somewhere suitable.

The advantage of the bag technique is that nothing drops onto the floor, so you don't lose any goodness, and the contents are kept clean. The drying time will depend on the contents – check them once a week to see how they're going.

Other heat sources

Most homes have a bunch of warm places, and all of these are options for drying. The back of your refrigerator, strangely, is a warm space, as the fridge gives off heat. A rack on top of your fridge (or cantilevered out from the back edge, if you can manage it) is a useful place for slow drying. We frequently use the top of our cooling woodstove to dry small quantities of food on wire cake racks overnight.

And don't forget your car! If the car is parked facing the equator, the dashboard can be an excellent drying space: light, heat and protection, all at once.

Zero-energy food preserving! These home-made racks are drying wild fruit on the verandah roof at Melliodora. They'll take two warm sunny days to dry sufficiently to be shelf-stable.

WILD FOOD AS MEDICINE

Many wild foods are strong medicine, as much as they are a tasty lunch – especially wild greens and wild berries, which are packed full of all sorts of goodness.

Wild food is potent and often bitter or sour, such as samphire, sorrel, dock or turkey tail mushrooms. These flavours have been largely forgotten in western cooking, but they are often a sign of medicinal strength and can be used judiciously for different health benefits. Some cooking cultures include bitter greens on a daily basis for this very reason.

Wild food can also be mild and sweet, such as liquorice root, plum and apple. These sweet flavours can become an essential part of tea brews, as well as desserts and lunch-box snacks. Adding sweetness from plants that you gathered down in the gully, rather than from a packet you bought in the supermarket, is a beautiful thing.

Turkey tail mushrooms growing on a willow stump next to a stream.

Making a tincture is a method of extracting goodness from a substance to make it available for ingestion in ways beyond a simple tea. Suitable ingredients include turkey tail mushrooms, elderberries or hawthorn berries, depending on the properties you're after. There are many different ways to make a tincture, but this is a basic home-friendly one that we use, based on alcohol that you can easily buy over the counter in any town.

This is a 'double extraction' tincture, commonly used for immune-stimulating herbs. The first extraction is with alcohol and the second is with water. The alcohol extracts useful non-soluble compounds from the substance you're using. The boiling water (also called the decoction) extracts soluble compounds like polysaccharides.

A SIMPLE TINCTURE METHOD

Dried turkey tail mushrooms, dried elderberries
  or dried hawthorn berries
Vodka (minimum 40% alcohol – 80 proof or higher)
  or similar spirit
Filtered water

1. First, prepare the dried medicinals. The greater the surface area, the greater possible extraction from that substance. If you're using turkey tails, finely chop them. Berries are fine to use whole.

2. Half-fill a large jar with the dried medicinals, then pour in enough vodka to fill the jar to the top. Seal and label the jar, and store in a dark, warm place, agitating it daily for 4–6 weeks.

3. Strain the vodka through a piece of muslin (cheesecloth) and measure how much liquid you have. Set this extraction aside. You'll be left with some seriously drunken medicinals (now called the marc). Add them to a pot with three times as much filtered water as the amount of vodka you've extracted. Bring to a gentle simmer and then cook, uncovered, until the liquid has reduced by half.

4. Let the liquid cool, then strain the marc a second time, pressing it firmly to extract all the goodness. This is the decoction. Compost the marc, or feed it to your chickens.

5. Now for the fun part: combining the extraction and the decoction to make the final tincture. You're aiming for an end product that contains 25% alcohol. If your vodka is 100 proof (50% alcohol), this makes things easy, as a 1:1 mix – 1 part extraction to 1 part decoction – of your two liquids will give you a 25% alcohol result. If your vodka is 80 proof (40% alcohol), you'll need a 5:3 mix – 5 parts extraction to 3 parts decoction. Mix well.

6. Label and store the tincture in a cool, dark place. It will keep for years, but is best consumed in the first year or so. A standard dose is ½ teaspoon, twice a day, for overall immune support. Check with your herbalist for intensive dosings.

TIPS

If you want an extra strong result and you have a large quantity of your chosen medicinal, use separate batches (in the same quantity) of medicinals for the extraction and decoction processes.

In some places, it's possible to get higher-strength alcohol (often grain alcohol) easily – up to 70 to 80%. This is great if you can access it. Adjust the ratio of the extraction to the decoction accordingly.

It's a good idea to decant some of the tincture into small, dark glass bottles with droppers for easy dosing.

RESOURCES

If you're interested in learning more about any of the subjects in this book, the following books and websites are a great place to start.

Firstly, head to our website: milkwood.net. It's jam-packed with how-tos and resources on all the subjects in this book.

THE TOMATO

The New Organic Grower: A Master's Manual of Tools and Techniques for the Home and Market Gardener, by Eliot Coleman. Chelsea Green Publishing, 1995.

The Heirloom Tomato: From Garden to Table, by Amy Goldman. Bloomsbury Publishing, 2008.

The Market Gardener: A Successful Grower's Handbook for Small-scale Organic Farming, by Jean-Martin Fortier. New Society Publishers, 2014.

Biointensive growing: *How to Grow More Vegetables*, by John Jeavons. Ten Speed Press; 9th edition, 2017.

No-dig Gardening & Leaves of Life, by Esther Deans. HarperCollins Publishers, 2001.

Permaculture Design: A Step-by-Step Guide, by Aranya. Permanent Publications, 2012.

Allsun Farm: www.allsun.com.au

MUSHROOM CULTIVATION

Growing Gourmet and Medicinal Mushrooms, by Paul Stamets. Ten Speed Press; 3rd edition, 2000.

All That the Rain Promises and More… A Hip Pocket Guide to Western Mushrooms, by David Arora. Ten Speed Press, 1991.

Organic Mushroom Farming and Mycoremediation: Simple to Advanced and Experimental Techniques for Indoor and Outdoor Cultivation, by Tradd Cotter. Chelsea Green Publishing, 2014.

Radical Mycology: A Treatise On Seeing & Working With Fungi, by Peter McCoy. Chthaeus Press, 2016.

NATURAL BEEKEEPING
Bee biology:

The Biology of the Honey Bee, by Mark L. Winston. Harvard University Press, 1991.

The Buzz about Bees: Biology of a Superorganism, by Jürgen Tautz. Springer, 2009.

Honeybee Democracy, by Thomas D. Seeley. Princeton University Press, 2010.

The Wisdom of the Hive: The Social Physiology of Honey Bee Colonies, by Thomas D. Seeley. Harvard University Press, 1996.

The Dancing Bees, by Karl von Frisch. Harcourt Brace, 1953.

Warré beekeeping:

Natural Beekeeping with the Warré Hive, by David Heaf. Northern Bee Books, 2013.

Beekeeping for All, by Emile Warré. Northern Bee Books, 2010 (English translation).

Tim Malfroy's Natural Beekeeping website: naturalbeekeeping.com.au

David Heaf's Warré resources and online forum: warre. biobees.com

Natural beekeeping:

The Bee-friendly Beekeeper: A sustainable approach, by David Heaf. Northern Bee Books, 2015.

Wisdom of the Bees, by Erik Berrevoets. SteinerBooks, 2009.

Top-Bar Beekeeping: Organic Practices for Honeybee Health, by Les Crowder and Heather Harrell. Chelsea Green Publishing, 2012.

The Barefoot Beekeeper, by Philip Chandler. Lulu.com, 2008.

History of bees and beekeeping:

The World History of Beekeeping and Honey Hunting, by Eva Crane. Routledge, 1999.

A Book of Honey, by Eva Crane. Scribner, 1980.

The Sacred Bee in Ancient Times and Folklore, by Hilda M. Ransome, Dover Publications, 2004.

Making mead:

Make Mead Like a Viking: Traditional Techniques for Brewing Natural, Wild-Fermented, Honey-Based Wines and Beers, by Jereme Zimmerman. Chelsea Green Publishing, 2015.

SEAWEED

Seaweeds: Edible, Available & Sustainable, by Ole G. Mouritsen. University Of Chicago Press, 2013.

Irish Seaweed Kitchen, by Prannie Rhatigan. Booklink, 2009.

Seaweeds of Australia, photographs by Bruce Fuhrer, text edited by I.G. Christianson, M.N. Clayton and B.M. Allender. Sydney: Reed, 1981.

Sea Vegetables, by Evelyn McConnaughey. Naturegraph Publishers, 2012.

Seaweed in the Kitchen, by Fiona Bird. Prospect Books, 2015.

Coastal Chef: Culinary Art of Seaweed & Algae in the 21st Century, by Claudine Tinellis. Harbour Publishing House, 2001.

Sunlight and Seaweed, by Tim Flannery. Text Publishing, 2017.

Galloway Wild Foods: gallowaywildfoods.com

Charles Dickens' journal on seaweeds in Scotland: djo.org.uk/household-words/volume-xiv/page-392.html

Seaweed innovators:

GreenWave ocean farmers: greenwave.org

Venus Shell Systems: venusshellsystems.com.au

Seaweed suppliers:

Sea Health Products: seahealthproducts.com.au

The Cornish Seaweed Company: cornishseaweed.co.uk

Atlantic Irish Seaweed: atlanticirishseaweed.com

WILD FOOD

Dark Emu, by Bruce Pascoe. Magabala Books, 2014.

Wild Food Plants of Australia, by Tim Low. HarperCollins Publishers, 1991.

The Rambunctious Garden: Saving Nature in a Post-Wild World, by Emma Marris. Bloomsbury Publishing, 2011.

The New Wildcrafted Cuisine, by Pascal Baudar. Chelsea Green Publishing, 2016.

Foraging and Feasting, by Dina Falconi. Botanical Arts Press LLC, 2013.

The Thrifty Forager, by Alys Fowler. Kyle Books, 2015.

The Solar Food Dryer, by Eben V. Fodor. New Society Publishers, 2006.

The Weed Forager's Handbook: A Guide to Edible and Medicinal Weeds in Australia, by Adam Grubb and Annie Raser-Rowland. Hyland House Publishing, 2012.

Kaukasis the Cookbook: A Culinary Journey through Georgia, Azerbaijan & Beyond, by Olia Hercules. Octopus Publishing Group, 2017.

A Year at Otter Farm, by Mark Diacono. Bloomsbury Publishing, 2014.

The Art of Fermentation: An In-depth Exploration of Essential Concepts and Processes from around the World, by Sandor Ellix Katz. Chelsea Green Publishing, 2012.

Wild Fermentation: The Flavor, Nutrition, and Craft of Live-Culture Foods, by Sandor Ellix Katz. Chelsea Green Publishing, 2016.

Turkeytail as cancer treatment: ncbi.nlm.nih.gov/pmc/articles/PMC4890100/

Index

A

A-frames, for tomatoes 31, 35
acidity
    in preserving tomatoes 53
    of soil 29
Agaricus bisporus 72
Agaricus compestris 279
Agrocybe aegerita 77
algae 182, 184
Amanita muscana 276
anaerobic organisms 103
Apis mellifera 128
apples
    apple scrap vinegar 240
    Spiced hawthorn and apple fruit
        leathers 258
    wild apples 239–40

B

basil 37
bee bread 169
bee space 129
beefsteak tomatoes 17
beekeeping 125–70
    backyard beekeeping with hives
        148–55
    beeswax 164–7
    equipment for 151, 153
    harvesting honey and honeycomb
        158–63
    history 126–7
    nadiring 145
    natural beekeeping 135–45
    overview 125
    processing honeycomb 162
    siting your hive 154–5
    through the seasons 146–7
    types of hives 138, 139, 148–50
bees
    biology 128–32
    hives in their natural state 136
    life cycle 130–1
    re-queening 142–3
    swarming of 142–3
beeswax 164–7
    making beeswax wraps 166–7
    processing 164–5
    rendering 165
berries, wild 244–58
bio-intensive double-dig method, of
    growing tomatoes 30
black salt 182
blackberries 244, 246–7
blackberry leaves, fermented 244
Blackberry wild-fermented young country
    wine 246–7
bladders (seaweed) 188
blades 188
blossom end rot 38
boletus of the steppes mushrooms 106
borage 37
Botany Bay spinach 267
brood cells 130–2
brown algae 184
bull kelp 182, 191, 201
bush tomatoes 18, 43
butter: Seaweed butter 214
button mushrooms 72
Buxton, Simon 127

C

cages, for tomatoes 35
capsicums: Shakshouka 60
Carpobrotus glaucescens 262
cellulose 81
cherry tomatoes 17, 37, 55
chickweed 271
chop and drop technique, for honey
    harvesting 161
cider 240
clearer boards 161
cleavers 270, 271
    Wild stock powder 272
climbing tomatoes 18, 19, 31, 43
coir fibre 22
cold frames 27
combs, in bee hives 128, 129, 141
companion plants, for tomatoes 36–7
compost seedbank method, for tomato
    seeds 46
container cultivation, of mushroom 81–96
country wine 246
Crataegus 257
crayweed 200

D

dandelion 268–9
    Wild stock powder 272
Dennett, Su 7
determinate tomatoes 18, 28, 38
DIY bag and filter system 86–7
dock 270, 271
drone bees 130–1
Drone Congregation Area 131
drying
apples 239
    mushrooms 111
    plums 241–2
    seaweed 202–3, 205
    tomatoes 55
    wild food 282–4
dulse 194, 195
Durvillaea potatorum 201

E

Ecklonia radiata 200, 201
elder 249–56
elderberries 253–4, 256
    Elderberry syrup 254
Elderberry syrup 254
elderflowers 249–50
    Wild fermented elderflower soda
        250
emergency cells 132
enokitake mushrooms 78, 106
equator-facing brick walls 27

F

feeding, of tomato plants 26, 29
fennel 261
fermentation method, for tomato seeds
    44–5
Fermented mushrooms 114
Fermented tomato salsa 58
fertiliser: seaweed fertiliser teas 221, 223
feta: Wild greens galette 274
field mushrooms 278, 279
Flammulina velutipes 106
Foeniculum vulgare 261
foraging guidelines 232–3, 235
frost protection 36
fruit fly 37

fruit trees, wild 239–43
fruiting chambers, for mushrooms 94–5
fruiting containers, for mushrooms 82, 85, 89
Fucales 200
Fucus spp. 194
fungi 69–70
    see also mushrooms; wild fungi

G

galette: Wild greens galette 274
Galium aparine 271
garden giant mushrooms 77, 106
garlic 37
    Wild stock powder 272
Geotrichum candidum 44
ginger
    Elderberry syrup 254
    Ginger seaweed salad 212
Ginger seaweed salad 212
gloves, for beekeeping 153
golden kelp 201
golden oyster mushrooms 76
grain spawn 75, 103
green algae 184
Green tomatoes in olive oil 56
greenhouses 26
greens *see* wild greens

H

hawthorn 257–8
hemlock 261
heritage tomatoes 17
hive tools 153
holdfasts 188
holey bucket cultivation technique 88
Holmgren, David 7
honey 143, 158, 162
    Elderberry syrup 254
honeycomb 158–63, 169
Hormosira banksii 183
hybrid seeds 42
hybrid tomatoes 17
hypha 71

I

indeterminate tomatoes 18, 28, 38

indigenous spinach 267
iodine 189

J

jam
    Pigface jam 263
    Plum jam 242–3

K

karakovan log hives 150
Katz, Sandor 246
kelp 194, 195, 200, 202
Kenyan top-bar hives 138, 150
kidney beans
    Slow-cooked kelp, bean, lamb and wild greens stew 216
king oyster mushrooms 76, 79, 81, 106
king stropharia mushrooms 77, 106
knots, for tying up tomatoes 31, 34
kōkihi 267

L

Lactarius deliciosus 276
lamb: Slow-cooked kelp, bean, lamb and wild greens stew 216
Laminaria spp. 194, 201
Langstroth hives 126, 150
laver 194, 195
Lenintula edodes 72, 77
lignin 81
lion's mane mushrooms 79
liqueur, wild 256
log cultivation, of mushrooms 99–102
log hives 126

M

Malfroy, Tim 148
mallow 270, 271
Malva spp. 271
mannite 202
marigolds 36
mead 170
melomel 170
mesh trellises 34
metheglin 170
misting 95
Mouritsen, Ole G. 202

mulch, seaweed as 219
mulching 31
mushroom cultivation
    container cultivation 81–96
    growing from spawn 75
    harvesting 96, 110
    importance of cleanliness 78, 81
    outdoor cultivation 99–107
    pasteurisation and sterilisation 82, 89, 90–3, 103
    species for beginners 76–7
    troubleshooting at fruiting stage 96
    types of cultures 74
mushroom gardens 103–6
mushroom scrolls 107
mushrooms 69–116
    biology 70
    cooking 110
    drying and rehydrating 111
    history 70, 72
    life cycle 71
    mushrooms and humans 72
    overview 69
    pickling 112, 115
    recipes for 114–16
    species for mushroom gardens 106
    types of 69
    wild fungi 276, 278–9
    see also mushroom cultivation
mycelium 71, 81, 82, 83, 94–6, 103
mychochitin 110
mycorrhizal fungi 69

N

nadiring 145
nasturtiums 36
natural beekeeping 135–45
natural comb 141
Neptune's necklace 183
nest scent 145
nettle 270, 271
    Wild stock powder 272
New Zealand spinach 267
newspaper method, for tomato seeds 46
no-dig method, of growing tomatoes 29
nori 194, 195

O

olive oil: Green tomatoes in olive oil 56
open-pollinated seeds 42
outdoor cultivation, of mushrooms
 99–107

P

Palmaria spp. 194
parsley: Wild stock powder 272
passata 49–50, 52–3
 Shakshouka 60
pasteurisation
 mushrooms 78, 82, 89, 90–3
 tomatoes 52
 woodchip substrate 103
pear tomatoes 17
pearl oyster mushrooms 73, 76, 79, 89
pectin 239
permaculture 7
pests and diseases 37–8
pH, of soil 29
pheromones 131, 132, 145
Phyllospora comosa 200
Pickled kelp stipe 214
pickling, of mushrooms 112, 115
pigface 262–3
Pigface jam 263
pine mushrooms 276
pink oyster mushrooms 76
planting out, of tomatoes 28–35
plastic containers, for mushroom
 cultivation 83
Pleurotus citrinopileatus 76
Pleurotus djamor 76
Pleurotus eryngii 76, 106
Pleurotus ostreatus 76
plug spawn 99–102
plugs, for seeds 21–2
Plum jam 242–3
Plum sauce 243
plum tomatoes 17
plums, wild 241–3
pollen 143, 169
Porphyra spp. 194
potatoes
 Wild greens galette 274
 Wild stock powder 272

pressure cookers 82
propolis 153, 168–9
propolis tincture 168
pruning: of tomatoes 38–9
Prunus 241

Q

queen bees 128, 130, 131–2, 136, 142–3
Quick tomato and wakame salad 60
quilt boxes 148

R

recipes
 Blackberry wild-fermented young
  country wine 246–7
 Botany Bay spinach 267
 Elderberry syrup 254
 Fermented mushrooms 114
 Fermented tomato salsa 58
 Ginger seaweed salad 212
 Green tomatoes in olive oil 56
 New Zealand spinach 267
 Pickled kelp stipe 214
 Pigface jam 263
 Plum jam 242–3
 Plum sauce 243
 Quick tomato and wakame salad 60
 Seaweed butter 214
 Seaweed tea with comfrey, borage and
  nettle 223
 Shakshouka 60
 Shiitake salt 116
 Simple tincture method 286
 Slow-cooked kelp, bean, lamb and
  wild greens stew 216
 Spiced hawthorn and apple fruit
  leathers 258
 Tomato passata 52–3
 Vinegar-pickled mushrooms 115
 Weedy gomasio 210
 Wild fermented elderflower soda 250
 Wild greens galette 274
 Wild stock powder 272
red algae 184
roma tomatoes 17
root knot nematodes 38
Rosaceae 239, 241

round and ribbed tomatoes 17
round and smooth tomatoes 17
royal jelly 131, 132
Rubus fruticosus 244
Rumex spp. 271
russet mite 37–8

S

saffron milkcaps 276, 278
salads
 Ginger seaweed salad 212
 Quick tomato and wakame salad 60
salsa: Fermented tomato salsa 58
Sambucus nigra 249, 253
samphire 264
saprotrophic fungi 69
sea lettuce 184, 191, 194, 195
seaweed 181–223
 anatomy of 188
 avoiding contamination 189
 foraging and harvesting 191–2, 194–5,
  197, 199
 habitat 186–7
 harvesting kit 199
 history 182–3
 live seaweed versus beach-cast
  seaweed 191–2
 nutritional benefits 189
 overview 181
 as part of the ecosystem 183
 preparing and drying 202–3, 205
 processing 205
 recipes for 209, 210, 212, 214, 216
 seaweed fertiliser teas 221, 223
 types of 184, 200–1
 uses in the garden 219, 221
Seaweed butter 214
Seaweed tea with comfrey, borage and
 nettle 223
seeds *see* tomato seeds
semi-determinate tomatoes 18, 38
sesame seeds
 Ginger seaweed salad 212
 Weedy gomasio 210
Shakshouka 60
shiitake mushrooms
 cultivation of 77

drying 111
    log cultivation of 99–102
    Shiitake salt 116
Shiitake salt 116
Simple tincture method 286
skeps 126, 150
slippery jack 278, 279
Slow-cooked kelp, bean, lamb and wild
    greens stew 216
slum gum 164
smokers 151
soil, for tomatoes 26, 29–30
Solanum lycopersicum 15
solar method, rendering beeswax 165
Sonchus oleraceus 271
sow thistle 271
spawn 75, 81, 89, 99, 103
Spiced hawthorn and apple fruit leathers
    258
spinach: Slow-cooked kelp, bean, lamb
    and wild greens stew 216
stakes 35
Stamets, Paul 103
Stellaria media 271
sterilisation 82
stew: Slow-cooked kelp, bean, lamb and
    wild greens stew 216
stipes 188
stock: Wild stock powder 272
stovetop method, rendering beeswax 165
Stropharia rugosoannulata 77, 106
substrate 75, 81, 89–91
Suillus luteus 279
suits, for beekeeping 153
sun-drying, of wild food 284
sun hives 150
sunlight 19
super-organisms 128
supercedure cells 132
swarm cells 132

T
tan oyster mushrooms 79
Taraxacum officinale 268
Tecticornia spp. 264
Tetragonia tetragonioides 267
Tetragonula bees 126
tincture: Simple tincture method 286

Tomato passata 52–3
tomato seeds
    compost seedbank method 46
    fermentation method 44–5
    germination of 26
    hybrid seeds versus open-pollinated
        seeds 42
    newspaper method 46
    saving seeds 42–6
    seed raising in plugs 21
    seed raising in trays 24–5
    seed-raising mix 22
    storing 46
tomatoes 15–60
    choosing which to grow 19
    companion plants for 36–7
    drying 55
    frost protection 36
    growing 20–35
    harvesting 41
    history 16
    life cycle 15
    making passata 49–50, 52–3
    pests and diseases 37–8
    preserving 49–50, 52–3
    pruning 38–9
    recipes for 52–3, 56, 58, 60
    ripening of 41
    seedlings 20–7
    Slow-cooked kelp, bean, lamb and
        wild greens stew 216
    soil heat 26
    soil preparation 29–30
    time to plant 35
    trellises for 31–2, 34–5
    types of 17–18
    watering 26, 36
    see also tomato seeds
Trametes versicolor 279
trellising 31–2, 34–5
turkey tail mushrooms 278, 279, 285
    Simple tincture method 286

U
Ulva lactuca 191
Ulva spp. 184, 194
Urtica dioica 271

V
veils, for beekeeping 153
velvet pioppini mushrooms 77
vinegar
    apple scrap vinegar 240
    Elderberry syrup 254
    Vinegar-pickled mushrooms 115
Vinegar-pickled mushrooms 115

W
wakame: Quick tomato and wakame
    salad 60
Ward, Paul 'Speedy' 107
Warré, Emile 126–7
Warré hives 126–7, 139, 148–55
warrigal greens 267
weeds 230
Weedy gomasio 210
Wild fermented elderflower soda 250
wild food 229–86
    berries 244–58
    dehydrating 282–4
    foraging guidelines 232–3, 235
    fruit trees 239–43
    fungi 276, 278–9
    greens 261–74
    legal access to sources of 232, 235
    mapping sources of 236–7
    as medicine 285–6
    overview 229–30
    toolkit for foraging 234
    weeds versus indigenous plants 230
wild fungi 276, 278–9
wild greens 261–74
    Slow-cooked kelp, bean, lamb and
        wild greens stew 216
    Wild greens galette 274
    Wild stock powder 272
Wild greens galette 274
wild liqueur 256
Wild stock powder 272
windowsills 27
wine: country wine 246
woodchip substrate 103–4
worker bees 130
worm castings 22
wracks 194, 195, 200, 202, 205

Acknowledgements

We are so lucky to be surrounded by inspiration and support in equally large measures, without which we could not have even begun to write this book.

Thank you firstly to our families for all the many, many forms that your love and support has taken – from sharing a farm with us to emergency seaweed foraging and recipe testing. We love you.

Thanks to David Holmgren and the late Bill Mollison for coming up with the concept of permaculture, which inspired us to start Milkwood in the first place. Extended thanks to David and his partner Su Dennett, who welcomed us with open hearts to Melliodora Permaculture Gardens, where we now live. Thanks to Jill Dupleix for suggesting we do a book all those years ago (sorry it took a while, Jill); and big thanks to Jane Morrow and Vivien Valk at Murdoch Books for making it all happen, as well as the Murdoch Books team for collectively helping us untangle our brains onto these pages.

Thanks to all our amazing students that we've learned so much from and with over the years, at farms, in cities and everywhere in between. Your presence and engagement has enabled us to continue to teach and share, and we are so grateful for that. Thanks to the many, many inspiring teachers we've worked with over the years, including David Holmgren, Bill Mollison, Joel Salatin, Sandor Katz, Hannah Moloney, David Asher, Alan Savory, Dave Jacke, Craig Sponholtz, Geoff Lawton, Rosemary Morrow, Tim Malfroy, Kirk Gadzia, Darren Doherty, Narelle Happ, Dan Palmer, Sam Vivers, Col Seis, Tim Heard, Eugenio Graz, Gillian Kozicki, Jean-Martin Fortier, Curtis Stone, Beck Lowe, Michael Hewins, Costa Georgiadis, Peter McCoy, Olivier Sofo, Brendan Morse, Floyd Constable, Joyce Wilkie, Michael Plane and more.

Thanks to the wonderful Heather McCabe, who keeps all Milkwood's courses running so smoothly, with such consistent good humour, and to Adam Kennedy for being with us from the beginning. Thanks to Kate Berry for the beautiful photos taken in all weathers, on land and sea and shore, and for being entirely unfazed by it all. Thanks to James McIntosh from Meanwhile Outside for all his help in the early stages of this book, and to the fabulous Brenna Quinlan for all the gorgeous illustrations and diagrams, as well as motivational water kefir and many good conversations.

Thanks to all our friends for their support during the tumbling process that is making a book, especially Fiona and Adam Walmsley, Paul 'Speedy' Ward, Heather McCabe, Sharon Flynn and the Artist as Family crew. Special thanks to Ashar Fox for always being up for every adventure, book related or otherwise, and for teaching us so much about the kind of parents and people that we want to be.

Regarding the tomato chapter, thanks firstly to Jaromir Rutar, Nick's opa, for teaching him the way of the tomato. Thanks to Joyce Wilkie and Michael Plane from Allsun Farm for their hard-won knowledge about growing great tomatoes; to Olivier Sofo, as well as his mum, Mary, for important intel on the proper way to make passata. Thanks to the fabulous Luisa Brimble for her passata day photos, and also to Hellene Algie for even more passata day photos.

Regarding the beekeeping chapter, a special word of thanks must be said to Tim Malfroy, Australian natural beekeeper and teacher who we've had the pleasure of knowing these last eight years. Tim's work as a full-time commercial beekeeper using innovative natural methods, as well as his work as an outspoken advocate and teacher of bee-centric beekeeping (the natural beekeeping principles this book are derived from his practice), have been invaluable to us, and many others also to the ongoing health of bee populations far and wide. Thanks, Tim.

Thanks also to Adam Kennedy for his generous spirit, knowledge and plentiful mead, and also to authors David Heaf and Thomas Seeley for their writings and inspiration.

Regarding the mushroom cultivation chapter, thanks to the many inspiring authors, mycologists and mushroom gatherers who have shared their knowledge with us along the way – people like Paul Stamets and Peter McCoy, as well as friends like Paul 'Speedy' Ward for inspiration, and the online mushroom community who share as they learn. Thanks to all our mushroom cultivation students for supporting us over the years, and to Will Borowski for getting us growing many years ago. Thanks to students-turned-growers Gabe Staats and Marita Smith, to Ryan Sharpley for gorgeous emergency mushrooms, and to Natalie McComas for the lovely photos she took during one of our mushroom courses.

Regarding the seaweed chapter, thanks to Dr Pia Winberg of Venus Shell Systems and to Jo Lane 'the kelp lady' for their knowledge. Thanks to Bruce Pascoe for his insights regarding indigenous uses of seaweed, and the awesome Stuart Whitelaw for his kelp salad recipe. Thanks to Nerissa Bradley and Oliver Brown for recipe testing, and to Fiona Walmsley and Penny Rushby-Smith for beach picnics and seaweed harvesting adventures.

Regarding Wild Food, a big thanks to Artist as Family – Patrick Jones, Meg Ulman, Woody Ulman-Jones and Zero the dog – for their friendship, knowledge and inspiration. Thanks to Paul 'Speedy' Ward, Bruce Pascoe, Sandor Katz, inspiring fellow foragers like Oliver Brown, Diego Bonetto, Adam Grubb and Annie Raser-Rowland, and to Tricia Hogbin for her assistance regarding various ecological points.

Finally, thanks to the generations of makers, finders, keepers and growers gone before us, from whom the roots of these skills have been passed on. May your hard-won knowledge thrive and nourish us all like the seaweed in springtime, for many centuries to come.

Published in 2018 by Murdoch Books, an imprint of Allen & Unwin

Murdoch Books Australia
83 Alexander Street
Crows Nest NSW 2065
Phone: +61 (0)2 8425 0100
murdochbooks.com.au
info@murdochbooks.com.au

Murdoch Books UK
Ormond House
26–27 Boswell Street
London WC1N 3JZ
Phone: +44 (0) 20 8785 5995
murdochbooks.co.uk
info@murdochbooks.co.uk

For Corporate Orders & Custom Publishing, contact our Business Development Team at
salesenquiries@murdochbooks.com.au.

Publisher: Jane Morrow
Editorial Manager: Julie Mazur Tribe
Design Manager: Vivien Valk
Design Concept: Alissa Dinallo
Designers: Vivien Valk and Susanne Geppert
Project Editor: Justine Harding
Photographers: Kate Berry and Kirsten Bradley
Illustrator: Brenna Quinlan
Production Director: Lou Playfair

A cataloguing-in-publication entry is available from the catalogue of the National Library
of Australia at nla.gov.au.

ISBN 978 1 74336 411 6 Australia
ISBN 978 1 74336 510 6 UK

A catalogue record for this book is available from the British Library.

Colour reproduction by Splitting Image Colour Studio Pty Ltd, Clayton, Victoria
Printed by C & C Offset Printing Co. Ltd., China

MIX
Paper from
responsible sources
FSC® C008047

The information provided within this book is for general inspiration and informational
purposes only. While we try to keep the information up-to-date and correct, the author and
publisher do not assume and hereby disclaim any liability to any party for any loss, damage
or disruption caused by errors or omissions, whether such errors or omissions result from
negligence, accident or any other cause. Be sure to check with your local council and use
common sense when handling any potentially harmful equipment or materials.